KU-260-058

THE ROUGH GUIDE TO

BANGKOK

by Paul Gray and Lucy Ridout

ROUGH
GUIDES

We set out to do something different when the first Rough Guide was published in 1982. Mark Ellingham, just out of university, was travelling in Greece. He brought along the popular guides of the day, but found they were all lacking in some way. They were either strong on ruins and museums but went on for pages without mentioning a beach or taverna. Or they were so conscious of the need to save money that they lost sight of Greece's cultural and historical significance. Also, none of the books told him anything about Greece's contemporary life – its politics, its culture, its people, and how they lived.

So with no job in prospect, Mark decided to write his own guidebook, one which aimed to provide practical information that was second to none, detailing the best beaches and the hottest clubs and restaurants, while also giving hard-hitting accounts of every sight, both famous and obscure, and providing up-to-the-minute information on contemporary culture. It was a guide that encouraged independent travellers to find the best of Greece, and was a great success, getting shortlisted for the Thomas Cook travel guide award, and encouraging Mark, along with three friends, to expand the series.

The Rough Guide list grew rapidly and the letters flooded in, indicating a much broader readership than had been anticipated, but one which uniformly appreciated the Rough Guide mix of practical detail and humour, irreverence and enthusiasm. Things haven't changed. The same four friends who began the series are still the caretakers of the Rough Guide mission today: to provide the most reliable, up-to-date and entertaining information to independent-minded travellers of all ages, on all budgets.

We now publish more than 150 titles and have offices in London and New York. The travel guides are written and researched by a dedicated team of more than 100 authors, based in Britain, Europe, the USA and Australia. We have also created a unique series of phrasebooks to accompany the travel series, along with an acclaimed series of music guides, and a best-selling pocket guide to the internet and World Wide Web. We also publish comprehensive travel information on our website: www.roughguides.com

Help us update

We've gone to a lot of trouble to ensure that this Rough Guide is as up to date and accurate as possible. However, things do change. All suggestions, comments and corrections are much appreciated, and we'll send a copy of the next edition (or any other Rough Guide if you prefer) for the best letters.

Please mark letters **"Rough Guide Bangkok Update"** and send to:

Rough Guides, 62–70 Shorts Gardens, London, WC2H 9AH, or Rough Guides, 4th Floor, 345 Hudson St, New York NY 10014.

Or send email to: mail@roughguides.co.uk
Online updates about this book can be found on
Rough Guides' website (see opposite)

The authors

Paul Gray has been a regular visitor to Thailand since 1987, when he taught English for a year in Chiang Mai. Now based in Dublin, he is co-author of the *Rough Guide to Thailand* and the *Rough Guide to Thailand's Beaches and Islands*, and has edited and contributed to many other guidebooks, including updating his native Northeast for the *Rough Guide to England*.

Lucy Ridout has spent the last 15 years travelling in and writing about Asia. She is co-author of the *Rough Guide to Thailand*, the *Rough Guide to Thailand's Beaches and Islands*, and the *Rough Guide to Bali and Lombok*, and has also co-written *First-Time Asia*, a handbook for travellers making their first visit to the region.

Acknowledgements

The authors jointly would like to thank: Julia Kelly, Nicky Agate and Narrell Leffman for additional Basics research; our editor, Richard Lim, for his insightful editing and resourceful enthusiasm; staff at the Bangkok Tourist Bureau and TAT, in particular Chris Lee and Abi Batalla at TAT's London office; Phil Cornwel-Smith; Randy Campbell; Andrew Spooner; Iain Stewart; Bangkok Airways. Thanks also to Karen Parker for proofreading, Rachel Holmes for typesetting, and Melissa Flack and Maxine Repath for the maps.

Reader's letters

Thanks to all the readers who have taken the time to write or email us with comments and suggestions for this edition:
Lisa Anderson, Caroline Bennett, Alan Booth, Hillary Brill, Peter Cunningham, Carolyn Bullock & Liz Donkin, Simon Chapman & Becky Edser, Richard Dion, Lynne Fender, Isabella Forrest, Lawrence Forrester, Vesa Frantsila, Emma Gervasio, Madeline Grove, Matt Günther & Simone von der Forst, Richard Harvey, Alan Hickey, Suzanne Kay, Henry Lew, Janet Lock, Roger Loxley, Padraig F. MacDonnchadha, Jamie MacSween, Bob & Ann Marshall, Keith McGhie, Martin Platt, Emily Prince, Polly Rashbrooke & Nic Macdonald, John Richardson, Lance Saunders, Steve Scott, Susan Shaw, Kerry Start & Tony Shilling, Hilary Sneller, Steve Taylor, Nic & Kim Walker, Jo Yuen, Rona Yuthasastrakosol, R.A. Zambardino.

CONTENTS

The Guide

Listings

Excursions from Bangkok

Contexts

MAP LIST

Introduction

The headlong pace and flawed modernity of Bangkok match few people's visions of the capital of exotic Siam. Spiked with scores of high-rise buildings of concrete and glass, it's a vast flatness which holds a population of at least nine million, and feels even bigger. But under the shadow of the skyscrapers you'll find a heady mix of chaos and refinement, of frenetic markets and hushed golden temples, of early-morning almsgiving ceremonies and ultra-hip designer boutiques.

Bangkok is a relatively young capital, established in 1782 after the Burmese sacked Ayutthaya, the former capital. A temporary base was set up on the western bank of the Chao Phraya River, in what is now Thonburi, before work started on the more defensible east bank, where the first king of the new dynasty, Rama I, built his fabulously ornate palace within a defensive ring of canals. He named this "royal island" **Ratanakosin**, and it remains the city's spiritual heart, not to mention its culturally most rewarding quarter. No visit to the capital would be complete without seeing Ratanakosin's star attractions – if necessary, the dazzling ostentation of **Wat Phra Kaeo** and the **Grand Palace**, the grandiose decay of **Wat Po** and the **National Museum**'s hoard of exquisite works of art can all be crammed into a single action-packed day.

Around the temples and palaces of the royal island spread
an amphibious city of shops and houses built on bamboo
rafts moored on the river and canals. Even though many of
the canals have since been built over, one of the great plea-
sures of the city is a ride on its remaining waterways; the
majestic **Chao Phraya River** is served by frequent ferries
and longtail boats, and is the backbone of a network of
canals and floating markets that remains fundamentally
intact in the west-bank **Thonburi** district. Inevitably the
waterways have earned Bangkok the title of "Venice of the
East", a tag that seems all too apt when you're wading
through flooded streets in the rainy season.

Bangkok began to assume its modern guise at the end of
the nineteenth century, when the forward-looking Rama V
relocated the royal family to a neighbourhood north of
Ratanakosin called **Dusit**, constructing grand European-style
boulevards, a new palace, Chitrlada (still used by the royal
family today), and **Wat Benjamabophit**, popularly known
as the "Marble Temple" because of its sumptuous use of
Italian marble. When political modernization followed in
1932, Dusit was the obvious choice of home for Thailand's
new parliament, which now sits in Parliament House.

Since Rama V's reign, Bangkok has attracted mass migra-
tion from all over Thailand, pushing the city's boundaries
ever eastwards in an explosion of modernization that has
blown away earlier attempts at orderly planning and left the
city without an obvious centre. The capital now sprawls
over 330 square kilometres and, with a population forty
times that of the second city, Chiang Mai, is far and away
the country's most dominant city. Bangkokians own four-
fifths of the nation's automobiles, and there's precious little
chance to escape from the pollution in green space: the city
has only 0.4 square metres of public parkland per inhabi-
tant, the lowest figure in the world, compared, for example,
to London's 30.4 square metres per person.

Modern Bangkok is not without its beauty however, the sleek glass towers and cool marble malls lending an air of energy and big-city drama to the eastern districts of **Silom**, **Siam Square** and **Sukhumvit**, which together form the hub of one of the liveliest and most fashionable cities in Asia. These areas shelter a few noteworthy tourist sights, too, best of which is **Jim Thompson's House**, a small, personal museum of Thai design. **Shopping** downtown varies from touristic outlets selling silks, handicrafts and counterfeit watches, to international fashion emporia and home-grown, street-wise boutiques. For livelier scenes, explore the dark alleys of the bazaars in **Chinatown** or the Indian district, **Pahurat**, or head out to the enormous, open-air **Chatuchak Weekend Market**. Similarly, the city offers wildly varied **entertainment**, ranging from traditional dancing and the orchestrated bedlam of Thai boxing, through hip bars and clubs playing the latest imported sounds, to the farang-only sex bars of the notorious Patpong district.

North and west of the city, the unwieldy urban mass of Greater Bangkok peters out into the vast, well-watered central plains, a region that for centuries has grown the bulk of the nation's food. The atmospheric ruins of Thailand's fourteenth-century capital **Ayutthaya** lie here, ninety minutes' train ride from Bangkok and, together with the ornate palace at nearby **Bang Pa-In**, make a rewarding excursion from the modern metropolis. Further west, the massive stupa at **Nakhon Pathom** and the traditional floating markets of **Damnoen Saduak** are also easily manageable as a day-trip, and combine well with a visit to the less touristed town of **Phetchaburi**, famous for its charming, historic temples. An overnight stay at **Kanchanaburi** is also well worth the effort: impressively sited on the River Kwai, it holds several moving **World War II sites**, including the notorious Death Railway.

CITY OF ANGELS

When Rama I was crowned in 1782, he gave his new capital a grand 43-syllable name to match his ambitious plans for the building of the city. Since then 21 more syllables have been added. Krungthepmahanakhornbowornrattanakosinmahintar-ayutthayamahadilokpopnopparatratchathaniburirom-udomratchaniwetmahasathanamornpimanavatarnsathit-sakkathattiyavisnukarprasit is Guinness-certified as the longest place name in the world and roughly translates as "Great city of angels, the supreme repository of divine jewels, the great land unconquerable, the grand and prominent realm, the royal and delightful capital city full of nine noble gems, the highest royal dwelling and grand palace, the divine shelter and living place of the reincarnated spirits". Fortunately, all Thais refer to the city simply as Krung Thep, though plenty can recite the full name at the drop of a hat. Bangkok – "Village of the Plum Olive" – was the name of the original village on the Thonburi side; with remarkable persistence, it has remained in use by foreigners since the 1660s, when the French built a short-lived garrison fort in the area.

When to visit

Bangkok's climate is governed by three seasons, though in reality the city sits firmly within the tropics and so enjoys warm days and nights year-round. The so-called **cool season**, which runs from November through February, is the pleasantest time to visit; days are invariably bright and clear, and temperatures average a manageable 27°C (though they can still reach a broiling 31°C at midday). Not surprisingly this is peak season for the tourist industry, so it's well worth booking accommodation and flights in advance over this period; prices for hotel rooms are at their highest during this time, rising to a climax at Christmas and New Year.

March sees the beginning of the **hot season**, when temperatures can rise to 36°C, and continue to do so beyond the end of April. During these sweltering months you'll probably be glad of an air-conditioned hotel room and may find yourself spending more money than anticipated, simply because it's more comfortable to travel across the city in an air-conditioned taxi rather than sweat it out on foot (though air-con buses are a good compromise option and the Skytrain the preferred alternative where available). The daily downpours that characterize the **rainy season** can come as a welcome relief, though being hot and wet is a sensation that doesn't appeal to everyone. The rainy season varies in length and intensity from year to year, but usually starts with a bang in May, gathers force between June and August, and comes to a peak in September and October,

	C°		RAINFALL
	AVERAGE DAILY		AVERAGE MONTHLY
	MAX	MIN	MM
Jan	28	21	11
Feb	28	21	28
March	29	21	31
April	30	22	72
May	31	23	190
June	31	23	152
July	30	23	158
Aug	31	23	187
Sept	31	23	320
Oct	30	23	231
Nov	29	23	57
Dec	28	22	9

when whole districts of the capital are flooded. Rain rarely lasts all day however, so as long as you're armed with an umbrella, there's no reason to reschedule your trip – and you'll get more for your money, too, as many hotels and airlines drop their prices right down at this time of year.

To find out the current weather situation and seven-day forecast in Bangkok, visit the Thai Meteorological Department website at Ⓦwww.tmd.motc.go.th/eng/index.html.

BASICS

BASICS

Getting there from Britain and Ireland

T he fastest and most comfortable way of reaching Bangkok from the UK is to fly nonstop from London with either Qantas, British Airways, EVA Airways or Thai International – a journey time of about twelve hours. Many scheduled airlines operate indirect flights (ie flights with one or more connections), which usually take up to four hours longer, but work out significantly cheaper. Prices for these vary throughout the year, but at the time of writing, airlines such as Lufthansa (who fly via Frankfurt) and Royal Jordanian (who stop off in Amman) offer good deals. There are no nonstop flights from any regional airports in Britain or from Dublin or Belfast, and rather than routing via London, you may find it convenient – and occasionally cheaper – to fly to another European hub such as Amsterdam, Frankfurt or Vienna, and take a connecting flight from there.

To make extra use of all that flying time and **stopover** on the way there or back, you'll probably have to go with the associated national airline – for example Air India for stops in Delhi or Bombay. This is an option which most airlines offer at the same price as their direct flights.

If you're planning a long trip with several stops in Asia or elsewhere, buying a **round-the-world (RTW) ticket** makes a lot of sense. A typical one-year ticket, costing from £1250 (plus tax), would depart and return to London, taking in Singapore, Bangkok, Bali, Sydney, Auckland, Tahiti, Los Angeles and New York, leaving you to cover the Singapore–Bangkok and LA–NYC legs overland.

RETURN FARES

The most expensive times to fly are July, August and December – you may have to book two to three months in advance for cheaper tickets during these peak periods. Discounted **nonstop London–Bangkok** return fares start at around £450 low season, rising to £550 during peak periods. For indirect flights, Lufthansa works out among the cheapest in high season, at about £440 inclusive of tax; the best low-season rate at the time of writing is £330 with Royal Jordanian. Some agents offer special discounts (around £400 return) with the more reputable airlines for full-time students and/or under-26s.

Bear in mind that the £20–30 **departure tax** applicable from British airports is not included in prices quoted by many travel agents; we have not included tax in the example fares detailed here. Also, you'll always have to pay an airport departure tax (B500) when leaving Thailand on an international flight.

The Tourism Authority of Thailand (TAT) has offices at 49 Albemarle St, London W1 (☏ 020/7499 7679, recorded information on ☏ 0839/300800; 🌐 www.thaismile.co.uk).

AIRLINES

British Airways
@ www.britishairways.com. In
the UK ☎ 0845/773 3377; in
the Irish Republic, call the UK
number ☎ 0141/222 2345.
Daily nonstop flights from
Heathrow to Bangkok.

EVA Airways In the UK
☎ 020/7380 8300,
@ www.evaair.com.tw. Three
nonstop Bangkok flights a
week from Heathrow.

Lauda Air In the UK
☎ 020/7630 5924,
@ www.laudaair.com. Flies
from Gatwick via Vienna twice
a week to Bangkok.

Lufthansa
@ www.lufthansa.co.uk. In the
UK ☎ 0845/773 7747, in the
Irish Republic ☎ 01/844 5544.
Five flights a week from
Heathrow via Frankfurt.

Qantas In the UK ☎ 0845/774
7767, @ www.qantas.com.au.
Daily nonstop flights to
Bangkok from Heathrow.

Royal Jordanian Airlines In the
UK ☎ 020/7878 6300,
@ www.rja.com.jo. Three
flights a week to Bangkok
from Heathrow, via Amman.

Thai Airways In the UK
☎ 0870/606 0911 or 0161/831
7861, @ www.thaiair.com.
Daily nonstop Bangkok flights
from Heathrow.

FLIGHT AGENTS

Britain

Bridge the World ☎ 020/7911
0900, @ www.bridgetheworld
.com.

Flightbookers ☎ 020/7757
3000, @ www.ebookers.com.

North South Travel
☎ 01245/608 291,
@ www.northsouthtravel.co.uk.

STA Travel
@ www.statravel.co.uk. In
London ☎ 020/7361 6144,
and over forty other branches
in British cities.

Trailfinders @ www.trailfinders
.co.uk. In London ☎ 020/7938
3939, plus branches in
Birmingham, Bristol, Glasgow
and Manchester.

GETTING THERE FROM BRITAIN AND IRELAND

5

Travelbag ⓣ 0870/737 7843, ⓦ www.travelbag.co.uk.

Travel Cuts ⓣ 020/7255 2082, ⓦ www.travelcuts.co.uk.

usit CAMPUS ⓦ www.usitcampus.co.uk. In London ⓣ 020/7730 8111, plus branches all over Britain.

Ireland

Joe Walsh Tours ⓦ www.joewalshtours.ie.

Dublin ⓣ 01/872 2555; Cork ⓣ 021/277 959

Silk Road Travel Dublin ⓣ 01/677 1029 or 677 1147.

Trailfinders Dublin ⓣ 01/677 7888, ⓦ www.trailfinders.ie

usit NOW ⓦ www.usitnow.ie. Dublin ⓣ 01/602 1700, Belfast ⓣ 028/9032 4073, plus branches in Cork, Derry, Galway, Limerick and Waterford.

GETTING THERE FROM BRITAIN AND IRELAND

Getting there from the US and Canada

There are no nonstop flights from North America to Bangkok, but plenty of airlines run daily flights there from major east- and west-coast cities with only one stop. Excluding layovers, the actual flying time from LA via Asia is approximately eighteen hours, and from New York via Europe it's around nineteen hours. From Canada, you can expect to spend something like sixteen hours in the air flying from Vancouver (via Tokyo) or at least twenty hours from Montreal (via Europe).

Circle Pacific deals allow you to make a certain number of **stopovers** and are generally valid for one year. On a Circle Pacific ticket booked through a discount travel agent, an itinerary starting out and ending in Los Angeles, taking in Tokyo, Hong Kong, Bangkok, Singapore, Jakarta, Denpasar (Bali) and Sydney costs around US$2100.

Typical off-the-shelf **round-the-world (RTW) tickets**, starting and ending in San Francisco with stops in Hong Kong, Bangkok, Delhi, Mumbai (Bombay), London and Boston cost around US$1500.

RETURN FARES

Fares depend on the season, and are highest in December and January and from June through August. From the **US**, expect to find regular, high-season published fares at around $1200 minimum from the West Coast and at least $1300 from the East Coast or the Midwest, while low-season fares can start at around $750 from the West Coast and $850 from the East Coast or Midwest. A discount travel agent, however, should be able to dig up, for instance, a high-season fare from LA for around $1050. Be on the lookout also for special limited-offer promotional fares from the major carriers like United Airlines or Thai, which can bring low-season fares down to as little as $600 from the West Coast or $750 from the East Coast.

Air Canada has the most convenient service to Bangkok from the largest number of **Canadian** cities. From Vancouver, expect to pay around CDN$2000 in low season (CDN$300 more in high season), from Toronto, CDN$2300 (CDN$400 more in high season).

The Tourism Authority of Thailand (TAT; ⓦ www.tat.or.th) has a tollfree service in North America on ⓣ 1-800-THAILAND; and offices at 1 World Trade Centre, Suite 3729, New York, NY10048 ⓣ 212/432-0433 or 432-0435, ⓔ ttny@aol.com; 611 North Larchmont Blvd, 1st Floor, Los Angeles, CA90004 ⓣ 323/461-9814; and 1393 Royal York Rd, #15, Toronto, Ontario, M9A 4Y9 ⓣ 416/614-2625.

AIRLINES

Air Canada ⓣ1-888/247 2262, ⓦwww.aircanada.ca. Daily flights to Bangkok from most major Canadian cities via Osaka, Hong Kong or London.

Cathay Pacific ⓣ1-800/233-2742, ⓦwww.cathaypacific.com. Daily flights via Hong Kong to Bangkok from New York, Los Angeles, San Francisco and Toronto.

China Air Lines ⓣ1-800/227-5118, ⓦwww.china-airlines.com. Flies to Bangkok via Taipei daily from Los Angeles and San Francisco, five times a week from New York, and four times a week (summer only) from Anchorage.

Delta Airlines ⓣ1-800/241 4141, ⓦwww.delta.com. Daily flights to Bangkok from most major US cities, via Seoul or Tokyo.

Finnair ⓦwww.finnair.fi; in the US ⓣ1-800/950-5000, in Canada ⓣ1-800/461-8651. Via Helsinki, three Bangkok flights a week from New York, and two summer-only flights a week from Toronto.

Japan Air Lines ⓣ1-800/525-3663, ⓦwww.japanair.com. Flies to Bangkok via Tokyo from Chicago, Dallas, Los Angeles, New York, San Francisco, Los Angeles and Vancouver.

KLM/Northwest ⓦwww.nwa.com; in the US ⓣ1-800/374 7747, in Canada ⓣ1-800/361 5073. Daily flights to Bangkok via Japan from San Francisco, Los Angeles, Chicago, Detroit, Seattle and New York, or via Amsterdam from New York.

Swissair ⓦwww.swissair.com; in the US ⓣ1-800/221 4750, in Canada ⓣ1-800/563 5954. Daily flights to Bangkok from Montréal, New York and Toronto via Zürich.

Thai Airways ⓦwww.thaiair.com; in the US ⓣ1-800/426-5204, in Canada ⓣ1-800/668-8103. Daily flights to Bangkok from Los Angeles via Osaka, and from New York via London.

United Airlines ⓣ1-800/241-6522, ⓦwww.ual.com. Daily flights to Bangkok from most major US cities, via Tokyo.

FLIGHT AGENTS

Air Brokers International ☎ 1-800/883-3273 or 415/397-1383, ⓦ www.airbrokers.com.

Airtech ☎ 212/219-7000, ⓦ www.airtech.com.

Council Travel ☎ 1-800/226 8624 or 617/528-2091, ⓦ www.counciltravel.com. Offices include: New York ☎ 212/822-2700; San Francisco ☎ 415/421-3473; Los Angeles ☎ 310/208-3551; Chicago ☎ 312/951-0585.

Educational Travel Center ☎ 1-800/747-5551 or 608/256-5551, ⓦ www.edtrav.com.

High Adventure Travel ☎ 1-800/350-0612 or 415/912-5600, ⓦ www.airtreks.com.

Now Voyager ☎ 212/431-1616, ⓦ www.nowvoyagertravel.com.

STA Travel ☎ 1-800/777 0112, ⓦ www.sta-travel.com. Branches include: New York ☎ 212/627-3111; Los Angeles ☎ 323/934-8722; San Francisco ☎ 415/391-8407; Boston ☎ 617/266-6014; Chicago ☎ 312/786-9050; Philadelphia ☎ 215/568-7999.

Travac ☎ 1-800/872-8800, ⓦ www.thetravelsite.com.

Travel Cuts ☎ 1-800/667-2887, ⓦ www.travelcuts.com. Branches include: Toronto ☎ 416/979-2406; Montréal ☎ 514/843-8511; Vancouver ☎ 1-888/FLY CUTS or 604/822-6890.

Getting there from Australia and New Zealand

There is no shortage of scheduled flights to Bangkok from Australia and New Zealand, with direct services being offered by Thai Airways, Qantas and Air New Zealand. Flight times are around nine hours from Perth and Sydney, or around eleven hours from Auckland. Many Asian airlines can take you there via their home cities, but this is often as expensive as a direct flight.

There are a variety of **round-the-world** (RTW) combinations that include Bangkok. Currently the cheapest is with Qantas/BA, allowing three free stops in each direction for around A$1700/NZ$2100. The most flexible are the mileage-based tickets such as the "Star Alliance 1" offered by the Star Alliance consortium of airlines (ⓦ www.star-alliance.com), and "One World Explorer" by Qantas, Cathay Pacific, British Airways and American Airlines. For example, prices for an RTW ticket from Sydney to

Bangkok, London, New York, Los Angeles, Auckland and back to Sydney start at around A$2400/NZ$3000.

The Tourism Authority of Thailand (TAT; ⓦ www.tat.or.th) has offices at 255 George St, Sydney, NSW 2000 (ⓣ 02/9247 7549); 2 Hardy Rd, South Perth, WA 6151 (ⓣ 08/9474 3646); and Floor 2, 87 Queen St, Auckland (ⓣ 09/379 8398).

RETURN FARES

Fares are structured according to **season**; for most airlines high season is from mid-November to mid-January and May to the end of August, when fares rise by about A/NZ$200–400. Generally airlines have a set fare from major eastern Australian cities (with Ansett and Qantas providing a shuttle service to the main point of departure), while fares from Darwin are around A$200 cheaper. From Christchurch and Wellington you'll pay NZ$150–300 more than from Auckland.

From **Australia**, the cheapest direct flights to Bangkok are with Olympic Airlines from Sydney (around A$850/A$1400 low/high season), while Thai Airways, Air New Zealand, BA and Qantas all weigh in around A$1000/A$1500. The best indirect deals are with Royal Brunei, via Bandar Seri Begawan (A$850/A$1100).

From **New Zealand**, Qantas offers the best direct low-season fares to Bangkok (around NZ$1100), with Thai Airways only marginally more expensive; Air New Zealand, however, charges a pricey NZ$1500. In high season, when fares on these airlines are pretty similar at NZ$1900–2100, it's slightly cheaper to get an indirect flight with Garuda to Bangkok.

AIRLINES

Air New Zealand
Ⓦ www.airnz.com; in Australia
Ⓣ 13/2476, in New Zealand
Ⓣ 09/357 3000 & 0800/737
000. Several flights a week
direct to Bangkok from
Auckland, Christchurch,
Brisbane and Sydney.

Ansett Ⓦ www.ansett.com.au;
in Australia Ⓣ 13/1414 or
02/9352 6707, in New
Zealand Ⓣ 09/336 2364.
Several flights a week from
major Australian cities and
from Auckland to Denpasar
and Bangkok.

Egypt Air In Australia
Ⓣ 02/9267 6979,
Ⓦ www.egyptair.com.eg. Two
flights a week direct to
Singapore from Sydney.

Garuda Ⓦ www.garuda-
indonesia.com; in Australia
Ⓣ 1300/365330, in New
Zealand Ⓣ 09/366 1862 &
0800/128510. Several flights a
week from major Australian
cities and from Auckland to
Bangkok, with a stopover in
either Denpasar or Jakarta.

Gulf Air Ⓦ www.gulfairco.com;
in Australia Ⓣ 02/9244 2199;
in New Zealand Ⓣ 09/308

3366. Three flights a week
direct to Singapore from
Sydney and Melbourne.

Malaysia Airlines
Ⓦ www.mas.com.my; in
Australia Ⓣ 13/2476, in New
Zealand Ⓣ 09/373 2741 &
0800/657472. Several flights a
week from Brisbane, Sydney,
Melbourne, Perth and
Auckland, via Kuala Lumpur,
to Bangkok.

Olympic Airways In Australia
Ⓣ 1800/221 663 & 02/9251
2044, Ⓦ www.olympic-
airways.com. Three direct
Sydney–Bangkok flights a
week.

Qantas Ⓦ www.qantas.com.au;
in Australia Ⓣ 13/1313, in
New Zealand Ⓣ 09/357 8900
& 0800/808 767. Several
flights a week direct to
Bangkok from major
Australasian cities.

Royal Brunei Airlines In
Australia Ⓣ 07/3221 7757,
Ⓦ www.bruneiair.com. Three
flights a week to Bangkok via
Bandar Seri Begawan from
Brisbane, Darwin and Sydney.

Singapore Airlines
Ⓦ www.singaporeair.com; in

GETTING THERE FROM AUSTRALIA AND NEW ZEALAND

Australia ⓣ 02/9350 0262 & 13/1011, in New Zealand ⓣ 09/303 2129 & 0800/808909. Flights to Bangkok via Singapore: daily from Sydney, Melbourne, Perth and Auckland; four flights a week from Cairns, Brisbane and Christchurch; and three flights a week from Darwin.

Thai Airways
ⓦ www.thaiair.com; in Australia ⓣ 1300/651960, in New Zealand ⓣ 09/377 3886. Flies direct to Bangkok three times a week from Sydney and Auckland, and twice a week from Brisbane, Melbourne, and Perth.

PACKAGE HOLIDAYS

If you can only manage a short visit, **package holidays**, offered by a whole host of operators through your travel agent, can be an economical and hassle-free way of sampling Bangkok. Example city-break prices, including international flights, are around A\$1200/NZ\$1600 for five nights in Bangkok (the exact price depends on the type of accommodation chosen). Package holidays departing from Darwin, where available, generally cost about A\$200 less per person.

TRAVEL AGENTS AND TOUR OPERATORS

Abercrombie and Kent In Australia ⓣ 03/9699 9766 or 1800/331 429, in New Zealand ⓣ 09/579 3369.

Anywhere Travel Sydney ⓣ 02/9663 0411, ⓔ anywhere@ozemail.com.au.

Asian Explorer Holidays Brisbane ⓣ 07/3832 4266.

Budget Travel ⓣ 0800/808 040, ⓦ www.budgettravel.co.nz. Auckland ⓣ 09/366 0061, plus branches around the country.

Destinations Unlimited Auckland ⓣ 09/373 4033.

Flight Centre ⓦ www.flightcentre.com.au. In

Australia: Sydney ⓣ 02/9235 3522, plus branches nationwide, nearest branch ⓣ 13/1600. In New Zealand: Auckland ⓣ 09/358 4310, plus branches nationwide.

Northern Gateway Darwin ⓣ 08/8941 1394, ⓔ oztravel@norgate.com.au.

San Michele Travel ⓣ 02/9299 1111 & 1800/222 244, ⓦ www.asiatravel.com.au.

STA Travel In Australia, nearest branch ⓣ 13/1776, fastfare telesales ⓣ 1300/360960, ⓦ www.statravel.com.au. In New Zealand, Auckland ⓣ 09/309 0458, fastfare telesales ⓣ 09/366 6673; plus branches nationwide.

Thai Binh Travel Sydney ⓣ 02/9724 2304.

Thailand Travel Adelaide ⓣ 08/8272 2166.

Thomas Cook In Australia: Sydney ⓣ 02/9231 2877; Melbourne ⓣ 03/9282 0222; local branch ⓣ 13/1771, telesales ⓣ 1800/801 002. In New Zealand, Auckland ⓣ 09/379 3920.

Trailfinders ⓦ www.trailfinders.co.au; Sydney ⓣ 02/9247 7666; Brisbane ⓣ 07/3229 0887; Cairns ⓣ 07/4041 1199.

Travel.com.au Sydney ⓣ 02/9249 5444 & 1300/130 482, ⓦ www.travel.com.au.

Travel Indochina Sydney ⓣ 02/9321 9133 & 1800/640 823.

usit BEYOND ⓦ www.usitbeyond.co.nz. Auckland ⓣ 09/379 4224 or 0800/788 336; plus branches nationwide.

OVERLANDING THROUGH ASIA

Indonesia's proximity to Australia and New Zealand makes it the obvious starting point for **overlanding** to Thailand through Asia. There are regular flights to Denpasar in Bali, where you can connect with boat, rail and bus links through Java and/or Sumatra. Northern Sumatra is just a short boat ride from Malaysia and Singapore, and there are regular ferry connections between

Medan and Penang, between Dumai and Melaka, and between the Riau islands and Johor Bahru and Singapore. Once in Malaysia or Singapore, you can proceed into Thailand by train, bus or plane (see p.20). Ansett, Qantas and Garuda fares to Denpasar start at A$800/NZ$1000.

Alternatively, you could fly to **Singapore** or **Malaysia** and then continue overland to Thailand by road or rail. From Australia, the best deals to Singapore are with Gulf Air, Egyptair or Royal Brunei (around A$700 low season/A$1200 high), with Royal Brunei flying to Kuala Lumpur for the same prices. From New Zealand, Singapore Airlines flies to Singapore for NZ1250/NZ$1900; Malaysia Airlines' fares to Kuala Lumpur are about ten percent cheaper.

Travel via Neighbouring Countries

T hailand has land borders with Burma, Laos, Cambodia and Malaysia, and works well as part of many overland itineraries, both across Asia and between Europe and Australia. Most passport holders should be able to get an on-the-spot thirty-day entry stamp into Thailand at any of the land borders described below; see p.22 for details. Bangkok is also an important transit point for flights between Europe and Vietnam, Laos and Cambodia; indeed on most flights from Europe to Indochina you have no choice but to be routed via Bangkok.

Contact details for Asian embassies in Bangkok are given on p.251.

TRAVEL VIA NEIGHBOURING COUNTRIES

17

BURMA

At the time of writing, there is no overland access from Burma into Thailand, and access in the opposite direction is restricted to day-trips. There are however numerous **flights** between Bangkok and Burma, and tourists who intend to enter Burma by air can buy four-week tourist **visas** at the Burmese embassy in Bangkok for B800 (issued within 24hr).

CAMBODIA

There are two legal **overland** border crossings from Cambodia into Thailand, both of which are currently open in both directions, but as regulations change quite frequently you should check latest developments with embassy officials and recent travellers. As for **flights**, Bangkok Airways runs daily Phnom Penh–Bangkok and Siem Reap–Bangkok services. At the time of writing, **visas** for Cambodia are issued to travellers on arrival at Phnom Penh and Siem Reap airports, and at both the land borders; if you do need to buy an advance thirty-day visa, you can do so from the Cambodian embassy in Bangkok (B1000; two working days) or from travel agents in Bangkok's Banglamphu district (for an extra B200).

The most commonly used land crossing is at **Poipet**, which lies just across the border from the Thai town of **Aranyaprathet** and has public-transport connections with Sisophon, Siem Reap and Phnom Penh. Note that the Thai border closes at 5pm every day, and that the last Aranyaprathet–Bangkok **bus** also leaves at 5pm; buses take about four and a half hours to reach Bangkok's Northern (Mo Chit) Bus Terminal. There are just two **trains** a day from Aranyaprathet to Bangkok (5hr 30min), departing at 6.30am and 1.35pm.

The other border crossing runs from Sihanoukville via

Koh Kong to **Ban Hat Lek** near Trat on Thailand's east coast. The usual route is to get the speedboat from Sihanoukville to Koh Kong, then a taxi-boat to the Hat Lek border post, but the Sihanoukville boat doesn't always arrive before the border closes at 5pm. Minibuses and songthaews run from Ban Hat Lek to Trat, 91km north-west, where you can pick up a **bus** straight to Bangkok's Eastern or Northern Bus Terminal (4–6hr). For a thorough guide to Koh Kong and how to reach it from both sides of the border, visit ⓦkohkong.com/kohkong.

LAOS AND VIETNAM

Tourists can cross into Thailand at five points along the **Lao border**: Houayxai (for Chiang Khong); Vientiane (for Nong Khai); Thakhek (for Nakhon Phanom); Savannakhet (for Mukdahan); and Pakxe (for Chong Mek). All these places have good rail and/or bus connections with Bangkok. With the right Lao visa and Vietnamese exit stamp, you can travel from **Vietnam's** Lao Bao border crossing via Savannakhet to Mukdahan in Thailand in a matter of hours.

Visas are required for all non-Thai visitors to Laos. A fif-teen-day visa on arrival can be bought (US$30 cash, plus 2 photos) at Vientiane Airport, Louang Phabang Airport and the Friendship Bridge in Nong Khai. Otherwise you must apply in advance for a visa at the Lao embassy in Bangkok (thirty-day visas for B750–1000, depending on nationality; allow three working days, or 24hr for an extra B300); at a tour agency, for example in Banglamphu (B2400–4000; three working days); or at a guest house in Chiang Khong. All travellers into Vietnam need to buy a visa in advance. Thirty-day visas take five working days to process at the embassy in Bangkok (B800–2000 depending on nationality, or B200 extra through a travel agent).

MALAYSIA AND SINGAPORE

It is possible to take a **train** all the way to Bangkok from **Singapore** (about 2000km), via **Malaysia**. The journey involves several changes, but the overall **Singapore–Bangkok** trip can be done in around thirty hours at a cost of about £60/$90; trains leave at least once a day from both ends. For the current timetable and ticket prices, visit the Malaysian Railways website Ⓦ www.ktmb.com.my.

Plenty of **buses** also cross the Thai–Malaysian border every day. The southern Thai town of Hat Yai is the major transport hub for international bus connections, including Singapore (18hr; £12/$18), Kuala Lumpur (12hr; £9/$13), and Penang (6hr; £9/$13); Hat Yai is fourteen to sixteen hours from Bangkok by frequent buses and trains. You'll also find long-distance buses and minibuses to Bangkok from Kuala Lumpur, Penang and Singapore, as well as in the reverse direction. **Ferries** connect Kuala Perlis and Langkawi in Malaysia with Satun in southern Thailand; there are two daily buses from Satun to Bangkok's Southern Bus Terminal and the journey takes 16 hours.

Most Western tourists can spend thirty days in Malaysia and fourteen days in Singapore without having bought a **visa** beforehand.

For details of timetables for trains to and from
Thailand's borders, consult the website of the
State Railway of Thailand Ⓦ www.srt.motc.go.th

THE EASTERN AND ORIENTAL EXPRESS

You can travel between Singapore and Bangkok in extreme style by taking the **Eastern and Oriental Express** train – a Southeast Asian version of the Orient Express – which transports its passengers in great comfort and luxury. The journey, via Kuala Lumpur, takes around 41 hours in all, departs approximately once a week from either terminus and costs from £800/$1300 per person all-inclusive. For details, go to to ⓦ www.orient-express.com or call ⓣ 020/7805 5100 (UK) or ⓣ 1-800/524-2420 (US); in Australia, Abercrombie and Kent (see p.14) can organize the journey for you.

TRAVEL VIA NEIGHBOURING COUNTRIES

Red tape and visas

There are three main entry categories for Thailand; for all of them your passport must be valid for at least six months from the date of entry. As visa requirements are often subject to change, you should always check with a Thai embassy or consulate, or a reliable travel agent, before departure.

Most foreign passport holders are allowed to enter the country for **stays of up to thirty days** without having to apply for a visa (New Zealanders are allowed up to ninety days). The period of stay will be stamped into your passport by immigration officials upon entry, but you're supposed to show proof of onward travel arrangements: unless you have a confirmed bus, train or air ticket out of Thailand, you may be put back on the next plane or sent back to get a sixty-day tourist visa from the nearest Thai Embassy. Such thirty-day stays cannot be extended under any but the most exceptional circumstances, though it's easy enough to get a new one by hopping across the border into a neighbouring country, most conveniently Malaysia, and back again.

If you're fairly certain you may want to stay longer than thirty days, then from the outset you should apply for a **sixty-day tourist visa** from a Thai embassy or consulate, accompanying your application – which always takes several days to process – with your passport and two photos. The sixty-day visa currently costs £8 per entry in the UK, for example – multiple-entry versions are available, which are handy if you're going to be leaving and re-entering Thailand.

Thai embassies also consider applications for the slightly more expensive **ninety-day non-immigrant visas** (£15 in the UK) as long as you can offer a good reason for your visit, such as study or business (there are different categories of non-immigrant visa for which different levels of proof are needed).

As it's quite a hassle to organize a ninety-day visa from outside the country (and generally not feasible for most tourists), you're better off applying for an **extension** to your tourist visa once inside Thai borders. All sixty-day tourist visas can be extended for a further thirty days, at the discretion of officials; extensions cost B500 and are issued over the counter at immigration offices (*kaan khao muang*) across Thailand. For details of Bangkok's immigration office, see p.252. You'll need two extra photos, plus two photocopies of the first four pages and latest Thai visa page of your passport.

Immigration offices also issue **re-entry permits** (B500) if you want to leave the country and come back again within the validity of your visa. If you **overstay** your visa limits, expect to be fined B100 per extra day when you depart Thailand, though an overstay of a month or more could land you in trouble with immigration officials.

THAI EMBASSIES AND CONSULATES ABROAD

For a full listing of Thai diplomatic missions abroad, check out the Thai Ministry of Foreign Affairs' website at Ⓦ www.mfa.go.th/embassy/.

Australia Optus Gate, 10 Moore St, Canberra ACT 2600 ☎02/6273 1141. Also consulates in Adelaide, Brisbane, Melbourne, Perth and Sydney.

Canada 180 Island Park Drive, Ottawa, Ontario K1Y 0A2 ☎613/722 4444, ⓦwww.magma.ca/~thaiott; plus consulates in Vancouver, Montréal, Calgary and Toronto.

Laos Embassy Consular Section, The Regent Centre, Route Luangprabang, Vientiane ☎021/217157–8.

Malaysia 206 Jalan Ampang, 50450 Kuala Lumpur ☎03/2148 8222; plus consulates in Kota Bharu and Penang.

New Zealand 2 Cook St, PO Box 17-226, Karori, Wellington ☎04/476 8618–19.

UK 29 Queens Gate, London SW7 5JB ☎0891/600150 or 020/7589 2944; plus consulates in Birmingham, Cardiff, Glasgow, Hull and Liverpool.

US 1024 Wisconsin Ave, NW, Suite 401, Washington, DC 20007 ☎202/944-3600 or 3608, ⓦwww.thaiembdc.org; plus consulates in Chicago, New York and Los Angeles.

RED TAPE AND VISAS

Health

Thailand's climate, wildlife and cuisine present Western travellers with fewer health worries than in many Asian destinations. Bangkok pharmacies (*raan khai yaa*; typically open daily 8.30am–8pm) are run by highly trained English-speaking pharmacists and are well stocked with local and international branded medicines. Hospital (*rong phayaabahn*) cleanliness and efficiency vary, but generally hygiene and health-care standards are good, and doctors usually speak English. In the event of a major health crisis, get someone to contact your embassy (see p.24) or insurance company – it may be best to get yourself flown home.

INOCULATIONS

There are no compulsory **inoculation** requirements for people travelling to Thailand from the West, but it makes sense to ensure your polio and tetanus boosters are up to date (they last ten years); most doctors also strongly advise vaccinations against typhoid and hepatitis A.

INOCULATION CENTRES AND INFORMATION

UK and Ireland

British Airways Travel Clinics
Call ☎ 01276/685040 or check ⓦ www.britishairways.com for locations in the UK.

Hospital for Tropical Diseases Travel Clinic, London
☎ 020/7388 9600. Recorded Health Line ☎ 09061/337733.

MASTA (Medical Advisory Service for Travellers Abroad, www.masta.org). Call their pre-recorded 24hr Travellers' Health Line (in the UK ☏ 0906/822 4100; in Ireland ☏ 1560/147000) to request printed health information tailored to your journey.

Travel Health Centre, Royal College of Surgeons in Ireland ☏ 01/402 2337.

USA

Travelers Medical Center, New York ☏ 212/982-1600.

Australia and New Zealand

Travellers' Medical and Vaccination Centres
www.tmvc.com.au. In Australia: Melbourne ☏ 03/9602 5788; Sydney ☏ 02/9221 7133 and branches in many other cities. In New Zealand: Auckland ☏ 09/373 3531; Christchurch ☏ 03/379 4000; Wellington ☏ 04/473 0991.

MOSQUITO-BORNE DISEASES

Only certain regions of Thailand are now considered malarial, and **Bangkok is malaria-free**, so if you are restricting yourself to the capital you do not have to take malaria prophylactics. If you're going to other parts of the country, check with official sources first. Bangkok does however have its fair share of **mosquitoes**; though nearly all the city's hotels and guest houses have screened windows, you will probably want to take mosquito repellent with you (or buy it there from any supermarket or pharmacy).

A further reason to protect yourself from mosquitoes is the (remote) possibility of contracting **dengue fever**, a viral disease spread, unlike malaria, by mosquitoes that bite during daylight hours. There's no inoculation against it, though it's rarely fatal; symptoms usually develop between five and eight days after being bitten and include fever, a rash, headaches, and severe joint pain. There are occasional outbreaks of dengue fever in Bangkok, particularly during and just after the rainy season; the only treatment is bed rest, liquids and non-aspirin-based painkillers, though more serious cases may require hospitalization.

DIGESTIVE PROBLEMS

Digestive troubles are often caused by contaminated food and water, or sometimes just by an overdose of unfamiliar foodstuffs. Break your system in gently by avoiding excessively spicy curries and too much raw fruit in the first few days, and then use your common sense about choosing where and what to eat: any crowded restaurant or popular noodle stall should be perfectly safe. Stick to **bottled water**, which is sold everywhere, or else opt for boiled water or tea.

Stomach trouble usually manifests itself as diarrhoea, which is best combated by drinking lots of fluids. If this doesn't work, you're in danger of getting **dehydrated** and should take some kind of rehydration solution, either a commercial sachet sold in all Thai pharmacies or a do-it-yourself version which can be made by adding a handful of sugar and a pinch of salt to every litre of boiled or bottled water (soft drinks are *not* a viable alternative).

OTHER DISEASES

Between four and seven percent of dogs in Bangkok are reported to be rabid, so steer clear of them whenever possible as **rabies** is transmitted by bites and scratches; cats and monkeys also carry rabies. If you are bitten or scratched, clean and disinfect the wound, preferably with alcohol, and seek medical advice right away.

AIDS is spreading fast in Thailand, primarily because of the widespread sex trade (see p.141). Condoms (*meechai*) are

HEALTH

sold in pharmacies, department stores, hairdressers, even on street markets. Due to rigorous screening methods, the country's **medical blood supply** is now considered safe.

HOSPITALS AND CLINICS IN BANGKOK

If you haven't picked up vaccinations in your home country, or if you need contraceptives or family planning advice, contact the Australian-run **Travmin Bangkok Medical Centre**, 8th Floor, Alma Link Building, next to Central Department Store at 25 Soi Chitlom, Thanon Ploenchit (☎ 655 1024–5); there's a general clinic here, too. Most expats rate the private **Bumrungrad Hospital** at 33 Soi 3, Thanon Sukhumvit (☎ 253 0250) as the best and most comfortable in the city. Other recommended hospitals and clinics include:

Bangkok Adventist Hospital (aka Mission Hospital), 430 Thanon Phitsanulok ☎ 281 1422.

Bangkok Christian Hospital, 124 Thanon Silom ☎ 233 6981–9.

Bangkok Nursing Home Hospital (BNH), 9 Thanon Convent ☎ 632 0550.

Dental Polyclinic, 211–13 Thanon Phetchaburi Mai ☎ 314 5070.

Pirom Pesuj Eye Hospital, 117/1 Thanon Phrayathai ☎ 252 4141.

Samitivej Sukhumvit Hospital, 133 Soi 49, Thanon Sukhumvit ☎ 392 0011–19.

HEALTH

Money, banks and costs

Thailand's unit of currency is the baht (abbreviated to "B"), which is divided into 100 satang. Notes come in B10, B20, B50, B100, B500 and B1000 denominations, and coins in 25 satang, 50 satang, B1, B5 and B10 denominations. At the time of writing the exchange rate was averaging B45 to US$1 and B64 to £1.

The Bangkok Bank's online currency converter
Ⓦ bbl.co.th/bankrates/fx_rates_curr.htm tells you
the day's rate in Thailand for 23 major currencies
against the Thai baht.

Banking hours are Monday to Friday 8.30am–3.30pm, but exchange kiosks in the main tourist centres are always open till at least 5pm, sometimes 10pm. Upmarket hotels will change money 24 hours a day; the **Don Muang airport exchange counters** also operate 24 hours.

MONEY, BANKS AND COSTS

TRAVELLER'S CHEQUES, DEBIT AND CREDIT CARDS

Sterling and dollar **traveller's cheques** are accepted at banks, exchange booths and many upmarket hotels across the city; generally, a total of B13 in commission and duty is charged per cheque. All issuers give you a list of numbers to call in the case of **lost or stolen cheques** and will issue replacements, usually within 24 hours, if you can produce the original receipts and a note of your cheque numbers.

American Express, Visa, MasterCard and Diners Club **credit cards** and Visa and MasterCard/Cirrus **debit cards** are accepted at top hotels as well as in some posh restaurants, department stores, tourist shops and travel agents, but surcharging of up to five percent is rife, and theft and forgery are major industries – always demand the carbon copies, and never leave cards in baggage storage. If you have a PIN for your card, you should also be able to **withdraw cash** from the city's numerous 24-hour ATMs ("automatic teller machines" or cashpoints). Almost every branch of the Bangkok Bank, Bank of Ayudhya, Siam Commercial and Thai Farmers Bank has ATMs that accept Visa cards, MasterCard and cards on the Cirrus network. There's usually a handling fee of 1.5 percent on every withdrawal.

COSTS

In a country where the daily minimum wage is under B165 a day, it's hardly surprising that Western tourists find Bangkok an extremely inexpensive place to visit. At the bottom of the scale, you could manage on a **daily budget** of about B400 (£7/US$10) if you're willing to opt for basic accommodation and eat, drink and travel as the locals do. With extras like air conditioning, taxis, and a meal and a couple of beers in a more touristy restaurant, a day's outlay would look more like B600–800 (£11–14/US$15–20). Staying in comfortable, upmarket hotels and eating in the more exclusive restaurants, you should be able to live extremely well for around B2000 a day (£35/US$50).

Because of severe currency fluctuations in the late 1990s, some tourist-oriented businesses now quote their prices in US dollars, particularly luxury hotels.

Bargaining is expected practice for a lot of commercial transactions, particularly at markets and when hiring tuk-tuks and taxis. It's a delicate art that requires humour, tact, patience – and practice. If your price is way out of line, the vendor's vehement refusal should be enough to make you increase your offer.

Opening hours and festivals

Most shops open at least Monday to Saturday from about 8am to 8pm, and department stores operate daily from around 10am to 9pm. Usual office hours are Monday to Friday 8am–5pm and Saturday 8am–noon, though at tourist-oriented businesses in the city centre these hours are longer, with no break at weekends. Government offices work Monday to Friday 8.30am–noon and 1–4.30pm.

Nearly all Thai **festivals** have some kind of religious aspect. The most theatrical are generally Brahmanic (Hindu) in origin, honouring elemental spirits with ancient rites and ceremonial parades. Buddhist celebrations usually revolve round the local temple (wat) and a light-hearted atmosphere prevails, as the wat grounds are swamped with food- and trinket-vendors and makeshift stages are set up to show *likay* folk theatre. Few of the **dates** for religious festivals are fixed (see p.33), so check with TAT for specifics.

Thais use both the Western Gregorian calendar and a Buddhist calendar – the Buddha is said to have died in the year 543 BC, so Thai dates start from that point: thus 2004 AD becomes 2547 BE (Buddhist Era).

NATIONAL HOLIDAYS AND FESTIVALS

Festivals marked with an asterisk are national holidays, when banks and offices close for the duration.

* **January 1** Western New Year's Day.
* **February Full Moon Day** Maha Puja: A day of merit-making marks the occasion when 1250 disciples gathered spontaneously to hear the Buddha preach. Best experienced at Wat Benjamabophit, where the festival culminates with a candlelit procession round the temple.
* **Late February to mid-April** Frequent kite fights and kite-flying contests in Sanam Luang. Kites are judged both for their beauty, and for their fighting prowess as one team tries to ensnare the other team's kite in mid-air.
* **April 6** Chakri Day. The founding of the Chakri dynasty.

* **April, usually 13–15** Songkhran, Thai New Year: The most exuberant of the national festivals welcomes the Thai New Year with massive public waterfights in the streets of the capital (and across the country), and big parades.
* **May 5** Coronation Day.
* **Early May** Raek Na, Royal Ploughing Ceremony: The royal ploughing ceremony marks the beginning of the rice-planting season. Ceremonially clad Brahmin priests parade sacred oxen and the royal plough across Sanam Luang and forecast the year's rice yield.
* **May Full Moon Day** Visakha Puja. The holiest day of the Buddhist year, commemorating the birth,

enlightenment and death of the Buddha all in one go. The most public and photogenic part is the candlelit evening procession around Wat Benjamabophit.

* **July Full Moon Day** Asanha Puja: Commemorates the Buddha's first sermon.

* **July, the day after Asanha Puja** Khao Pansa: The start of the annual three-month Buddhist rains retreat, when new monks are ordained.

* **August 12** Queen's birthday.

* **October 23** Chulalongkorn Day. The anniversary of Rama V's death.

October Full Moon Day Tak Bat Devo: Devotees at temples across the city make offerings to monks and there's general merrymaking to celebrate the end of the Buddhist retreat period.

Late October or early November Loy Krathong: One of Thailand's most picturesque festivals, when banana-leaf baskets of flowers and lighted candles are floated on khlongs, ponds and rivers all over Thailand to honour water spirits and celebrate the end of the rainy season.

First week of November Ngan Wat Saket: Probably Thailand's biggest temple fair, held around Wat Saket (see p.102) and the Golden Mount, with all the usual festival trappings.

* **December 5** King's birthday.

* **December 10** Constitution Day.

* **December 31** Western New Year's Eve.

Cultural hints

—————————

Tourist literature has so successfully marketed Thailand as the "Land of Smiles" that a lot of foreigners arrive in the country expecting to be forgiven any outrageous behaviour. This is just not the case: there are some things so universally sacred in Thailand that even a hint of disrespect will cause deep offence.

THE MONARCHY

The worst thing you can possibly do is to bad-mouth the **royal family**. The monarchy might be a constitutional one, but almost every household displays a picture of King Bhumibol and Queen Sirikit, and respectful crowds mass whenever either of them makes a public appearance. You should also be prepared to stand when the **king's anthem** is played at the beginning of every cinema programme. A less obvious point: as the king's head features on all Thai currency, you should never step on a coin or banknote, which is tantamount to kicking the king in the face.

RELIGION

Buddhism plays an essential part in the lives of most Thais, and Buddhist monuments should be treated accordingly –

which basically means wearing long trousers or knee-length skirts, covering your upper arms, and removing your shoes whenever you visit one. All **Buddha images** are sacred and should never be clambered over or treated in any manner that could be construed as disrespectful.

Monks come only just beneath the monarchy in the social hierarchy, and are treated with deference. Theoretically, monks are forbidden to have any close contact with **women**, which means, if you're female, you mustn't sit or stand next to a monk, or even brush against his robes; if it's essential to pass him something, put the object down so that he can then pick it up – never hand it over directly. **Nuns**, however, get treated like women rather than like monks.

THE BODY

The Western liberalism embraced by the Thai sex industry is very unrepresentative of the majority Thai attitude to the body. **Clothing** – or the lack of it – is what bothers Thais most about tourist behaviour. You should dress modestly in all public places (see above) and, stuffy and sweaty as it sounds, keep shorts and vests for the beach.

According to ancient religious belief, the head is the most sacred part of the **body** and the feet the most unclean. This means that it's very rude to touch a Thai person's head or to point your feet either at a human being or at a sacred image – when sitting on a temple floor, for example, you should tuck your legs beneath you rather than stretch them out towards the Buddha.

On a more practical note, the **left hand** is used for washing after defecating, so Thais never use it to put food in their mouth, pass things or shake hands – as a foreigner though, you'll be assumed to have different customs, so left-handers shouldn't worry unduly.

SOCIAL CONVENTIONS

In fact, Thais very rarely shake hands anyway, using the **wai** to greet and say goodbye and to acknowledge respect, gratitude or apology. A prayer-like gesture made with raised hands, the wai changes according to the relative status of the two people involved: Thais can instantaneously assess which wai to use when, but as a foreigner your safest bet is to go for the "stranger's" wai, which requires that your hands be raised close to your chest and your fingertips placed just below your chin. If someone makes a wai at you, you should definitely wai back, but it's generally wise not to initiate.

Public displays of **physical affection** in Thailand are much more acceptable between friends of the same sex than between lovers, whether hetero- or homosexual. Holding hands and hugging is as common among male friends as with females, so if you're given fairly intimate caresses by a Thai acquaintance of the same sex, don't assume you're being propositioned.

THE GUIDE

THE GUIDE

Introducing the city

Bangkok can be a tricky place to get your bearings as it's huge and ridiculously congested, with largely featureless modern buildings and no obvious centre. The boldest line on the map is the Chao Phraya River, which divides the city into Bangkok proper on the east bank, and Thonburi, part of Greater Bangkok, on the west.

The historical core and site of the original royal palace is **Ratanakosin**, which nestles into a bend in the river. The city's most important and extravagant sights are found here, and this is the place to start your tour of the capital. Three concentric canals radiate eastwards around Ratanakosin: the southern part of the area between the canals is the vibrant, old-style trading enclave of **Chinatown** and Indian **Pahurat**, linked to the old palace by Thanon Charoen Krung (aka New Road); the northern part is characterized by quirky religious architecture and the **Democracy Monument**, west of which is the backpackers' ghetto of **Banglamphu**. Beyond the canals to the north, the modern-day royal district of **Dusit** is quieter and more European in ambience; it's the site of many government buildings and the nineteenth-century palace, which is connected to Ratanakosin by the two stately avenues, Thanon Rajdamnoen Nok and Thanon Rajdamnoen Klang.

BANGKOK ADDRESSES

Thai addresses can be confusing as property is often numbered twice, firstly to show which real-estate lot it stands in, and then to distinguish where it is on that lot. Thus 154/7–10 Thanon Rajdamnoen means the building is on lot 154 and occupies numbers 7–10.

A minor road running off a major road is often numbered as a soi ("lane" or "alley", though it may be a sizeable thoroughfare), rather than given its own street name. Thanon Sukhumvit, for example, has minor roads numbered Soi 1 to Soi 103, with odd numbers on one side of the road and even on the other; so a Thanon Sukhumvit address could read something like 27/9–11 Soi 15, Thanon Sukhumvit, which would mean the property occupies numbers 9–11 on lot 27 on minor road number 15 running off Thanon Sukhumvit.

The modern high-rise jungle that is "New", **downtown** Bangkok begins to the east of the canals and beyond the main rail line, and stretches as far as the eye can see to the east and north. It's here that you'll find the best **shops**, **bars**, **restaurants** and **nightlife**, as well as a couple of worthwhile sights. The main business district and most of the embassies are south of **Thanon Rama IV**, with the port of Khlong Toey at the southern edge. The diverse area north of Thanon Rama IV includes the sprawling campus of Chulalongkorn University, huge shopping centres around **Siam Square** and a variety of other businesses. A couple of blocks northeast of Siam Square stands the tallest building in Bangkok, the 84-storeyed *Baiyoke Sky Hotel*, whose golden spire makes a good point of reference. To the east stand the skyscraper office blocks and fashionable residences of **Thanon Sukhumvit**.

Very little of old Bangkok remains, but the back canals of **Thonburi**, a couple of minutes' boat ride across the river from Ratanakosin and Chinatown, retain a traditional feel quite at odds with the modern metropolis.

Greater Bangkok now covers an area some 30km in diameter and though unsightly urban development predominates, an expedition to the **outskirts** is made worthwhile by **Chatuchak**, the city's largest market, a couple of interesting outdoor museums, and the chance to visit the varied suburbs of **Nonthaburi** and **Ko Kred** upriver.

The telephone code for Bangkok is ☎02. Thai area codes must be dialled, even to call a number within the same area. Calling Bangkok from abroad, dial your international access number, followed by ☎66-2, then the subscriber's number.

Arrival

Getting to your guest house or hotel on arrival in gridlocked Bangkok is unlikely to put you in a good mood, and unless you arrive by train, you should be prepared for a long slog into the centre. For most travellers, however, their first sight of the city is Don Muang Airport, 25km to the north.

BY AIR

Once you're through immigration at either of **Don Muang Airport's** two international terminals – queues are often horrendous, owing to the availability of free shortstay visas on the spot – you'll find 24-hour exchange booths, a couple of helpful TAT information desks (daily 8am–midnight; ☎523 8972), post offices and international telephone facilities, a pricey left-luggage depot (B70 per item per day), an emergency clinic and, on the fourth floor of the newer Terminal 2 opposite *Pizza Hut*, an expensive cybercafé. Among a wide variety of food and drink outlets – particularly in Terminal 2, which boasts Chinese and Japanese restaurants, and a British pub that offers 24-hour breakfasts – the cheapest and most interesting options are two food centres serving simple Thai dishes, one on the south side of Terminal 2 on the walkway to the domestic terminal, the other on the fourth floor, accessible from Terminals 1 and 2.

Note that you'll have problems checking in at some of the smaller, more budget-orientated guest houses after 10pm (nightwatchmen aren't usually authorized to admit new arrivals), so if you're arriving after about 8pm, either make straight for the backpackers' district of Banglamphu and hope to get lucky, or stay near the airport (see below), or else resign yourself to shelling out for a pricey down-town hotel room for your first night: a round-the-clock Thai Hotels Association **accommodation desk**, with prices generally cheaper than rack rates, can help with bookings.

Airport accommodation

If you've got time to kill and money to spare between flights, you can rest and clean up at the *Amari Airport Hotel* (☏566 1020, 🖷566 1941, 🅦www.amari.com; ➒), just across the road from the international terminal, which rents out very upmarket **bedrooms** for three-hour periods from 8am to 6pm ($20, no reservations) – far better than the international terminals' day rooms, which are twice the price and designed for transit passengers. If you need to stay near the airports and can't afford the *Amari*'s regular overnight rates, the *Comfort Inn* is a more economical choice (☏552 8929, 🖷552 8920, 🅔pinap@loxinfo.co.th; ➑) and will pick you up for the five-minute journey from the terminals if you call. Another good option is the huge *Asia Airport Hotel*, less than ten minutes' drive north of the international terminal, just south of the Rangsit interchange on Thanon Phaholyothin (℡992 6653, ℻992 6828; ⓦwww.asiahotel.co.th; ❼). All rooms here are air-conditioned and comfortably furnished, there's a hotel restaurant, a swimming pool and a shopping complex, and free transport to and from the airport; book over the internet for significant discounts. Cheaper still is the *We-Train* guest house, about 3km west of the airport (℡929 2301–10, ℻929 2300, ⓦwww.wetrain.linethai.co.th), run by the Association for the Promotion of the Status of Women, where proceeds go to help distressed women and children; in a peaceful lakeside setting, there are dorms (B140), comfortable fan or aircon rooms (❹) and a swimming pool.

The domestic terminal at Don Muang is 500m away from Terminal 2, connected by an air-conditioned covered walkway and by a free shuttle bus (daily 5am–midnight; every 15min).

Getting into town from the airport

The most economical way of getting into the city is by **public bus**, but this can be excruciatingly slow and the invariably crowded vehicles are totally unsuitable for heavily laden travellers. The bus stop is on the main highway which runs north–south just outside the airport buildings: to find it, head straight out from the northern end of arrivals. Most of the buses run all day and night, with a reduced service after 10pm; see the box on pp.56–58 for a rough sketch of the most useful routes – the TAT office in arrivals has further details.

Unless you're already counting your baht, you're better off getting into the city by air-con **airport bus**. Four routes are covered, each with a departure every half-hour between about 4.30am and half past midnight from outside Terminal 1, Terminal 2 and the domestic terminal (clearly signposted outside each building); the set fare of B100 is paid on the bus. Route AB1 runs along to the west end of Thanon Silom, via Pratunam and Thanon Rajdamri; route AB2 goes to Sanam Luang, via Victory Monument, Democracy Monument, Thanon Tanao (for Thanon Khao San), Thanon Phra Sumen and Thanon Phra Athit; route AB3 runs down the Dindaeng Expressway and along Thanon Sukhumvit to Soi Thonglor via the Eastern Bus Terminal; and route AB4 runs down the Dindaeng Expressway and west along Thanon Ploenchit to Siam Square, then down to Hualamphong train station. A handy colour leaflet available from the TAT desks details which major hotels each route passes.

The **train** to Hualamphong station is the quickest way into town, and ideal if you want to stay in Chinatown, but services are irregular. To reach the station at Don Muang follow the signs from arrivals in Terminal 1 (if in doubt head towards the big *Amari Airport Hotel*, across the main highway, carry on through the hotel foyer and the station is in front of you). Over thirty trains a day make the fifty-minute trip to Hualamphong, with fares starting from B5 in third class (though express trains command surcharges of up to B80), but they're not evenly spaced, with concentrations around the early morning – at other times of the day you might have to wait over an hour.

Taxis to the centre are comfortable, air-conditioned and not too extravagantly priced, although the driving can be hairy. A wide variety is on offer, from pricey limousines, through licensed metered cabs, down to cheap unlicensed and unmetered vehicles – avoid the last-mentioned, as newly arrived travellers are seen as easy victims for robbery, and the cabs are untraceable. Metered taxis, the best option, are operated from counters that are signposted clearly outside Terminal 1. Even including the B50 airport pick-up fee and B70 tolls for the overhead expressways, a journey to Thanon Ploenchit downtown, for example, should set you back around B250, depending on the traffic.

BY TRAIN

Travelling to Bangkok by **train** from Malaysia and most parts of Thailand, you arrive at **Hualamphong Station**, which is centrally located and served by numerous **city buses**. The most useful of these are bus #53 (non-air-con), which stops on the east side (left-hand exit) of the station and runs to the budget accommodation in Banglamphu; and the #25 and #40 (both non-air-con), which run east to Siam Square (for Skytrain connections) and along Thanon Sukhumvit to the Eastern Bus Terminal; the westbound #25 runs to Tha Thien (for the Grand Palace), while the westbound #40 heads over the river to the Southern Bus Terminal. For bus route details, see pp.56–58.

Station **facilities** include a post office, an exchange booth and a Cirrus/MasterCard cashpoint machine (to get to the nearest Visa ATM walk 100m left along Thanon Rama IV to the bank next to *You Sue Vegetarian Restaurant*). There are two **left-luggage** offices at Hualamphong station. The more secure but pricier option is inside the postal service centre at the main entrance (Mon–Fri & Sun 7am–7pm, Sat 8am–4pm; B30 per day). Alternative storage is available at a cabin halfway down Platform 12 (daily 4am–10.30pm; B10 per day for 1–5 days, B15 per day for more than 5 days), next to the Eastern and Oriental check-in counter, but it's not fully enclosed and so doesn't look as secure as the other place.

Anyone who comes up to you on or around Hualamphong's
station concourse and offers help/information/transport or
ticket-booking services is almost certainly a con-artist,
however many official-looking ID tags are hanging around
their necks. This is a well-established scam to fleece new
arrivals; avoid them at all costs.

The efficient VC Travel and Tour **travel agent** and
accommodation-booking service (daily 5am–8pm;
☎613 6725) on the mezzanine floor above *Coffee Bucks* is
the best place to buy onward rail tickets (no commission) as
well as domestic and international flights; they can also
arrange discounted accommodation at many hotels (**❹** and
up) in Bangkok and other major tourist destinations around
the country.

BY BUS

Long-distance **buses** to Bangkok come to a halt at a number of far-flung spots. All services from the north and
northeast terminate at the **Northern Bus Terminal** (**Mo
Chit**) on Thanon Kamphaeng Phet 2, as do a few east-
coast buses from Chanthaburi and Trat (near the
Cambodian border). The quickest way into the city centre
from Mo Chit is by **Skytrain** (see p.62) from the Mo Chit
BTS station, five minutes' walk from the bus terminal on
Thanon Phaholyothin. Otherwise, it's a long bus or taxi
ride into town: **city buses** from the Mo Chit area include
#2 and #77 to Thanon Silom; air-con and ordinary #3,
and air-con #9, #12 and #32 to Banglamphu; and both
air-con and ordinary #29 to Hualamphong Railway
Station; for details see pp.56-58.

Bus services from Malaysia and the south, as well as from
Kanchanaburi, use the **Southern Bus Terminal** (**Sai Tai**

Mai) at the junction of Thanon Borom Ratchonni and the Nakhon Chaisri Highway, west of the Chao Phraya River in Thonburi. Numerous **city buses** run across the river, including air-con #7 to Banglamphu and Hualamphong Station, and air-con #11 to Banglamphu and Thanon Sukhumvit (see pp.56–57 for routes). City buses are especially useful here as the Southern Bus Terminal is renowned for its belligerent **taxi** drivers, nearly all of whom refuse to use the meter and quote anything from B250 to B650 for the trip into central Bangkok.

Most buses from the east coast (for the Cambodian border) use the **Eastern Bus Terminal** (**Ekamai**) at Soi 40, Thanon Sukhumvit. Right beside the Ekamai **Skytrain** stop (see p.62), the bus station is also served by lots of **city buses**, including air-con #11 to Banglamphu and non-air-con #59 to the Northern Bus Terminal (see pp.56–58 for details), or you can take a taxi down Soi 63 to Tha Ekamai, a pier on Khlong Sen Seb, to pick up the **canal boat service** to the Golden Mount near Banglamphu (see p.60).

Information and maps

The **Bangkok Tourist Bureau** (BTB) provides excellent information for tourists on all budgets both from its headquarters, the **Bangkok Information Centre**, located next to Phra Pinklao Bridge at 17/1 Thanon Phra Athit in Banglamphu (daily 9am–7pm; ☏225 7612–4), and from its dozen strategically placed information booths around the capital. They all provide reasonable city maps for free, and also run a variety of interesting city tours by boat, bus and bicycle (see p.55). The city's branches of the nationwide

BANGKOK ON THE INTERNET

General resources

Accommodating Asia: Thailand ⓦwww.accomasia.com/thailand.htm. Features a particularly good "Travellers' Notes" section, with links to the diaries, travelogues and homepages of recent travellers to Thailand.

Bangkok Post ⓦwww.bangkokpost.net.
The day's main stories from Thailand's leading English-language daily, plus archive headlines for the last two months, and travel stories.

René Hasekamp's Homepage ⓦwww.hasekamp.demon.nl/thaiindex.htm. Practical tips for travellers to Thailand, plus info on selected sights and a handy list of FAQs.

Siam Net ⓦwww.siam.net/guide.
Decent jumping-off point, with general background on Thailand and its main tourist centres, plus hotel bookings services and useful information on visas, prices etc.

Thai Focus ⓦwww.thaifocus.com.
Wide-ranging portal site, offering hotel-booking service, domestic and international air tickets, car rental, plus a basic introduction to Thailand's main destinations.

Tourism Authority of Thailand (TAT) ⓦwww.tat.or.th.
The official TAT site has general background on Thailand, plus links to accommodation and other standard stuff.

Tourism Authority of Thailand, London
ⓦwww.thaismile.co.uk. The official website for the London TAT office offers special deals on flights to Thailand, has a page for tourist tips, a travellers' bulletin board and an innovative section on Thai culture in the UK.

Travellers' resources and bulletin boards

Internet Travel Information Service Ⓦwww.itisnet.com.
Specifically aimed at budget travellers, this fairly new site includes weekly reports from the road, so there's heaps of up-to-the-minute info on things like current airfares and visa requirements.

Journeywoman Ⓦwww.journeywoman.com.
Highly recommended site for women travellers. Highlights include travelogues, advice for solo travellers, and "What Should I Wear?", which features first-hand tips on acceptable dress in over a hundred different countries,.

Lonely Planet Thorn Tree Ⓦthorntree.lonelyplanet.com.
Recommended and popular travellers' forums, divided into regions (eg Mainland Southeast Asia) and topics (Travelling with Kids).

Rough Guides Ⓦwww.roughguides.com.
Regularly updated travel site, with forums, features plus online travel guides.

Thailand Tips Ⓦwww.thailandtips.com.
Thailand-specific forum for travellers' queries and advice about everything from elephants to the best airport hotel.

Bangkok listings

Bangkok Metro Ⓦbkkmetro.com.
The online version of Bangkok's monthly listings magazine includes archives of features, plus exhaustive coverage of restaurants, shops and clubs.

Groovy Map Ⓦwww.groovymap.com.
Lively site from the company who publish wacky, annotated maps of Bangkok, with top-ten lists of things to do by day and night in the city, plus a what's on calendar.

INFORMATION AND MAPS

Tourism Authority of Thailand (TAT) can also be useful: as well as the booth in the airport arrivals concourse, TAT maintains a Tourist Service Centre within walking distance of Banglamphu, at 4 Thanon Rajdamnoen Nok (daily 8.30am–4.30pm; ☎282 9773–4; 24hr freephone tourist assistance ☎1155), a twenty-minute stroll from Thanon Khao San, or accessible by air-con buses #3 and #9. Other useful sources of information, especially about what to avoid, are the travellers' **noticeboards** in many of the Banglamphu guest houses.

If you're staying in Bangkok for more than a couple of days, it's well worth getting hold of *Metro*, a monthly **listings magazine** available in bookstores, hotel shops and 7-11 shops. For B100, you get a mixed bag of lively articles and especially useful sections on restaurants, cinemas, nightlife and gay life. The two English-language dailies, the *Nation* and the *Bangkok Post*, also give limited information about what's on across the city and carry details of cinema showings. Thailand is well represented on the internet, and some of the most useful **websites** are listed in the box on pp.50–51.

Maps

To get around Bangkok without spending much money, you'll need to buy a **bus map**. Of the several available at bookshops, hotels and some guest houses, the most useful is Bangkok Guide's *Bus Routes & Map*, which not only maps all major air-conditioned and non-air-conditioned bus routes but also carries detailed written itineraries of some two hundred bus routes on its flip-side. If you can't find a copy, opt for the long-running bright blue and yellow bus map published by Tour 'n' Guide, which maps bus routes as well as the names of dozens of smaller sois; its street locations are not always reliable however, and exact routings can be hard to decipher. *Litehart's Groovy Map and Guide* colour-codes its bus routes for ease of use, but only gives selected routes; they also publish a *Bangkok By Night* map, which highlights their recommended bars, restaurants and clubs. The most accurate map for locating small streets and places of interest in the city is *GeoCenter's Bangkok 1:15,000*, best bought before you leave home, though it's also available in some Bangkok bookshops. Serious shoppers might also want to buy a copy of *Nancy Chandler's* idiosyncratic map of Bangkok, which has lots of annotated recommendations on shops and markets across the city; it's available in most tourist areas.

City transport

There can be few cities in the world where **transport** is such a headache as it is in Bangkok. Bumper-to-bumper vehicles create fumes so bad that some days the city's carbon monoxide emissions come close to the international danger level, and it's not unusual for residents to spend three hours getting to work – and these are people who know where they're going. However, the opening in December 1999 of the elevated train network called the Bangkok Transit System, or BTS Skytrain, has radically improved public transport in a few parts of the city, notably the Siam Square, Silom and Sukhumvit areas. Unfortunately for tourists, the Skytrain system does not stretch as far as Ratanakosin or Banglamphu, where boats still provide the fastest means of hopping from one sight to another.

For each sight in the city, we've given numbers of the most useful buses that run past, or at least within a fifteen-minute walk, and details of nearby Skytrain stations and boat transport, if any. The routes of all the bus numbers mentioned in the box on pp.56–58, but for the full, highly complex, picture you'll need to get hold of a bus map (see pp.52–53), or log on to the Bangkok Mass Transportation website at wwww.bmta.motc.go.th, which also gives details on every city bus route in English.

The main form of transport in the city are **buses**, and once you've mastered the labyrinthine complexity of the route map you'll be able to get to any part of the city, albeit slowly. Catching the various kinds of **taxi** can make a serious dent in your budget, and you'll still get held up by the daytime traffic jams. **Boats** are obviously more limited in their range, but they're regular and as cheap as buses, and you'll save a lot of time by using them whenever possible – a journey between Banglamphu and the GPO, for instance, will take around thirty minutes by water, half what it would take on land. The **Skytrain** has a similarly limited range but is also worth using whenever suitable for all or part of your journey; its network coincides with the Chao Phraya River express boats at the vital hub of Sathorn Bridge (Saphan Taksin). **Walking** might often be quicker than travelling by road, but the heat can be unbearable, distances are always further than they look on the map, and the engine fumes are stifling. **Renting a car** is possible (see p.249), but is best kept for out-of-town trips – city traffic jams are just too much to cope with, and parking is impossible. As there are some novel rules of the road, it would be better to get a car with driver from a travel agent or hotel for about B1000 a day.

BUSES

Bangkok has three types of bus service, and it's not uncommon for one route to be served by the full trio. **Ordinary** (non-air-conditioned) buses come in a variety of colours and sizes, and fares for most journeys range from B3.5 to B5, payable to a conductor; most routes maintain a 24-hour service. **Air-conditioned** buses (denoted **AC** in this book, and also staffed with conductors) subdivide into three varieties: blue (B6–18 according to distance travelled) and orange (B8–20) public buses, and smaller blue private buses (B8–20); most stop at around 10pm, but some of the more popular services run all night. As buses can only go as fast as the car in front (averaging 4kph at the moment), you'll probably be spending a long time on each journey, so you'd be well advised to pay the extra for cool air – and the air-conditioned buses are usually less crowded, too. It's also possible during the day to travel certain routes on flashy, air-conditioned private **microbuses**, which were designed with the commuter in mind and offer the use of an on-board telephone and newspapers, plus the certainty of a seat (no standing allowed) for a B25 fare (exact money only), which is dropped into a box beside the driver's seat.

The open-topped, double-decker Bangkok Sightseeing Bus does a ninety-minute guided tour of Ratanakosin, taking in the Grand Palace and Vimanmek (5 daily, B200; contact the Bangkok Tourist Bureau for details). The BTB also run several quite unusual tours of the capital, including a night-time bicycle tour of Ratanakosin (every Sat 7–9.30pm; B290 including bicycle), and a highly recommended 35-kilometre ride along the canal towpaths of Thonburi (see p.117).

USEFUL BUS ROUTES

Because of various one-way systems and other idiosyncrasies, some of the following bus routes may not be exactly the same in reverse. Check official bus maps to be sure.

#2 (AC): *Oriental Hotel*–Thanon Silom–Thanon Rama IV–MBK department store (for Siam Square)–Thanon Phayathai–Chatuchak Weekend Market–Lard Phrao–Suwinthawong.

#3 (ordinary): Northern Bus Terminal–Chatuchak Weekend market–Thanon Phaholyothin–Thanon Samsen–Thanon Phra Athit (for Banglamphu guest houses)–Thanon Sanam Chai–Thanon Triphet–Memorial Bridge (for Pak Khlong Talat)–Taksin Monument–Wat Suwan.

#3 (AC): Southern Bus Terminal–Thanon Borom Ratchonni–Phra Pinklao Bridge (for Banglamphu guest houses)–Democracy Monument–Rajdamnoen Nok (for TAT and boxing stadium)–Wat Benjamabophit–Thanon Sri Ayutthaya (for Thewes guest houses)–Victory Monument–Chatuchak Weekend Market–Rangsit.

#4 (AC): Airport–Thanon Rajaprarop–Thanon Silom–Thanon Charoen Krung–Thonburi.

#7 (AC): Southern Bus Terminal–Thanon Borom Ratchonni–Phra Pinklao (for Banglamphu guest houses)–Sanam Luang–Thanon Charoen Krung–Thanon Chakrawat–Thanon Yaowarat (for Chinatown and Wat Traimit)–Hualamphong Station–Thanon Rama IV–Bang Na Intersection–Pak Nam (for Ancient City buses).

#8 (AC): Wat Po–Grand Palace–Giant Swing (for Wat Suthat)–Thanon Yaowarat–Siam Square–Thanon Ploenchit–Thanon Sukhumvit–Eastern Bus Terminal–Pak Nam (for Ancient City buses).

#9 (AC): Nonthaburi–Chatuchak Weekend Market–Victory Monument–Thanon Phitsanulok–Democracy Monument–Rajdamnoen Klang (for Banglamphu guest houses)–Phra Pinklao–Thonburi.

#10 (AC): Airport–Chatuchak Weekend Market–Victory Monument–Dusit Zoo–Thanon Rajwithi–Krung Thon Bridge (for Thewes guest houses)–Thonburi.

#11 (AC): Southern Bus Terminal–Thanon Borom Ratchonni–Phra Pinklao–Rajdamnoen Klang (for Banglamphu guest houses)–Democracy Monument–Thanon Sukhumvit–Eastern Bus Terminal–Pak Nam (for Ancient City buses).

#12 (AC): Northern Bus Terminal–Chatuchak Weekend Market–Thanon Phetchaburi–Thanon Larn Luang–Democracy Monument (for Banglamphu guest houses)–Tha Chang–Pak Khlong Talat.

#13 (AC): Airport–Victory Monument–Thanon Rajaprarop–Thanon Sukhumvit–Eastern Bus Terminal–Sukhumvit Soi 62.

#15 (ordinary): Bamrung Muang–Thanon Phra Athit (for Banglamphu guest houses)–Grand Palace–Sanam Luang–Democracy Monument– Phanfa (for Khlong Sen Seb and Golden Mount)–Siam Square–Thanon Rajdamri–Thanon Silom–Thanon Charoen Krung–Krung Thep Bridge–Thanon Rajadapisek.

#16 (ordinary): Thanon Srinarong–Thanon Samsen–Thewes (for guest houses)–Thanon Phitsanulok–Siam Square–Thanon Henri Dunant–GPO–Tha Si Phraya.

#25 (ordinary): Eastern Bus Terminal–Thanon Sukhumvit–Siam Square–Hualamphong Station–Thanon Yaowarat (for Chinatown)–Pahurat–Wat Po and the Grand Palace–Tha Chang.

#29 (AC and ordinary): Airport–Chatuchak Weekend Market–Victory Monument–Siam Square–Hualamphong Station.

USEFUL BUS ROUTES

#32 (AC): Thanon Phra Pinklao–Rajdamnoen Klang (for Thanon Khao San guest houses) – Democracy Monument–Victory monument–Northern Bus Terminal.

#38 (ordinary): Chatuchak Weekend Market–Victory Monument–Thanon Sri Ayutthaya (for Suan Pakkad)–Thanon Phetchaburi–Soi Asoke–Eastern Bus Terminal.

#39 (AC and ordinary): Chatuchak Weekend Market–Victory Monument–Thanon Sri Ayutthaya–Thanon Larn Luang–Democracy Monument–Rajdamnoen Klang (for Thanon Khao San guest houses)–Sanam Luang.

#40 (ordinary): Eastern Bus Terminal–Thanon Sukhumvit–Thanon Rama I (for Siam Square)–Hualamphong Station–Thanon Yaowarat (for Chinatown)–Southern Bus Terminal.

#53 (ordinary): Hualamphong Station–Thanon Krung Kasem–Thanon Samsen and Thanon Phra Athit (for Banglamphu guest houses)–Sanam Luang (for National Museum and Wat Mahathat)–Thanon Mahathat (for Grand Palace and Wat Po)–Pahurat–Thanon Krung Kasem.

#56 (ordinary): Circular route; Phra Sumen–Wat Bowoniwes–Thanon Ratchasima (for Vimanmek Palace)–Thanon Rajwithi–Krung Thon Bridge–Thonburi–Memorial Bridge–Thanon Chakraphet (for Chinatown)–Thanon Mahachai–Democracy Monument–Thanon Tanao (for Khao San guest houses)–Thanon Phra Sumen.

#59 (ordinary): Airport–Chatuchak Weekend Market–Victory Monument–Phanfa (for Khlong Sen Seb and Golden Mount)–Democracy Monument (for Banglamphu guest houses)–Sanam Luang.

#124 and #127 (ordinary): Southern Bus Terminal–Tha Pinklao (for ferry to Phra Athit and Banglamphu guest houses).

USEFUL BUS ROUTES

EXPRESS BOATS

The Chao Phraya Express Boat Company operates the vital **express-boat** (*reua duan*) service, using large water buses to plough up and down the river, between clearly signed piers (*tha*) which appear on all Bangkok maps – the important central stops are outlined in the box on p.60 and marked on map 2. Its usual route, ninety minutes in total, runs between Wat Rajsingkorn, just upriver of Krung Thep Bridge, in the south and Nonthaburi in the north. These **"daily standard"** boats set off every ten to fifteen minutes or so from about 6am to 6.30pm, with the last boat in each direction flying a blue flag. Boats do not necessarily stop at every landing – they'll only pull in if people want to get on or off. And when they do stop, it's not for long – when you want to get off, be ready at the back of the boat in good time for your pier. During rush hours (roughly 6–9am & 4–7pm), certain **"special express"** boats operate limited-stop services on set routes, flying either a **yellow** (Nonthaburi to Rajburana, far downriver beyond Krung Thep Bridge) or a **red and orange flag** (Nonthaburi to Wat Rajsingkorn).

    Tickets can be bought on board, and cost B6–12 according to distance travelled, or B15–25 on yellow-flag boats. Don't discard your ticket until you're off the boat, as the staff at some piers impose a B1 fine on anyone disembarking without one.

CROSS-RIVER FERRIES

Smaller than express boats are the slow **cross-river ferries** (*reua kham fak*), which shuttle back and forth between the same two points. They can be found at every express stop and plenty of other piers in between and are especially useful

CENTRAL EXPRESS-BOAT STOPS

Numbers correspond to those on map 2.

1 Thewes (all daily standard and special express boats) –
  for Thewes guest houses.

2 Banglamphu (daily standard) – for Thanon Khao San and
  Banglamphu guest houses.

3 Phra Pinklao Bridge (all daily standard and special
  express boats) – for Thonburi shops and city buses to the
  Southern Bus Terminal.

4 Bangkok Noi (daily standard) – for trains to Kanchanaburi.

5 Wang Lang (or Prannok; all daily standard and special
  express boats) – for Siriraj Hospital.

6 Chang (daily standard and red and orange flag) – for
  the Grand Palace.

7 Thien (daily standard) – for Wat Po, and the cross-river
  ferry to Wat Arun.

for connections to Chao Phraya special express-boat stops
during rush hours. Fares are B2, which you usually pay at
the entrance to the pier.

LONGTAIL BOATS

Longtail boats (*reua hang yao*) ply the khlongs of
Thonburi like buses, stopping at designated shelters (fares
are in line with those of express boats), and are available
for individual rental here and on the river (see p.116). On
the Bangkok side, **Khlong Sen Seb** is well served by
longtails, which run at least every fifteen minutes during
daylight hours from the Phanfa pier at the Golden Mount

8 Ratchini (aka Rajinee; daily standard).

9 Saphan Phut (Memorial Bridge; daily standard and red and orange flag) – for Pahurat, Pak Khlong Talat (and Wat Prayoon in Thonburi).

10 Rachavongse (aka Rajawong; all daily standard and special express boats) – for Chinatown.

11 Harbour Department (daily standard).

12 Si Phraya (all daily standard and special express boats) – walk north past the *Sheraton Royal Orchid Hotel* for River City shopping complex.

13 Wat Muang Kae (daily standard) – for GPO.

14 Oriental (all daily standard and special express boats) – for Thanon Silom.

15 Sathorn (all daily standard and special express boats) – for Thanon Sathorn.

(handy for Banglamphu, Ratanakosin and Chinatown), and head way out east to Wat Sribunruang, with useful stops at Thanon Phrayathai, aka Saphan Hua Chang (for Jim Thompson's House and Ratchathewi Skytrain stop), Pratunam (for the World Trade Centre and Gaysorn Plaza), Soi Chitlom, Thanon Witthayu (Wireless Rd), and Soi Nana Nua (Soi 3), Soi Asoke (Soi 21), Soi Thonglo (Soi 55) and Soi Ekamai (Soi 63), all off Thanon Sukhumvit. This is your quickest and most interesting way of getting between the west and east parts of town, if you can stand the stench of the canal. You may have trouble actually locating the piers as none are signed in English and they all look very unassuming and

EXPRESS BOATS • LONGTAIL BOATS

rickety; see the map 2 for locations and keep your eyes peeled for a plain wooden jetty – most jetties serve boats running in both directions. Once on the boat, state your destination to the conductor when he collects your fare, which will be between B7 and B15. Due to the recent construction of some low bridges, all passengers change on to a different boat at Pratunam and then again at the stop way out east on Sukhumvit Soi 71 – just follow the crowd.

SKYTRAIN

The long-awaited elevated railway known as the **BTS Skytrain** or *rot fai faa* (ⓦwww.bts.co.th) is now operating in Bangkok, after over thirty years of planning, fudging and building. Although the network – if indeed it can be called that – is limited, it provides a much faster alternative to the bus, it's clean, efficient and vigorously air-conditioned, and – because fares are comparatively high for Bangkokians – rarely crowded. There are only two Skytrain lines, both running every few minutes from 6am to midnight, with **fares** of around B15–45 per trip depending on distance travelled. Currently, the only **passes** available that are likely to appeal to visitors cost B250 for ten trips (B160 for students), B300 for fifteen trips (B210 for students), but watch out for new deals being introduced.

The **Sukhumvit Line** runs from Mo Chit (stop #N8) in the northern part of the city (near Chatuchak Market and the Northern Bus Terminal), south via Victory Monument (N3) to the interchange, **Central Station** (CS), at Siam Square, and then east along Thanon Ploenchit and Thanon Sukhumvit, via the Eastern Bus Terminal (Ekamai; E7), to On Nut (Sukhumvit Soi 77; E9); the whole journey to the eastern end of town from

BTS SKYTRAIN

Sukhumvit Line
Silon Line

Mo Chit (for Chatuchak Market & Northern Bus Terminal) N8
Saphan Khwai (for Chatuchak Market) N7
Sena Ruam (planned) N6
Ari N5
Sanam Pao N4
Victory Monument N3
Phaya Thai (for Suan Pakkad) N2
Ratchathewi (for Khlong Sen Seb) N1
National Stadium (for Jim Thompson's House) W1
Central Station (Siam) CS
Chit Lom (for Erawan Shrine) E1
Phloen Chit E2
Nana (for Landmark Hotel) E3
Asok (for Ban Kamthieng) E4
Phrom Phong (for Emporium) E5
Thong Lo (for Soi 55) E6
Ekkamai (for Eastern Bus Terminal) E7
Phra Khanong (for Soi 71) E8
On Nut (for Soi 77) E9

Ratchadamri (for Regent Hotel) S1
Sala Daeng (for Patpong, Silom 4 etc) S2
Chong Nonsi S3
Surasak S5
Saphan Taksin (for Chao Phraya express boats) S6

THANON PHAHOLYOTHIN
PHAYA THAI
RAJDAMRI
SILOM
SATHORN
PLOENCHIT
THANON SUKHUMVIT

Mo Chit takes around thirty minutes. The **Silom Line** runs from the National Stadium (W1), just west of Siam Square, through Central Station, and then south along Thanon Rajdamri, Thanon Silom and Thanon Sathorn, via Sala Daeng near Patpong (S2), to Saphan Taksin (Sathorn Bridge; S6), to link up with the full gamut of express boats on the Chao Phraya River. Free feeder buses,

SKYTRAIN

currently covering seven circular routes mostly along Thanon Sukhumvit, are geared more for commuters than visitors, but pick up a copy of the ubiquitous free BTS **map** if you want more information.

The Skytrain network is just the first phase of a planned integrated city transport programme that will be greatly enhanced by the opening of an underground rail system, currently due in 2002. The subway will run from the central Hualamphong Railway Station, east along Thanon Rama IV, then north up Soi Asoke/Thanon Ratchadapisek before terminating at Mo Chit in the north of the city.

TAXIS

Bangkok **taxis** come in three forms, and are so plentiful that you rarely have to wait more than a couple of minutes before spotting an empty one of any description. Neither tuk-tuks nor motorbike taxis have meters, so you should agree on a price before setting off, and expect to do a fair amount of haggling. Rates for all rise after midnight, and during rush hours when each journey takes far longer.

The most sedate option, Bangkok's metered, air-conditioned **taxi cabs**, is also the most expensive, but well worth the extra in the heat of the day; look out for the "TAXI METER" sign on the roof, which should be illuminated when the cab is available for hire. Fares start at B35, on a clearly visible meter in the front of the vehicle which the driver should reset at the start of each trip, and increase in stages on a combined speed/distance formula. Occasionally, drivers will refuse long, slow, less profitable journeys across town (especially in the middle of the afternoon, when many cabs have to return to the depot for a change of drivers), or, at quieter times of day, will take you on a roundabout, more expensive route to your destination. If a string of metered-cab drivers don't like the sound of your destination, you'll have to try to negotiate a flat fare with one of them, or with one of the now-rare unmetered cabs (denoted by a "TAXI" sign on the roof).

Tuk-tuks

Slightly less stable but typically Thai, **tuk-tuks** can carry three passengers comfortably and are the standard way of making shortish journeys (Banglamphu to Patpong will cost at least B80). These noisy, three-wheeled, open-sided buggies fully expose you to the worst of Bangkok's pollution, but are the least frustrating type of city transport – they are a lot nippier than taxi cabs, and the drivers have no qualms about taking semi-legal measures to avoid gridlocks. Be aware, however, that tuk-tuk drivers tend to speak less English than taxi drivers – and there have been cases of robberies and attacks on women passengers late at night. Even during the day it's quite common for tuk-tuk drivers to try and con their passengers into visiting a jewellery or expensive souvenir shop with them, for which they get a hefty commission; the usual tactic involves falsely informing tourists that the Grand Palace is closed (see p.68), and offering instead a ridiculously cheap or even free round-city tour – always bear in mind that fuel is around B17/litre and that no honest tuk-tuk driver would make even a short journey for less than B30. Because of the rise in these scams, the Bangkok Tourist Board now advises tourists to take metered taxis instead of tuk-tuks or, failing that, to make sure they take a tuk-tuk with a white "TAXI" sign on the roof, which at least means it's registered to take passengers.

TAXIS

Motorbike taxis

Least costly (a short trip, say from Banglamphu to Wat Po, should cost B20) and quickest of the trio are **motorbike taxis**, though these are rarely used by tourists as they carry only one passenger and are too dangerous to recommend for cross-city journeys. Still, if you've got nerves of steel, pick the riders out by their numbered, coloured vests or find their taxi rank, often at the entrance to a long soi. Crash helmets are compulsory on all main roads in the capital and passengers should insist on wearing one (traffic police fine non-wearers on the spot), though the local press has reported complaints from people who've caught head-lice this way (they suggest wearing a headscarf under the helmet).

Ratanakosin

When Rama I developed **Ratanakosin** as his new capital in 1782, after the sacking of Ayutthaya and a temporary stay across the river in Thonburi, he paid tribute to its precursor by imitating Ayutthaya's layout and architecture – he even shipped the building materials downstream from the ruins of the old city. Like Ayutthaya, the new capital was sited for protection beside a river and turned into an artificial island by the construction of defensive canals, with a central **Grand Palace** and adjoining royal temple, **Wat Phra Kaeo**, fronted by an open cremation field, **Sanam Luang**; the Wang Na (Palace of the Second King), now doing service as the **National Museum**, was also built at this time. **Wat Po**, which predates the capital's founding, was further embellished by Rama I's successors, who consolidated Ratanakosin's pre-eminence by building several grand European-style palaces (now housing government institutions); **Wat Mahathat**, the most important centre of Buddhist learning in southeast Asia; and the National Theatre and Thammasat University.

Bangkok has expanded eastwards away from the river, leaving the Grand Palace a good 5km from the city's commercial heart, and the royal family have long since moved their residence to Dusit, but Ratanakosin remains the ceremonial centre of the whole kingdom – so much so that it feels as if it might sink into the boggy ground under the weight of its own mighty edifices. The heavy, stately feel is lightened by noisy **markets** along the riverside strip and by Sanam Luang, still used for cremations and royal ceremonies, but also functioning as a popular open park and the hub of the modern city's bus system. Despite containing several of the country's main sights, the area is busy enough in its own right not to have become a swarming tourist zone, and strikes a neat balance between liveliness and grandeur.

Ratanakosin is within easy walking distance of Banglamphu, but is best approached from the river, via the **express-boat** piers of Tha Chang (for the Grand Palace) or Tha Thien (for Wat Po). A **word of warning**: when you're heading for the Grand Palace or Wat Po, you may well be approached by someone pretending to be a student or an official, who will tell you that the sight is closed when it's not, because they want to lead you on a shopping trip. Although the opening hours of the Grand Palace in particular are sometimes erratic because of state occasions or national holidays, it's far better to put in a bit of extra legwork and check it out for yourself.

There are no hotels in Ratanakosin, but it's only a stone's throw from the accommodation in Banglamphu (see p.157). The best spots for refreshment in Ratanakos are in *Na Pralan Café* (see p.194) and the evening riverside bar *Boh* (see p.213).

WAT PHRA KAEO AND THE GRAND PALACE

Map 4, C6–D8. Daily 8.30am–3.30pm, palace halls closed Sat & Sun; B200, including brochure with map, as well as admission to the Vimanmek Palace in Dusit; Ⓦwww.palaces.thai.net. Free tours in English at 10am, 10.30am, 1.30pm & 2pm; personal audioguide B100, with passport or credit card as surety. Express boat to Tha Chang; or bus AC#8 or #25, plus dozens of others to Sanam Luang.

THANON SANAM CHAI

Sanam Luang

THANON NA PHRA LAN

N

50 m

0

Wat Phra Kaeo

Inner Palace
(not open to the public)

10

9

5

11

8 13 12

7 14

6

15

4

3

2

22

16

17

Offices of the Royal Household
(not open to the public)

Grand Palace

20

21

18

19

THANON MAHARAT

To Tha Chang

Gate of Glorious Victory	1	Phra Mondop	12
Ticket office	2	Angkor Wat model	13
Coins Museum	3	Phra Si Ratana Chedi	14
Entrance to Wat Phra Kaeo	4	Exit from Wat Phra Kaeo	15
Chapel of the Gandhara Buddha	5	Phra Thinang Amarin Winichai	16
The bot and Emerald Buddha	6	Chakri Maha Prasat	17
Royal mausoleum	7	Dusit Maha Prasat	18
Porcelain viharn	8	Mount Krailas model	19
Library	9	Wat Phra Kaeo Museum	20
Prangs	10	Café	21
Royal Pantheon	11	Exit from Grand Palace	22

WAT PHRA KAEO & THE GRAND PALACE

WAT PHRA KAEO AND THE GRAND PALACE

Hanging together in a precarious harmony of strangely beautiful colours and shapes, **Wat Phra Kaeo** is the apogee of Thai religious art and the holiest Buddhist site in the country, housing the most important image, the **Emerald Buddha**. Built as the private royal temple, Wat Phra Kaeo occupies the northeast corner of the huge **Grand Palace**, whose official opening in 1785 marked the founding of the new capital and the rebirth of the Thai nation after the Burmese invasion. Successive kings have all left their mark here, and the palace complex now covers 61 acres, though very little apart from the wat is open to tourists.

The Silpakorn University Gallery (Mon–Fri 9am–7pm, Sat 9am–4.30pm; free; ☏880 7374–6) on Thanon Na Phra Lan, across the road from the entrance to the Grand Palace, stages regular exhibitions of modern Thai work – see *Bangkok Metro* magazine for details.

The only **entrance** to the complex in 2km of crenellated walls is the Gate of Glorious Victory in the middle of the north side, on Thanon Na Phra Lan. This brings you onto a driveway with a tantalizing view of the temple's glittering spires on the left and the dowdy buildings of the Offices of the Royal Household on the right: this is the powerhouse of the kingdom's ceremonial life, providing everything down to chairs and catering, and even lending an urn when someone of rank dies.

As the Grand Palace is Thailand's most sacred site, you have to show respect by **dressing in smart clothes** – no vests, shorts, see-through clothes, sarongs, mini-skirts, fisherman's trousers, slip-on sandals or flip-flops allowed. If your rucksack won't stretch that far, head for the office to the right just inside the Gate of Glorious Victory, where suitable garments or shoes can be provided (free, socks B15) as long as you leave some identification (passport or credit card) as surety. If you haven't dressed in the right clothes and haven't brought any ID with you, all is not lost: street-sellers opposite the entrance rent out the required attire (sandals with straps, for example, for B50, with a B50 deposit).

Wat Phra Kaeo

Entering the temple is like stepping onto a lavishly detailed stage set, from the immaculate flagstones right up to the gaudy roofs. Although it receives hundreds of foreign sight-seers and at least as many Thai pilgrims every day, the temple, which has no monks in residence, maintains an unnervingly sanitized look, as if it were built only yesterday. Its jigsaw of structures can seem complicated at first, but the basic layout is straightforward: the turnstiles in the west wall open onto the back of the bot, which contains the Emerald Buddha; to the left, the upper terrace runs parallel to the north side of the bot, while the whole temple compound is surrounded by arcaded walls, decorated with extraordinary murals of scenes from the *Ramayana* (see "The Murals", p.76).

The approach to the bot

Immediately inside the turnstiles, you're confronted by six-metre tall *yaksha*, gaudy demons from the *Ramayana*, who watch over the Emerald Buddha from every gate of the temple and ward off evil spirits. Less threatening is the toothless old codger, cast in bronze and sitting on a plinth by the back wall of the bot, who represents a Hindu hermit credited with inventing yoga and herbal medicine.

Skirting around the bot, you'll reach its **main entrance** on the eastern side, in front of which stands a cluster of grey **statues** which have a strong Chinese feel: next to Kuan Im, the Chinese Goddess of Mercy, are a sturdy pillar topped by a lotus flower, which Bangkok's Chinese community presented to Rama IV during his 27 years as a monk, and two handsome cows which commemorate Rama I's birth in the Year of the Cow. Worshippers make their offerings to the Emerald Buddha in among the statues, where they can look at the image through the open doors of the bot without messing up its pristine interior with candle wax and joss-stick ash.

Nearby in the southeastern corner of the temple precinct, look out for the beautiful country scenes painted in gold and blue on the doors of the **Chapel of the Gandhara Buddha**, a building which was crucial to the old royal rain-making ritual. Adorning the roof are thousands of nagas (serpents), symbolizing water; inside the locked chapel, among the paraphernalia used in the ritual, is kept the Gandhara Buddha, a bronze image in the gesture of calling down the rain with its right hand, while cupping the left to catch it. In times of drought the king would order this week-long ceremony to be conducted, during which he was bathed regularly and kept away from the opposite sex while Buddhist monks and Hindu Brahmins chanted continuously.

The bot and the Emerald Buddha

The **bot**, the largest building of the temple, is one of the few original structures left at Wat Phra Kaeo, though it has been augmented so often it looks like the work of a wildly inspired child. Eight *sema* stones mark the boundary of the consecrated area around the bot, each sheltering in a psychedelic fairy castle, joined by a low wall decorated with Chinese porcelain tiles which depict delicate landscapes. The walls of the bot itself, sparkling with gilt and coloured glass, are supported by 112 golden garudas (birdmen) holding nagas, representing the god Indra saving the world by slaying the serpent-cloud which had swallowed up all the water. The symbolism reflects the king's traditional role as a rainmaker.

Inside the bot, a nine-metre high pedestal supports the tiny **Emerald Buddha**, a figure whose mystique draws pilgrims from all over Thailand – here especially you must act with respect, sitting with your feet pointing away from the Buddha. The spiritual power of the sixty-centimetre jadeite image comes from its legendary past. Reputed to have been created in Sri Lanka, it was discovered when lightning cracked open an ancient chedi in Chiang Rai in northern Thailand in the early fifteenth century. The image was then moved around the north, dispensing miracles wherever it went, before being taken to Laos for two hundred years. The future Rama I snatched it back when he captured Vientiane in 1779, as it was believed to bring great fortune to its possessor, and installed it at the heart of his new capital as a talisman for king and country.

To this day the king himself ceremonially changes the Buddha's costumes, of which there are three sets, one for each season: the crown and ornaments of an Ayutthayan king for the hot season; a gilt monastic robe dotted with blue enamel for the rainy season, when the monks retreat into the temples; and a full-length gold shawl to wrap up in for the cool season. (The Buddha was granted three new sets of these costumes in 1997, with the old sets put on display in the Wat Phra Kaeo Museum – see p.79.) Among the paraphernalia in front of the pedestal is the tiny, black Victory Buddha, which Rama I always carried with him into war for luck. The two lowest Buddhas were both put there by Rama IX: the one on the left on his sixtieth birthday in 1987, the other when he became the longest-reigning Thai monarch in 1988.

The upper terrace

The eastern end of the **upper terrace** is taken up with the **Prasat Phra Thep Bidorn**, known as the **Royal Pantheon**, a splendid hash of styles. The pantheon has its

THE RAMAYANA

The Ramayana is generally thought to have originated as an oral epic in India, where it appears in numerous dialects. The most famous version is that of the poet Valmiki, who as a tribute to his king drew together the collection of stories over two thousand years ago. From India, the *Ramayana* spread to all the Hindu-influenced countries of South Asia and was passed down through the Khmers to Thailand, where as the Ramakien it has become the national epic, acting as an affirmation of the Thai monarchy and its divine Hindu links. As a source of inspiration for literature, painting, sculpture and dance-drama, it has acquired the authority of holy writ, providing Thais with moral and practical lessons, while its appearance in the form of films and comic strips shows its huge popular appeal. The version current in Thailand was composed by a committee of poets sponsored by Rama I, and runs to three thousand pages.

The central story of the *Ramayana* concerns Rama (in Thai, Phra Ram), son of the king of Ayodhya, and his beautiful wife Sita, whose hand he wins by lifting and stringing a magic bow. The couple's adventures begin when they are exiled to the

roots in the Khmer concept of *devaraja*, or the divinity of kings: inside are bronze and gold statues, precisely life-size, of all the kings since Bangkok became the Thai capital. The building is open only on special occasions, such as Chakri Day (April 6), when the dynasty is commemorated.

From here you get the best view of the **royal mausoleum**, the **porcelain viharn** and the **library** to the north, all of which are closed to the public, and, running along the east side of the temple, a row of eight bullet-like **prangs**, each with a different nasty ceramic colour.

WAT PHRA KAEO AND THE GRAND PALACE

forest, along with Rama's good brother, Lakshaman (Phra Lak), by the hero's father under the influence of his evil step-mother. Meanwhile, in the city of Lanka (in Thai, Longka), the demon king Totsagan (also known as Ravana) has conceived a passionate desire for Sita and, disguised as a hermit, sets out to kidnap her. By transforming one of his subjects into a beautiful deer, which Rama and Lakshaman go off to hunt, Totsagan catches Sita alone and takes her back to Lanka. Rama then wages a long war against the demons of Lanka, into which are woven many battles, spy scenes and diversionary episodes, and eventually kills Totsagan and rescues Sita.

The Thai version shows some characteristic differences from the Indian. Hanuman, the loyal monkey king, is given a much more playful role in the *Ramakien*, with the addition of many episodes which display his cunning and talent for mischief, but the major alteration comes at the end of the story, when Phra Ram doubts Sita's faithfulness after rescuing her from Ravana. In the Indian story, this ends with Sita being swallowed up by the earth so that she doesn't have to suffer Rama's doubts any more; in the *Ramakien* the ending is a happy one, with Phra Ram and Sita living together happily ever after.

Described by Somerset Maugham as "monstrous vegetables", they represent, from north to south, the Buddha, Buddhist scripture, the monkhood, the nunhood, the Buddhas who attained enlightenment but did not preach, previous emperors, the Bodhisattva and the future Buddha.

In the middle of the terrace, dressed in deep-green glass mosaics, the **Phra Mondop** was built by Rama I to house the *Tripitaka*, or Buddhist scripture. It's famous for the mother-of-pearl cabinet and solid-silver mats inside, but is never open. Four tiny **memorials** at each corner of the mondop show the symbols of each of the nine Chakri kings, from the ancient crown representing Rama I to the present king's sun symbol, while the bronze statues surrounding the memorials portray each king's lucky white elephants, labelled by name and pedigree. A contribution of Rama IV, on the north side of the mondop, is a **scale model of Angkor Wat**, the prodigious Cambodian temple, which during his reign was under Thai rule. At the western end of the terrace, you can't miss the golden dazzle of the **Phra Si Ratana Chedi**, which Rama IV (1851–68) erected to enshrine a piece of the Buddha's breastbone.

The murals

Extending for over a kilometre in the arcades which run inside the wat walls, the **murals of the Ramayana** depict every blow of this ancient story of the triumph of good over evil, using the vibrant buildings of the temple itself as backdrops, and setting them off against the subdued colours of richly detailed landscapes. Because of the damaging humidity, none of the original work of Rama I's time survives: maintenance is a never-ending process, so you'll always find an artist working on one of the scenes.

The story is told in 178 panels, labelled and numbered in Thai only, starting in the middle of the northern side: in the first episode, a hermit, while out ploughing, finds the baby Sita, the heroine, floating in a gold urn on a lotus leaf and brings her to the city. Panel 109 shows the climax of the story, when Rama, the hero, kills the ten-headed demon Totsagan, and the ladies of the enemy city weep at the demon's death. Panel 110 depicts his elaborate funeral procession, and in 113 you can see the funeral fair, with acrobats, sword jugglers, and tightrope walkers. In between, Sita – Rama's wife – has to walk on fire to prove that she has been faithful during her fourteen years of imprisonment by

Totsagan. If you haven't the stamina for the long walk round, you could sneak a look at the end of the story, to the left of the first panel, where Rama holds a victory parade and distributes thank-you gifts.

The palace buildings

The exit in the southwest corner of Wat Phra Kaeo brings you to the palace proper, a vast area of buildings and gardens, of which only the northern edge is on show to the public. Though the king now lives in the Chitrlada Palace in Dusit, the Grand Palace is still used for state receptions and official ceremonies, during which there is no public access to any part of the palace; in addition the interiors of the Phra Thinang Amarin Winichai and the Dusit Maha Prasat are closed at weekends.

Phra Maha Monthien

Coming out of the temple compound, you'll first be confronted by a beautiful Chinese gate covered in innumerable tiny porcelain tiles. The **Phra Maha Monthien**, which extends in a straight line behind the gate, was the grand residential complex of earlier kings. Only the **Phra Thinang Amarin Winichai**, the main audience hall at the front of the complex, is open to the public. The supreme court in the era of the absolute monarchy, it nowadays serves as the venue for the king's birthday speech; dominating the hall is the *busbok*, an open-sided throne with a spired roof, floating on a boat-shaped base. The rear buildings are still used for the most important part of the elaborate coronation ceremony, and each new king is supposed to spend a night there to show solidarity with his forefathers.

Chakri Maha Prasat and Inner Palace

Next door you can admire the facade – nothing else – of

the "farang with a Thai hat", as the **Chakri Maha Prasat** is nicknamed. Rama V, whose portrait you can see over the entrance, employed an English architect to design a purely Neoclassical residence, but other members of the royal family prevailed on the king to add the three Thai spires. This used to be the site of the elephant stables: the large red tethering posts are still there and the bronze elephants were installed as a reminder. The building displays the emblem of the Chakri dynasty on its gable, which has a trident (*ri*) coming out of a *chak*, a discus with a sharpened rim.

The **Inner Palace** (closed to the public), which used to be the king's harem, lies behind the gate on the left-hand side of the Chakri Maha Prasat. The harem was a town in itself, with shops, law-courts and a police force for the huge all-female population: as well as the current queens, the minor wives and their servants, it was home to the daughters and consorts of former kings, and the daughters of the aristocracy who attended the harem's finishing school. Today, the Inner Palace houses a school of cooking, fruit-carving and other domestic sciences for well-bred young Thais.

Dusit Maha Prasat

On the western side of the courtyard, the delicately proportioned **Dusit Maha Prasat**, an audience hall built by Rama I, epitomizes traditional Thai architecture. Outside, the soaring tiers of its red, gold and green roof culminate in a gilded *mongkut*, a spire shaped like the king's crown which symbolizes the thirty-three Buddhist levels of perfection. Each tier of the roof bears a typical *chofa*, a slender, stylized bird's head finial, and several *hang hong* (swan's tails), which represent three-headed nagas. Inside, you can still see the original throne, the **Phra Ratcha Banlang Pradap Muk**, a masterpiece of mother-of-pearl inlaid work. When a senior member of the royal family dies, the hall is used for the lying-in-state: the body, embalmed and seated in a huge sealed urn, is placed in the west transept, waiting up to two years for an auspicious day to be cremated.

To the right and behind the Dusit Maha Prasat rises a strange model mountain, decorated with fabulous animals and topped by a castle and prang. It represents **Mount Krailas**, a version of Mount Meru, the centre of the Hindu universe, and was built as the site of the royal tonsure ceremony. In former times, Thai children had shaved heads except for a tuft on the crown which, between the age of five and eight, was cut in a Hindu initiation rite to welcome adolescence. For the royal children, the rite was an elaborate ceremony that sometimes lasted five days, culminating with the king's cutting of the hair knot. The child was then bathed at the model Krailas, in water representing the original river of the universe flowing down the central mountain.

The Wat Phra Kaeo Museum

In front of the Dusit Maha Prasat, beside a small, basic **café**, the air-conditioned **Wat Phra Kaeo Museum** (B50) is currently under renovation, though it should still be possible to get in to see its mildly interesting collection of artefacts associated with the Emerald Buddha, and architectural elements rescued from the Grand Palace grounds. Highlights include the Emerald Buddha's original costumes, the bones of various kings' white elephants, and two useful scale models of the Grand Palace, one as it is now, the other as it was when first built.

WAT PO

Map 4, D8. Daily 8am–5pm; B20. Express boat to Tha Thien; or bus AC#8 or #25, plus dozens of others to Sanam Luang.

Where Wat Phra Kaeo may seem too perfect and shrink-

WAT PO

THANON SANAM CHAI

THANON THAI WANG

SOI CHETUPHON

THANON MAHARAT

To Tha Thien

N

0   50 m

Visitors' entrances   1
Entrances to Bot   2
Bot   3
Massage Pavilions   4
Traditional Medicine Pavilions   5
Rama II Chedi   6
Phra Si Sanphet Chedi   7
Rama III Chedi   8
Rama IV Chedi   9
Chapel of the Reclining Buddha   10
Chinese Pavilion   11
Library   12
European Pavilion   13
Monks' Quarters   14
Grand Palace   15

WAT PO

wrapped for some, **Wat Po**, covering twenty acres to the south of the Grand Palace, is lively and shambolic, a complex arrangement of lavish structures which jostle with classrooms, basketball courts and a turtle pond. Busloads of tourists shuffle in and out of the **north entrance**, stopping only to gawp at the colossal Reclining Buddha, but you can avoid the worst of the crowds by using the **main entrance** on Soi Chetuphon to explore the huge compound, where you'll more than likely be approached by friendly young monks wanting to practise their English.

Wat Po is the oldest temple in Bangkok and older than the city itself, having been founded in the seventeenth century under the name Wat Potaram. Foreigners have stuck to the contraction of this old name, even though Rama I, after enlarging the temple, changed the name in 1801 to Wat Phra Chetuphon, which is how it is generally known to Thais. The temple had another major overhaul in 1832, when Rama III built the chapel of the Reclining Buddha, and turned the temple into a public centre of learning by decorating the walls and pillars with inscriptions and diagrams on subjects such as history, literature, animal husbandry and astrology.

Dubbed Thailand's first university, the wat is still an important centre for traditional medicine, notably **Thai massage**, which is used against all kinds of illnesses, from backaches to viruses; thirty-hour training courses in English, usually held over fifteen days, cost B6000 (☎221 2974 or ✉WatpoTTM@netscape.net for more information). Alternatively you can simply turn up and suffer a massage yourself in the ramshackle buildings (open until 6pm) on the east side of the main compound; allow two hours for the full works (B200 per hr; foot reflexology massage B200 for 45min).

WAT PO

The eastern courtyard

The main entrance on Soi Chetuphon is one of a series of sixteen monumental gates around the main compound, each guarded by stone **giants**, many of them comic Westerners in wide-brimmed hats – ships which exported rice to China would bring these statues back as ballast.

The entrance brings you into the eastern half of the main complex, where a courtyard of structures radiate from the bot – the principal congregation and ordination hall – in a disorientating symmetry. To get to the bot at the centre, turn right and cut through the two surrounding cloisters, which are lined with 394 Buddha images, many of them covered with stucco to hide their bad state of repair – anyone can accrue some merit by taking one away and repairing it.

The elegant **bot** has beautiful teak doors decorated with mother-of-pearl, showing stories from the *Ramayana* in minute detail. Look out also for the stone bas-reliefs around the base of the bot, which narrate a longer version of the *Ramayana* in 152 action-packed panels. The plush interior has a well-proportioned altar on which ten statues of disciples frame a graceful Buddha image containing the remains of Rama I, the founder of Bangkok (Rama IV placed them there so that the public could worship him at the same time as the Buddha).

Back outside the entrance to the double cloister, keep your eyes open for a miniature mountain covered in statues of naked men in tall hats who appear to be gesturing rudely: they are *rishis* (hermits), demonstrating various positions of healing massage. Skirting the southwestern corner of the cloisters, you'll come to a pavilion between the eastern and western courtyards, which displays plaques inscribed with the precepts of traditional medicine, as well as anatomical pictures showing the different pressure points and the illnesses that can be cured by massaging them.

WAT PO

The western courtyard

Among the 95 chedis strewn about the grounds, the four **great chedis** in the western courtyard stand out as much for their covering of garish tiles as for their size. The central chedi is the oldest, erected by Rama I to hold the remains of the most sacred Buddha image of Ayutthaya, the Phra Si Sanphet. Later, Rama III built the chedi to the north for the ashes of Rama II and the chedi to the south to hold his own remains. Rama IV built the fourth, with bright blue tiles, for an uncertain purpose.

In the northwest corner of the courtyard stands the chapel of the **Reclining Buddha**, a 45-metre-long gilded statue of plaster-covered brick which depicts the Buddha entering Nirvana, a common motif in Buddhist iconography. The chapel is only slightly bigger than the statue – you can't get far enough away to take in anything but a surreal close-up view of the beaming five-metre smile. As for the feet, the vast black soles are beautifully inlaid with delicate mother-of-pearl showing the 108 *lakshanas* or auspicious signs which distinguish the true Buddha. Along one side of the statue are 108 bowls, which will bring you good luck and a long life if you put 25 satang in each.

LAK MUANG

Map 4, E5. Express boat to Tha Chang; or bus AC#8 or #25, plus dozens of others to Sanam Luang.

At 6.54am on April 21, 1782 – the astrologically determined time for the auspicious founding of Bangkok – a pillar containing the city's horoscope was ceremonially driven into the ground opposite the northeast corner of the Grand Palace. This pillar, the **lak muang** – all Thai cities have one, to provide a home for their guardian spirits – was made from a four-metre tree trunk carved with a lotus-shaped crown, and is now sheltered in an elegant shrine surrounded by immaculate gardens. It shares the shrine with the taller *lak muang* of Thonburi, which was recently incorporated into Greater Bangkok.

Hundreds of worshippers come here every day to pray and offer flowers, particularly childless couples seeking the gift of fertility. In one corner of the gardens you can often see short performances of **classical dancing**, paid for by well-off families when they have a piece of good fortune to celebrate.

SANAM LUANG

Map 4, E4. Express boat to Tha Chang; or bus AC#8 or #25, plus dozens of others.

Sanam Luang, a bare field to the north of the Grand Palace, is one of the last open spaces left in Bangkok, where residents of the capital gather in the evening to meet, eat and play. The nearby pavements are the marketplace for some exotic spiritual salesmen: on the eastern side sit astrologers and palm readers, and sellers of bizarre virility potions and contraptions; on the western side and spreading around Thammasat University and Wat Mahathat, scores of small-time hawkers sell amulets. In the early part of the year, the sky is filled with kites, which every afternoon are flown in kite-fighting contests.

As it's in front of the Grand Palace, the field is also the venue for national ceremonies, such as the **Ploughing Ceremony**, held every May at a time selected by astrologers to bring good fortune to the rice harvest. The elaborate Brahmin ceremony is led by an official from the Ministry of Agriculture, who stands in for the king in case the royal power were to be reduced by any failure in the ritual. At the designated time, the official cuts a series of circular furrows with a plough driven by two oxen, and

KITE FLYING

Flying intricate and colourful kites is now done mostly for fun in Thailand, but it has its roots in more serious activities. Filled with gunpowder and fitted with long fuses, kites were deployed in the first Thai kingdom at Sukhothai (1240–1438) as machines of war. In the same era, special *ngao* kites, with heads in the shape of bamboo bows, were used in Brahmin rituals: the string of the bow would vibrate in the wind and make a noise to frighten away evil spirits (nowadays noisy kites are still used, though only by farmers to scare birds). By the height of the Ayutthayan period (1351–1767) kites had become largely decorative: royal ceremonies were enhanced by fantastically shaped kites, adorned with jingling bells and ornamental lamps.

In the nineteenth century Rama V, by his enthusiastic lead, popularized kite flying as a wholesome and fashionable recreation. Contests are now held all over the country between February and April, when winds are strong and farmers have free time after harvesting the rice. These contests fall into two broad categories: those involving manoeuvrable flat kites, often in the shapes of animals; and those in which the beauty of static display kites is judged. The most popular contest of all, which comes under the first category, matches two teams, one flying star-shaped *chulas*, two-metre-high "male" kites, the other flying the smaller, more agile *pakpaos*, diamond-shaped "females". Each team uses its skill and teamwork to ensnare the other's kites and drag them back across a dividing line.

scatters rice which has been sprinkled with lustral water by the Brahmin priests of the court. When the ritual is over, spectators rush in to grab handfuls of the rice, which they then plant in their own paddies for good luck.

In a tiny park by the hectic bus stops at the northeast corner of Sanam Luang stands the abundant but rather neglected figure of **Mae Toranee**, the earth goddess, wringing the water from her ponytail. Originally part of a fountain built here by Rama V's queen, Saowaba, to provide Bangkokians with fresh drinking water, the statue illustrates a Buddhist legend featured in the murals of many temples. While the Buddha was sitting in meditation at a crucial stage of his enlightenment, Mara, the force of evil, sent a host of earthly temptations and demons to try to divert him from his path. The Buddha remained cross-legged and pointed his right hand towards the ground – the most popular pose of Buddha statues in Thailand – to call the earth goddess to bear witness to his countless meritorious deeds, which had earned him an ocean of water stored in the earth. Mae Toranee obliged by wringing her hair and engulfing Mara's demons in the deluge.

WAT MAHATHAT

Map 4, C4. Daily 9am–5pm; free. Express boat to Tha Chang; or bus AC#8 or #25, plus dozens of others to Sanam Luang.

On Sanam Luang's western side, with its main entrance on Thanon Maharat, **Wat Mahathat**, founded in the eighteenth century, provides a welcome respite from the surrounding tourist hype, and a chance to engage with the eager monks studying at **Mahachulalongkorn Buddhist University** here. As the nation's centre for the Mahanikai monastic sect, and housing one of the two Buddhist universities in Bangkok, the wat buzzes with purpose. It's this activity, and the chance of interaction and participation, rather than any special architectural features, which make a visit so rewarding. The many university-attending monks at the wat are friendly and keen to practise their English, and are more than likely to approach you: diverting topics might range from the poetry of Dylan Thomas to English football results gleaned from the BBC World Service.

Every day the twenty-acre grounds host an interesting **herbal medicine market**, and outside, along the pavements of Maharat and surrounding roads, vendors set up stalls to sell some of the city's most reasonably priced **amulets** (though the range and quality are not as good as at the main market at Wat Rajnadda), taking advantage of the spiritually auspicious location.

Situated in Section Five of the wat is its **International Buddhist Meditation Centre**, where Vipassana meditation practice is available in English (daily 7–10am, 1–4pm & 6–9pm; ☏222 6011 or 01/694 1527 for further information). Participants are welcome to stay in the simple surroundings of the meditation building itself (donation requested) or at a quiet house nearby (B200 per day).

THE NATIONAL MUSEUM

Map 4, E3. Wed–Sun 9am–4pm; B40 including free leaflet and map. Express boat to Tha Chang; or bus AC#8 or #25, plus dozens of others to Sanam Luang.

The **National Museum** houses a colossal hoard of Thailand's chief artistic riches, ranging from sculptural treasures in the north and south wings, through bizarre decorative objects in the older buildings, to outlandish funeral chariots and the exquisite Buddhaisawan Chapel, as well as occasionally staging worthwhile temporary exhibitions (details on ☏224 1370). Should you linger longer than anticipated (and most people do), the simple **cafeteria** serves good, inexpensive Thai food.

The free guided museum tours (in English Wed & Thurs 9.30am; details on ☏215 8173) are worth making time for: they're generally entertaining, and their explication of the choicest exhibits provides a good introduction to Thai religion and culture.

History and prehistory

The building which houses the information office and bookshop provides a quick whirl through the **history** of Thailand, a display in which a couple of gems are hidden. The first is a black stone inscription, credited to King Ramkhamhaeng of Sukhothai, which became the first capital of the Thai nation in the thirteenth century. Discovered in 1833 by the future Rama IV, it's the oldest extant inscription using the Thai alphabet. This, combined with the description it records of prosperity and piety in Sukhothai's Golden Age, has made the stone a symbol of Thai nationhood. Further on is a four-foot-tall carved *kinnari*, a graceful half-human, half-bird creature said to live in one of the Himalayan heavens. This delicate masterpiece is from the best period of Thai woodcarving, the seventeenth and early eighteenth centuries, before the fall of Ayutthaya.

The **prehistory** room is entered through a separate door at the back end of the building. Prominent here are bronze artefacts from Ban Chiang in the northeast of Thailand, one of the earliest Bronze Age cultures ever discovered, including the world's oldest socketed tool, an axe head set in a sandstone mould (3600–2300 BC).

The main collection: southern building

At the back of the compound, two large modern buildings, flanking an old converted palace, house the museum's **main collection**, kicking off on the ground floor of the **southern building**. Look out here for some historic sculptures from the rest of Asia, including one of the earliest representations of the Buddha, from Gandhara in northwest India. Alexander the Great left a garrison at Gandhara, which explains why the image is in the style of Classical Greek sculpture: for example, the *ushnisha*, the supernatural bump on the top of the head, which symbolizes the Buddha's intellectual and spiritual power, is rationalized into a bun of thick, wavy hair.

Upstairs, in the **Dvaravati** rooms (sixth to eleventh centuries), the pick of the stone and terracotta Buddhas is a small head in smooth, pink clay, whose downcast eyes and faintly smiling full lips typify the serene look of this era. You can't miss a voluptuous Javanese statue of elephant-headed Ganesh, Hindu god of wisdom and the arts, which, being the symbol of the Fine Arts Department, is always freshly garlanded. As Ganesh is known as the clearer of obstacles, Hindus always worship him before other gods, so by tradition he has grown fat through getting first choice of the offerings – witness his trunk jammed into a bowl of food in this sculpture.

Room 9 contains the most famous piece of **Srivijaya** art (seventh to thirteenth centuries), a bronze Bodhisattva Avalokitesvara found at Chaiya in southern Thailand – according to Mahayana Buddhism, a *bodhisattva* is a saint who has postponed his passage into Nirvana to help ordinary believers gain enlightenment. With its pouting face and sinuous torso, this image has become the ubiquitous emblem of the south.

The rough chronological order of the collection continues back downstairs with an exhibition of **Khmer** and **Lopburi** sculpture (seventh to fourteenth centuries), most notably some dynamic bronze statuettes and stone lintels. Look out for an elaborate lintel which depicts Vishnu reclining on a dragon in the sea of eternity, dreaming up a new universe after the old one has been annihilated in the Hindu cycle of creation and destruction. Out of his navel comes a lotus, and out of this emerges four-headed Brahma, who will put the dream into practice. Nearby, a smooth, muscular stone statue with a sweet smile and downcast eyes shows King Jayavarman VII, last of the great Khmer emperors. Such royal statues are very rare, and the features borrowed from Buddha images suggest that Jayavarman believed that he was close to Buddhahood himself.

The main collection: northern building

The second half of the survey, in the northern building, begins upstairs with the **Sukhothai** collection (thirteenth to fifteenth centuries), which is short on Buddha images but has some chunky bronzes of Hindu gods and a wide range of ceramics. The **Lanna** rooms (thirteenth to sixteenth centuries) include a miniature set of golden regalia, contain tiny umbrellas and a cute pair of filigree flip-flops, which would have been enshrined in a chedi.

An ungainly but serene Buddha head, carved from grainy, pink sandstone, represents the **Ayutthaya** style of sculpture (fourteenth to eighteenth centuries): the faintest incision of a moustache above the lips betrays the Khmer influences which came to Ayutthaya after its conquest of Angkor. A sumptuous scripture cabinet, showing a cityscape of old Ayutthaya, is a more unusual piece, one of a surviving handful of such carved and painted items of furniture.

Downstairs in the **Bangkok** rooms (eighteenth century onwards), a stiffly realistic standing bronze brings you full circle: in his zeal for Western naturalism, Rama V had the statue made in the Gandhara style of the earliest Buddha image displayed in the first room of the museum.

The funeral chariots

To the east of the northern building, beyond the café on the left, stands a large garage where the fantastically elaborate **funeral chariots** of the royal family are stored. Preeminent among these is the Vejayant Rajarot, built by Rama I in 1785 for carrying the urn at his own funeral.

The thirteen-metre-high structure symbolizes heaven on Mount Meru, while the dragons and divinities around the sides – piled in five golden tiers to suggest the flames of the cremation – represent the mythological inhabitants of the mountain's forests. Weighing forty tonnes and pulled by three hundred men, the teak chariot was used as recently as 1985 for the funeral of Queen Rambhai Bharni, wife of Rama VII.

Wang Na (Palace of the Second King)

The sprawling central building of the compound was originally part of the **Wang Na**, a huge palace stretching across Sanam Luang to Khlong Lod, which housed the "second king", appointed by the reigning monarch as his heir and deputy. When Rama V did away with the office in 1887, he turned the "Palace of the Second King" into a museum, which now contains a fascinating array of Thai *objets d'art*.

As you enter (room 5), the display of sumptuous rare gold pieces behind heavy iron bars includes a well-preserved armlet taken from the ruined prang of fifteenth-century Wat Ratburana in Ayutthaya. In adjacent room 6, an intricately carved ivory seat turns out, with gruesome irony, to be a *howdah*, for use on an elephant's back. Among the masks worn by *khon* actors next door (room 7), look out especially for a fierce Hanuman, the white monkey-warrior in the *Ramayana* epic, gleaming with mother-of-pearl.

The huge and varied ceramic collection in room 8 includes some sophisticated pieces from Sukhothai, while the room above (9) holds a riot of mother-of-pearl items, whose flaming rainbow of colours comes from the shell of the turbo snail from the Gulf of Thailand. It's also worth seeking out the display of richly decorated musical instruments in room 15, where you can hear tapes of the unfamiliar sounds they produce.

THE NATIONAL MUSEUM

The Buddhaisawan Chapel

The second holiest image in Thailand, after the Emerald Buddha, is housed in the **Buddhaisawan Chapel**, the vast hall in front of the eastern entrance to the Wang Na. Inside, the fine proportions of the hall, with its ornate coffered ceiling and lacquered window shutters, are enhanced by painted rows of divinities and converted demons, all turned to face the chubby, glowing **Phra Sihing Buddha**, which according to legend was magically created in Sri Lanka and sent to Sukhothai in the thirteenth century. Like the Emerald Buddha, the image was believed to bring good luck to its owner and was frequently snatched from one northern town to another, until Rama I brought it down from Chiang Mai in 1795 and installed it here in the second king's private chapel. Two other images (in Nakhon Si Thammarat and Chiang Mai) now claim to be the authentic Phra Sihing Buddha, but all three are in fact derived from a lost original – this one is in a fifteenth-century Sukhothai style. It's still much loved by ordinary people, and at Thai New Year is carried out onto Sanam Luang, where worshippers sprinkle it with water as a merit-making gesture.

The careful detail and rich, soothing colours of the surrounding 200-year-old **murals** are surprisingly well preserved; the bottom row between the windows narrates the life of the Buddha, beginning in the far right-hand corner with his parents' wedding.

Tamnak Daeng

On the south side of the Buddhaisawan Chapel, the sumptuous **Tamnak Daeng** (Red House) stands out, a large, airy Ayutthaya-style house made of rare golden teak, surmounted by a multi-tiered roof decorated with carved foliage and swan's-tail finials. Originally part of the private quarters of Princess Sri Sudarak, elder sister of Rama I, it was moved from the Grand Palace to the old palace in Thonburi for Queen Sri Suriyen, wife of Rama II; when her son became second king to Rama IV, he dismantled the edifice again and shipped it here to the Wang Na compound. Inside, it's furnished in the style of the early Bangkok period, with some of the beautiful objects that once belonged to Sri Suriyen, a huge, ornately carved box bed, and the uncommon luxury of an indoor toilet and bathroom.

THE NATIONAL GALLERY

Map 4, F2. Wed–Sun 8am–4pm; B30; ☎281 2224. Express boat to Tha Banglamphu; or bus AC#3 or #53, plus dozens of others to Sanam Luang.

Thailand's **National Gallery**, across the hectic Phra Pinklao Road from Sanam Luang, accommodates a permanent collection of largely uninspiring and derivative twentieth-century Thai art, but its temporary exhibitions can be pretty good – see *Bangkok Metro* magazine for details. The fine old wooden building that houses the gallery is also worth more than a cursory glance – it used to be the Royal Mint, and is constructed in typical early twentieth-century style, around a central courtyard.

Banglamphu and the Democracy Monument area

Best known as the site of the travellers' mecca, Thanon Khao San (see p.157), the **Banglamphu** district (map 3) also holds a couple of noteworthy temples and still boasts a good number of wooden shophouses and narrow alleyways alongside the purpose-built guest houses, travel agents and jewellery shops. But the most interesting sights in this part of the city are found in the neighbourhoods to the south and east of the huge stone **Democracy Monument**, which forms the centrepiece of an enormous roundabout that siphons traffic from the major Rajdamnoen Klang artery. Most of these areas, within walking distance of the Khao San guest houses and equally accessible from the Grand Palace, retain a traditional flavour, and there is as yet hardly any high-rise architecture. The string of temple-supply shops around **Wat Suthat** and **Sao Ching Cha** make this a rewarding area to explore, and the amulet market in the grounds of **Loh Prasat** is also well worth seeking out.

- -

Banglamphu boasts a mouthwatering range of
eating places, from guest-house cafés on Thanon
Khao San (see p.189) to bohemian Thai restaurants
favoured by local students on Thanon Phra Athit
(see p.191). Nightlife here is pretty lively too, attracting a
good mix of Thais and tourists to the easy-going but
not at all sleazy bars and clubs (see p.212).

- -

The fastest and least stressful way of getting to this area is by **boat**. Longtail canal boats run along Khlong Sen Seb from various spots in downtown Bangkok (see p.60) to the Phanfa terminus right next to the Golden Mount compound, just 30m from Wat Rajnadda, while the Chao Phraya Express boats (see p.59) operate an equally efficient service to Tha Banglamphu, just a few hundred metres west of Thanon Khao San. For access from anywhere else, you'll need to make use of the **bus** network: Democracy Monument is served by dozens of buses from all parts of the city, and as a landmark is hard to miss; if you're coming from eastern or northern parts of the city (such as Hualamphong Station, Siam Square or Sukhumvit), get off the bus as soon as you see it – it's almost impossible to cross the road at the *Royal Hotel* (westernmost) bus stop on Rajdamnoen Klang.

WAT CHANA SONGKHRAM

Map 3, C10. Express boat to Tha Banglamphu; or bus #53 or #56.
Sandwiched between Thanon Khao San and the Chao Phraya River at the heart of the Banglamphu backpackers' ghetto stands the lusciously renovated eighteenth-century **Wat Chana Songkhram**. As with temple compounds

throughout the country, Wat Chana Songkhram is used for all sorts of neighbourhood activities (including car-parking and football games) and is not at all an ivory tower; in this instance, part of the temple yard has been appropriated by stallholders selling secondhand books and travellers' clothes, making the most of the constant stream of tourists who use the wat as a shortcut between the river and Khao San. It's worth slowing down for a closer look though, as the gables of the bot roof are beautifully ornate, embossed with a golden relief of Vishnu astride Garuda enmeshed in an intricate design of red and blue glass mosaics, and the golden finials are shaped like nagas (mythical serpents). Peeking over the compound walls on to the guest houses and internet cafés of Soi Ram Bhuttri are a row of *kuti* or monks' quarters, elegantly simple wooden cabins on stilts with steeply pitched roofs.

PHRA SUMEN FORTRESS AND THE CHAO PHRAYA WALKWAY

Map 3, C8–A10. Express boat to Tha Banglamphu; or bus #53 or #56.

The crenellated whitewashed tower beside the Chao Phraya River at the junction of Phra Athit and Phra Sumen roads is **Phra Sumen Fortress** (aka Phra Sumeru Fortress), a renovated corner of the original eighteenth-century city walls. It was the northernmost of fourteen octagonal towers built by Rama I in 1783 to protect the royal island of Ratanakosin and originally contained 38 rooms for storing ammunition. (The only other surviving tower, also renovated, is Phra Mahakan Fortress, a few hundred metres east of Democracy Monument, next to the Golden Mount; see p.102.) Nowadays there's nothing to see inside the Phra Sumen tower, but it makes a striking landmark, and the area around it has been made into a pleasant grassy riverside park, with English-language signs describing the history of the fortifications.

The fort also marks the northernmost limit of a **riverside walkway** which at time of writing only ran as far as the Bangkok Information Centre at Phra Pinklao Bridge, but is due to be extended all the way down to Tha Chang, in front of the Grand Palace. As well as providing a good view of the boats and barges on the Chao Phraya, the Phra Sumen–Phra Pinklao walkway takes you past the front entrances of two very grand old buildings, both of them beautifully restored and currently occupied by international organizations. The United Nations' Food and Agriculture Organization (FAO) now uses the early-twentieth-century mansion known as **Baan Maliwan** as its library (unfortunately closed to casual visitors), while the nearby UNICEF office is housed in the late nineteenth-century palace of one of the wives of Rama IV, which also served as the headquarters of the clandestine Seri Thai resistance movement during World War II. Both these mansions have their most attractive features facing the river, as most visitors would have arrived by boat in those days.

On the eastern side of Thanon Phra Athit, there's another fine early twentieth-century mansion, Baan Phra Athit, at no. 201/1; most of this building is now occupied by a private company, but one wing has been turned into the café-bar *Coffee and More*, with views on to the courtyard.

WAT INDRAVIHARN

Map 3, G6. Express boat to Tha Thewes; or bus #3 or #16.

North of Democracy, at the edge of the Banglamphu district on Thanon Wisut Kasat, **Wat Indraviharn** (also known as

Wat In) features on some tourist itineraries by virtue of the enormous standing Buddha that dominates its precincts. Commissioned by Rama IV in the mid-nineteenth century to enshrine a Buddha relic from Sri Lanka, the 32-metre-high image certainly doesn't rate as a work of art: its enormous, overly flattened features give it an ungainly aspect, while the gold mirror-mosaic surface only emphasizes its faintly kitsch effect. But the beautifully pedicured foot-long toenails peep out gracefully from beneath devotees' garlands of fragrant jasmine, and you can get reasonable views of the neighbourhood by climbing the stairways of the tower supporting the statue from behind; when unlocked, the doorways in the upper part of the tower give access to the interior of the hollow image, affording vistas from shoulder level. Elsewhere in the wat's compact grounds are the usual amalgam of architectural and spiritual styles, including a Chinese shrine and statues of Ramas IV and V.

Wat Indraviharn is a favourite hangout for con-artists, and the popular scam here is to offer tourists a tuk-tuk tour of Bangkok for the ridiculously cheap price of B20. The catch is that you will be taken to a nearby jewellery shop and find it extremely difficult to come away empty-handed. Ignore any persistent tuk-tuk drivers and flag down a passing metered taxi instead.

DEMOCRACY MONUMENT

Map 3, F13. Longtail boat to Tha Phanfa; or bus AC#3, AC#9, AC#11, AC#15, #15, #39, #56, or #59.

Begun in 1939, the **Democracy Monument** was conceived as a testament to the ideals that fuelled the 1932 revolution and the changeover to a constitutional monarchy, hence its symbolic positioning between the royal residences.

Its **dimensions** are also significant: the four stone wings, set in a circle, tower to a height of 24m, the same as the radius of the monument – an allusion to June 24, the date the system was changed; the 75 cannons around the perimeter refer to the year, 2475 BE (1932 AD). The monument contains a copy of the constitution and is a focal point for public events and demonstrations – it was a rallying-point during the pro-democracy protests of May 1992 and, more cheerfully, gets decked out with flowers every year on December 5, in honour of the king's birthday. If you're prepared to brave the traffic that streams round Democracy day and night, you can climb the steps at the base of the monument and inspect its facades at closer quarters. Each wing is carved with friezes showing heroic scenes from Thailand's history.

The monument was designed by **Corrado Feroci**, an Italian sculptor invited to Thailand by Rama VI in 1924 to encourage the pursuit of Western art. He changed his name to Silpa Bhirasi and stayed in Thailand until his death, producing many of Bangkok's statues and monuments – including the Rama I statue at Memorial Bridge and Victory Monument in the Phrayathai district – as well as founding the first Institute of Fine Arts.

WAT RAJNADDA, LOH PRASAT AND THE AMULET MARKET

Map 3, H14. Longtail boat to Tha Phanfa; or bus AC#3, AC#9, AC#11, AC#15, #15, #39, #56, or #59.

Five minutes' walk southeast of Democracy Monument, at the point where Rajdamnoen Klang meets Thanon Mahachai, stands the assortment of religious buildings known collectively as **Wat Rajnadda**. It's immediately recognizable by the dusky-pink, multi-tiered, castle-like structure called

AMULETS

To protect themselves from malevolent spirits and physical misfortune, Thais wear or carry at least one amulet at all times. The most popular images are copies of sacred statues, while others show holy men, kings, or a many-armed monk closing his eyes, ears and mouth to concentrate better on reaching Nirvana. On the reverse is often inscribed a *yantra*, a combination of letters and figures designed to ward off evil; these can be very specific, protecting your durian orchards from storms, for example, or your tuk-tuk from oncoming traffic.

Amulets can be made from bronze, clay, plaster or gold, and some have sacred ingredients added, such as the ashes of burned holy texts. But what really determines an amulet's efficacy is its history: where and by whom it was made, who or what it represents, and who consecrated it. Monks are often involved in making the images, and are always called upon to consecrate them – the more charismatic the monk, the more powerful the amulet. In return, the proceeds from the sale of amulets contributes to wat funds.

The belief in amulets probably originated in India, where tiny images were sold to pilgrims who visited the four holy sites associated with the Buddha. But not all amulets are Buddhist-related – there's a whole range of other enchanted objects, including tigers' teeth, tamarind seeds, coloured threads and miniature phalluses. The latter are of Hindu origin; worn around the waist, they are associated with fertility and provide protection for the genitals.

Loh Prasat or "Iron Monastery" – a reference to its numerous metal spires. The only structure of its kind in Bangkok, Loh Prasat is the dominant and most bizarre of Wat Rajnadda's components. Each tier is pierced by passageways running north–south and east–west (fifteen in each direction at ground level), with small meditation cells at each point of intersection. The Sri Lankan monastery on which it is modelled contained a thousand cells; this one probably has half that number.

In the southeast (Thanon Mahachai) corner of the temple compound, Bangkok's biggest amulet market, the **Wat Rajnadda Buddha Centre**, comprises at least a hundred stalls selling tiny Buddha images of all designs, materials and prices. Alongside these miniature charms are statues of Hindu deities, dolls and carved wooden phalluses, also bought to placate or ward off disgruntled spirits, as well as love potions and tapes of sacred music.

Though the amulet market at Wat Rajnadda is probably the best in Bangkok, you should also check out the amulet flea market that sets up daily on the pavements in front of Wat Mahathat (map 4, C4). Prices at these stalls start as low as B10 and rise into the thousands.

THE GOLDEN MOUNT

Map 3, I14. Longtail boat to Tha Phanfa; or bus AC#3, AC#9, AC#11, AC#15, #15, #39, #56, or #59.

The dirty yellow hill crowned with a gleaming gold chedi just across the road from Loh Prasat is the grandiosely named Golden Mount, or Phu Khao Tong. It rises within the compound of **Wat Saket**, a dilapidated late eighteenth-century temple built by Rama I just outside his new city walls to serve as the capital's crematorium. During the following hundred years the temple became the dumping ground for some sixty thousand plague victims – the majority of them too poor to afford funeral pyres, and thus left to the vultures.

The **Golden Mount** was a late addition to the compound. Early in the nineteenth century, Rama III built a huge chedi here, but the ground proved too soft to support it, and the whole thing collapsed. Since Buddhist law states that a religious building can never be destroyed, however tumbledown, the hill of rubble was left in place; fifty years later Rama V topped it with a more sensibly sized chedi in which he placed a few relics, believed by some to be the Buddha's teeth.

To reach the base of the mount, follow the renovated crenellations of the eighteenth-century Phra Mahakan Fortress and the old city wall, going past a small market selling caged birds, before veering left at the sign. Climbing to the top, you'll pass remnants of the collapsed chedi and plaques commemorating donors to the temple. The **terrace** surrounding the base of the new chedi is a good place for landmark-spotting: immediately to the west are the gleaming roofs of Wat Rajnadda and the salmon-pink Loh Prasat; behind them you can see the spires of the Grand Palace (see p.70) and, even further beyond, the beautifully proportioned prangs of Wat Arun on the other side of the river (see p.118).

Wat Saket hosts an enormous annual temple fair in the first week of November, when the mount is illuminated with coloured lanterns and the whole compound seethes with funfair rides, food sellers and travelling performers.

WAT SUTHAT AND SAO CHING CHA

Map 2, C4. Daily 9am–9pm; B20. Bus AC#7, AC#8, #25 or #56.
Located about 700m southwest of the Golden Mount, and a similar distance directly south of Democracy Monument along Thanon Dinso, **Wat Suthat** is one of Thailand's six most important temples and contains Bangkok's tallest **viharn**, built in the early nineteenth century to house the

meditating figure of **Phra Sri Sakyamuni Buddha**. This eight-metre-high statue was brought all the way from Sukhothai by river, and now sits on a glittering mosaic dais surrounded with surreal **murals** that depict the last 24 lives of the Buddha rather than the more usual ten. The galleries that encircle the viharn contain 156 serenely posed Buddha images, making a nice contrast to the **Chinese statues** dotted around the viharn's courtyard and that of the bot in the adjacent compound, most of which were brought over from China during Rama I's reign, as ballast in rice boats: check out the depictions of gormless Western sailors and the pompous Chinese scholars.

The area just in front of Wat Suthat is dominated by the towering, red-painted teak posts of **Sao Ching Cha**, otherwise known as the **Giant Swing**, once the focal point of a Brahmin ceremony to honour Shiva's annual visit to earth. Teams of two or four young men would stand on the outsized seat (now missing) and swing up to a height of 25m to grab between their teeth a bag of gold suspended on the end of a bamboo pole. The act of swinging probably symbolized the rising and setting of the sun, though legend also has it that Shiva and his consort Uma were banned from swinging in their heavenly abode because doing so caused cataclysmic floods on earth – prompting Shiva to demand that the practice be continued on earth as a rite to ensure moderate rains and bountiful harvests. The terrestrial version led to so many accidents that it was outlawed in the 1930s.

The streets leading up to Wat Suthat and Sao Ching Cha are renowned as the best place in the city to buy **religious paraphernalia**, and are well worth a browse. Thanon Bamruang in particular is lined with shops selling everything a good Buddhist could need, from household offertory tables to temple umbrellas and two-metre-high Buddha images. They also sell special alms packs for devotees to donate to monks; a typical pack is contained within a holy

WAT SUTHAT AND SAO CHING CHA

saffron-coloured plastic bucket (which can be used by the monk for washing his robes, or himself), and comprises such daily necessities as soap, toothpaste, soap powder, toilet roll, candles and incense.

WAT RAJABOPHIT

Map 4, G7. Bus AC#7, AC#8 or #25.

From Wat Suthat, walk south down Thanon Titong for a few hundred metres before turning right (west) on to Thanon Rajabophit, on which stands **Wat Rajabophit**, one of the city's prettiest temples and another example of Chinese influence. Built by Rama V, it is characteristic of this progressive king in its unusual design, with the rectangular bot and viharn connected by a circular cloister that encloses a chedi. Every external wall in the compound is covered in the pastel shades of Chinese *bencharong* ceramic tiles, creating a stunning overall effect, while the interior of the bot looks like a tiny banqueting hall, with gilded Gothic vaults and intricate mother-of-pearl doors.

If you now head west towards the Grand Palace from Wat Rajabophit, you'll pass a gold **statue of a pig** as you cross the canal. The cute porcine monument was erected in tribute to one of Rama V's wives, born in the Chinese Year of the Pig. Alternatively, walking in a southerly direction down Thanon Banmo takes you all the way down to the Chao Phraya River and Memorial Bridge, passing some fine old Chinese shophouses and the exuberant flower and vegetable market, Pak Khlong Talat, en route (see p.113).

Chinatown
and Pahurat

When the newly crowned Rama I decided to move his capital across to the east bank of the river in 1782, the Chinese community living on the proposed site of his palace was given no choice but to relocate downriver, to the **Sampeng** area. Two hundred years on, **Chinatown** has grown into the country's largest Chinese district, a sprawl of narrow alleyways, temples and shophouses packed between Charoen Krung (also known as New Road) and the river, separated from Ratanakosin by the Indian area of **Pahurat** – famous for its cloth and dressmakers' trimmings – and bordered to the east by Hualamphong train station. Real estate in this part of the city is said to be the most valuable in the country, with land prices on the Charoen Krung and Yaowarat arteries reputed to fetch over a million baht per square metre; not surprisingly, there are almost a hundred gold shops in the Sampeng quarter.

For the tourist, Chinatown is chiefly interesting for its markets, shophouses, open-fronted warehouses and remnants of colonial-style architecture, though it also has a few

THE CHINESE IN THAILAND

The Chinese have been a dominant force in the shaping of Thailand, and commerce is the foundation of their success. When the capital was moved from Ayutthaya to Bangkok in 1782 it was to an already flourishing Chinese trading post and, as the economy began to boom, both Rama I and Rama II encouraged Chinese immigration to boost the indigenous workforce. Thousands of migrants came, most of them young men eager to earn money that could be sent back to families impoverished by civil wars and persistently bad harvests.

By the close of the nineteenth century, the Chinese dominated Thailand's commercial and urban sector, while the Thais remained in firm control of the political domain. It was an arrangement that apparently satisfied both parties – as the old Chinese proverb goes, "We don't mind who holds the head of the cow, providing we can milk it" – and one that still holds true today.

Because so few Chinese women had emigrated, intermarriage between the two communities was common until the beginning of the twentieth century – indeed, there is some Chinese blood in almost every Thai citizen today, including the king. But in the early 1900s Chinese women started to arrive in Thailand, making Chinese society more self-sufficient and enclosed. Anti-Chinese feelings grew and discriminatory laws ensued, including the closing of some jobs to Chinese citizens, a movement that increased in fervour as communism began to be perceived as a threat. Since the 1970s, strict immigration controls have limited the number of new settlers to one hundred per nationality per year, a particularly harsh imposition on the Chinese.

noteworthy temples. The following account covers Chinatown's main attractions and most interesting neighbourhoods, sketching a meandering and quite lengthy route which could easily take a whole day to complete on foot.

Chinatown is an enjoyably untouristed area to stay in, though the choice of hotels is limited (see p.164). Eating options, on the other hand, proliferate, and a selection of the more formal Chinese restaurants are listed on p.195.

Easiest access is to take the Chao Phraya Express **boat** to Tha Rajavongse (Rajawong) at the southern end of Thanon Rajawong, which runs through the centre of Chinatown. This part of the city is also well served by **buses** from downtown Bangkok, as well as from Banglamphu and Ratanakosin; your best bet is to take any Hualamphong-bound bus (see box on pp.56–58) and then walk from the train station. The non-air-con bus #56 is also a useful link from Banglamphu, as it runs along Thanon Tanao at the end of Thanon Khao San and then goes all the way down Mahachai and Chakraphet roads in Chinatown – get off just after the Merry King department store for Sampeng Lane. Coming from downtown Bangkok and/or the Skytrain network, jump on a non-air-con #25 or #40, both of which run from Sukhumvit, via Siam Square, to Hualamphong, then Thanon Yaowarat and on to Pahurat.

Orientation in Chinatown can be quite tricky: the alleys (known as *trok* rather than the more usual soi) are extremely narrow, their turn-offs and other road signs often obscured by the mounds of merchandise that clutter the pavements and the surrounding hordes of buyers and sellers.

CHINATOWN AND PAHURAT

WAT TRAIMIT AND THE GOLDEN BUDDHA

Map 5, H6. Daily 9am–5pm; B20. Bus AC#4, AC#7, #25, #29, #40 or #53.

Given the confusing layout of the district, it's worth starting your explorations at the eastern edge of Chinatown, just west of Hualamphong station, with the triangle of land occupied by **Wat Traimit**. Cross the khlong beside the station and walk 200m down (signed) Thanon Tri Mit to enter the temple compound. Outwardly unprepossessing, the temple boasts a quite stunning interior feature: the world's largest solid gold Buddha is housed here, fitting for a community so closely linked with the gold trade, even if the image has nothing to do with China's spiritual heritage. Over 3m tall and weighing five and a half tonnes, the **Golden Buddha** gleams as if coated in liquid metal, seated amid candles and surrounded with offerings of lotus buds and incense.

Cast in the thirteenth century, the image was brought to Bangkok by Rama III, completely encased in stucco – a common ruse to conceal valuable statues from would-be thieves. The disguise was so good that no one guessed what was underneath until 1955 when the image was accidentally knocked in the process of being moved to Wat Traimit, and the stucco cracked to reveal a patch of gold (sections of the stucco casing are now on display alongside the Golden Buddha). The discovery launched a country-wide craze for tapping away at plaster Buddhas in search of hidden precious metals, but Wat Traimit's is still the most valuable – it's valued, by weight alone, at US$14 million. A fine example of the curvaceous grace of Sukhothai art, the beautifully proportioned figure is best appreciated by comparing it with the much cruder Sukhothai Buddha in the next-door bot, to the east.

SAMPENG LANE AND SOI ISSARANUPHAP

Map 5, C2–F6. Express boat to Tha Rajavongse (Rajawong); or bus AC#4, AC#7, #25, #40, #53 or #56.

Leaving Wat Traimit by the Charoen Krung/Yaowarat exit (at the back of the temple compound), walk northwest along Thanon Yaowarat and make a left turn onto Thanon Songsawat to reach **Sampeng Lane** (also signposted as Soi Wanit 1), an area that used to thrive on opium dens, gambling houses and brothels, but now sticks to more reputable (if tacky) commerce. Stretching southeast–northwest for about a kilometre, Sampeng Lane is a fun place to browse and shop, unfurling itself like a ramshackle department store selling everything at bargain-basement rates. Among other things, this is the cheapest place in town to buy Chinese silk pyjama pants, electronic pets and other computer games, sarongs, alarm clocks, underwear and hair accessories. And, to complete this perfect shopping experience, there are food stalls every few steps to help keep up your energy.

For a rather more sensual experience, take a right about halfway down Sampeng Lane, into **Soi Issaranuphap** (also signed in places as Soi 16). Packed with people from dawn till dusk, this long, dark alleyway, which also traverses Charoen Krung, is the place to come in search of ginseng roots (essential for good health), quivering fish heads, cubes of cockroach-killer chalk, and pungent piles of cinnamon sticks. Alleys branch off in all directions to gaudy Chinese temples and market squares. You'll see Chinese grandfathers discussing business in darkened shops, and ancient pharmacists concocting bizarre potions to order. Soi Issaranuphap finally ends at the Thanon Plaplachai intersection amid a flurry of shops specializing in paper **funeral art**. Believing that the deceased should be well provided for in their afterlife, Chinese buy miniature paper replicas of necessities to be burned with the body: especially popular are houses, cars, suits of clothing and, of course, money.

The only time you'll find Chinese-run shops, hotels and restaurants closed is over the annual three-day holiday at Chinese New Year. This is the community's most important festival, but is celebrated much more as a family affair than in the Chinatowns of other countries.

WAT MANGKON KAMALAWAT

Map 5, F3. Bus AC#4, AC#7, #25, #40, #53 or #56.

If Soi Issaranuphap epitomizes traditional Chinatown commerce, then **Wat Mangkon Kamalawat** (also known as Wat Leng Nee Yee, or "Dragon Flower Temple") stands as a superb example of the community's spiritual practices. Best approached via its dramatic multi-tiered gateway 10m northwest up Charoen Krung from the Soi Issaranuphap junction, Wat Mangkon receives a constant stream of devotees, who come to leave offerings at one or more of the small altars inside this important Mahayana Buddhist temple. As with the Theravada Buddhism espoused by the Thais, Mahayana Buddhism (see Religion, p.316) fuses with other ancient religious beliefs, notably Confucianism and Taoism, and the statues and shrines within Wat Mangkon cover the whole spectrum. Passing through the secondary gateway, under the glazed ceramic gables topped with undulating Chinese dragons, you're greeted by a set of four outsized statues of bearded and rather forbidding sages, each clasping a symbolic object: a parasol, a pagoda, a snake's head and a mandolin. Beyond them, a series of Buddha images swathed in saffron netting occupies the next chamber, a lovely open-sided room of gold paintwork, red-lacquered wood, lattice lanterns and pictorial wall panels inlaid with mother-of-pearl. Elsewhere in the compound you'll find a fortune-teller, a Chinese medicine stall, and little booths selling devotional paraphernalia.

WAT GA BUANG KIM

Map 5, D4. Express boat to Tha Rajavongse (Rajawong); or bus AC#4, AC#7, #25, #40, #53 or #56.

Less than 100m northwest up Charoen Krung from Wat Mangkon, a left turn into Thanon Rajawong, followed by a right turn into Thanon Anawong and a further right turn into the narrow, two-pronged Soi Krai brings you to the typical neighbourhood temple of **Wat Ga Buang Kim**. Here, as at Thai temples upcountry, local residents socialize in the shade of the tiny, enclosed courtyard and the occasional worshipper drops by to pay homage at the altar. This particular wat is remarkable for its exquisitely ornamented "vegetarian hall", a one-room shrine with a central altarpiece framed by intricately carved wooden tableaux – gold-painted miniatures arranged as if in sequence, with recognizable characters reappearing in new positions and in different moods. The hall's outer wall is adorned with small tableaux, too, the area around the doorway at the top of the stairs peopled with finely crafted ceramic figurines drawn from Chinese opera stories. The other building in the wat compound is a stage used for Chinese opera performances.

WAT CHAKRAWAT

Map 5, C4. Express boat to Tha Rajavongse (Rajawong); or bus #56.

About another 100m to the south, the temple of **Wat Chakrawat** overlooks the Chao Phraya River. The compound is home to several long-suffering crocodiles, not to mention monkeys, dogs and chess-playing local residents. **Crocodiles** have lived in the tiny pond behind the bot for about fifty years, ever since one was brought here after being hauled out of the river, where it had been endangering the limbs of bathers. The original crocodile, stuffed, sits in a glass case overlooking the current generation in the pond.

Across the other side of the wat compound is a grotto housing two unusual **Buddhist relics**. The first is a black silhouette on the wall, decorated with squares of gold leaf and believed to be the Buddha's shadow; nearby, the statue of a fat monk looks on. The story goes that this monk was so good-looking that he was forever being tempted by the attentions of women; the only way he could deter them was to make himself ugly, which he did by gorging himself into obesity.

PAHURAT

Map 5, B2. Express boat to Tha Saphan Phut (Memorial Bridge); or bus AC#7, #53 or #56.

The small square south of the intersection of Chakraphet and **Pahurat** roads is the focus of the capital's sizeable Indian community. Curiosity-shopping is not as rewarding here as in Chinatown, but if you're interested in buying **fabrics** other than Thai silk, this is definitely the place. Thanon Pahurat is chock-a-block with cloth merchants specializing in everything from curtain and cushion materials, through saree and sarong lengths to wedding outfits and *lakhon* dance costumes complete with accessories. Also here, at the Charoen Krung/Thanon Triphet intersection, is the Old Siam Plaza: its mint-green and cream exterior, resplendent with shutters and balustraded balconies, is redolent of a colonial summer palace, and its airy, three-storey interior is filled with a strange combination of shops selling either upmarket gifts or hi-tech consumer goods. Most rewarding are the half-dozen shops on the ground floor that carry an excellent range of silk from north and northeast Thailand; many of them offer

PAHURAT

dressmaking services as well. But most of the ground floor is taken up by a permanent food festival and is packed with stalls selling snacks, sweets and sticky desserts. Pahurat is also renowned for its **Indian restaurants**, and a short stroll along Thanon Chakraphet will take you past a choice selection of curry houses and street vendors.

PAK KHLONG TALAT

Map 5, A4. Express Boat to Tha Saphan Phut (Memorial Bridge); or Bus #3, AC#12, #53 or #56.

A browse through **Pak Khlong Talat**, a 24-hour **flower and vegetable market**, is a fine and fitting way to round off a day in Chinatown, though if you're an early riser it's also a great place to come before dawn, when market gardeners from Thonburi boat and truck their freshly picked produce across the Chao Phraya, ready for sale to the shopkeepers, restaurateurs and hoteliers. Occupying an ideal position close to the river, the market has been operating from covered halls between the southern ends of Thanon Banmo, Thanon Chakraphet and the river bank since the nineteenth century, and is the biggest wholesale market in the capital. The flower stalls, selling twenty different varieties of cut orchids and myriad other tropical blooms, spill on to the streets along the riverfront as well and, though prices are lowest in the early morning, you can still get some good bargains here in the afternoon.

For the most interesting approach to the market from the Old Siam Plaza, turn west across Thanon Triphet to reach Thanon Banmo, and then follow this road south down towards the Chao Phraya River. As you near the river, notice the facing rows of traditional Chinese shophouses, still in use today, which retain their characteristic (peeling) pastel-painted facades, shutters and stucco curlicues; there's an entrance into the market on the right.

Thonburi

Bangkok really began across the river from Ratanakosin in the town of **Thonburi**. It's hard to imagine Thonburi, devoid of grand ruins and isolated from central Bangkok, as a former capital of Thailand, but so it was for fifteen years, between the fall of Ayutthaya in 1767 and the establishment of Bangkok in 1782. General Phrya Taksin chose to set up his capital here, strategically near the sea and far from the marauding Burmese, but the story of his brief reign is a chronicle of battles that left little time and few resources to devote to the building of a city worthy of its predecessor. When General Chao Phraya displaced the demented Taksin to become Rama I, his first decision as founder of the Chakri dynasty was to move the capital to the more defensible site across the river. It wasn't until 1932 that Thonburi was linked to its replacement by the **Memorial Bridge** (Saphan Phut), built to commemorate the one-hundred-and-fiftieth anniversary of the foundation of the Chakri dynasty and of Bangkok, and dedicated to Rama I, whose bronze statue sits at the Bangkok approach. Thonburi retained its separate identity for another forty years until, in 1971, it officially became part of Bangkok.

While Thonburi may lack the fine monuments of Thailand's other ancient capitals, it nevertheless contains some of the most traditional parts of Bangkok, making it a pleasant and evocative place in which to wander (or even cycle; see p.117). As well as the imposing riverside structure of **Wat Arun**, Thonburi offers a fleet of royal barges and several moderately interesting temples. In addition, life on this side of the river still revolves around the **khlongs**, on which vendors of food and household goods paddle their boats through the residential areas, and canalside factories transport their wares to the Chao Phraya River artery. **Architecture** along the canals ranges from ramshackle, makeshift homes balanced just above the water – and prone to flooding during the monsoon season – to villa-style residences where the river is kept at bay by lawns, verandas and concrete. Venture on to the Thonburi backroads just three or four kilometres west of the river and you find yourself surrounded by market gardens, nurseries and rural homes, with no hint of the throbbing metropolis across on the other bank. Modern Thonburi, on the other hand, sprawling to each side of Thanon Phra Pinklao, consists of the prosaic line-up of department stores, cinemas, restaurants and markets found all over urbanized Thailand.

Getting there is simply a matter of crossing the river – use one of the numerous bridges (Memorial and Phra Pinklao are the most central), take a cross-river ferry, or hop on the express ferry, which makes three stops around the riverside Bangkok Noi station, just south of Phra Pinklao Bridge.

Thonburi has no obvious places to stay, but the guest houses and restaurants of Banglamphu (see p.157 and p.189) are within easy reach, just across the Chao Phraya River.

EXPLORING THONBURI BY BOAT AND BIKE

One of the most popular ways of seeing the sights of Thonburi is by longtail boat, taking in Wat Arun and the Royal Barge Museum, then continuing along Thonburi's network of small canals. The easiest place to organize boat tours is at the Bangkok Information Centre, where staff help hire a boat for you at Tha Wang Nah pier, next to their office on Thanon Phra Athit in Banglamphu (B400 per boat per hour, with a maximum of six people per boat). Most people however hire boats from Tha Chang, which is conveniently located in front of the Grand Palace, but is renowned for its aggressive and unscrupulous touts and boatmen; if you do go for this option, try to bargain the price down to B400 per hour, but expect to be charged up to B1500 per boat for a two-hour tour.

A less expensive option is to use the public longtails that run bus-like services along back canals from central Bangkok-side piers, departing every ten to thirty minutes and charging B15–30 a round trip. Potentially interesting routes include the Khlong Bangkok Noi service from Tha Chang; the Khlong Mon service from Tha Thien, in front of Wat Po; the Khlong Bang Waek service (along the canal that runs northwest off Khlong Bangkok Yai) from Tha Saphan Phut, at Memorial Bridge; and the Khlong Om service from Tha Nonthaburi. There have however been recent reports that taxi-boat drivers are making it impossible for tourists to board the public services from Tha Chang and Tha Thien, so the tourist office suggests starting in Nonthaburi instead.

A fixture of the upper-bracket tourist round is the organized canal tour to see Thonburi's Wat Sai floating market. This has become so commercialized and land-based that it can't be recommended in preference to the two-hour trip out to the floating market of Damnoen Saduak (see p.279), but if you're short on time and set on seeing fruit- and flower-laden paddle boats, then join the longtail Wat Sai market tours from Tha Chang or from Tha Oriental (at the *Oriental Hotel*); these tours leave at around 7am and cost from B400 per person. Also worth considering is the fairly contrived but still picturesque Taling Chan floating market, which operates every Saturday and Sunday from 9am to 4pm on Khlong Chakphra in front of Taling Chan District Office, a couple of kilometres west of Bangkok Noi station. It can be visited as part of a chartered longtail tour, or you can make your own way there on bus #79 from Democracy Monument/Rajdamnoen Klang, getting out at Khet Taling Chan, and either watching from the banks or hiring a longtail from the market. Alternatively, the Mitchaophya Boat Company (☎225 6179) runs a boat tour that departs from Tha Chang at 9am on Saturdays and Sundays, taking in the Royal Barge Museum, floating markets and the island of Ko Kred, returning at 4pm (B200, children B150).

The most peaceful and least touristed way to enjoy the canals of Thonburi is to join the monthly **bicycle tour** organized by the Bangkok Tourist Bureau on Thanon Phra Athit in Banglamphu (☎225 7612–4; B650 including bike rental). You need to be reasonably fit to tackle the 35-kilometre route, which is specially designed to follow canal towpaths wherever possible; on the way you're guided through exceptionally scenic parts of both Thonburi and Nonthaburi, taking in khlong-side settlements, water-borne market traders, market gardens, orchid nurseries and neighbourhood temples. The tour currently takes place from 7am to 4.30pm on the first Sunday of every month, but there are plans to make it a weekly event, so call ahead to check.

EXPLORING THONBURI

WAT ARUN

Map 4, A9. Daily 7am–5pm; B20. Cross-river ferry from Tha Thien.

Almost directly across the river from Wat Po rises the enormous five-pranged **Wat Arun,** the Temple of Dawn, probably Bangkok's most memorable landmark and familiar as the silhouette used in the TAT logo. It looks particularly impressive best from the river, as you head downstream from the Grand Palace towards the *Oriental Hotel*, but is ornate enough to merit stopping off for a closer look. All boat tours include half an hour here, but – despite the claims of tour operators who'll try to persuade you otherwise – it's easy to visit Wat Arun independently: just take a B2 cross-river ferry from the pier adjacent to the Chao Phraya Express Boat pier at Tha Thien.

A good way to enjoy the night-time, floodlit view of Wat Arun and Bangkok's other riverside sights is to join one of the restaurant boats that travel up and down the Chao Phraya River every evening; see p.195 for recommendations.

A wat has occupied this site since the Ayutthaya period, though it only became known as the Temple of Dawn in 1768, when General Phrya Taksin reputedly reached his new capital at the break of day. The temple served as his royal chapel and housed the recaptured Emerald Buddha for several years until the image was moved to Wat Phra Kaeo in 1785. Despite losing its special status after the relocation, Wat Arun continued to be revered, and was reconstructed and enlarged to its present height of 104m by Rama II and Rama III.

The Wat Arun that you see today is a classic prang structure of Ayutthayan style, built as a representation of Mount Meru, the home of the gods in Khmer mythology. Climbing the two tiers of the square base that supports the

central prang, you not only get a good view of the river and beyond, but also a chance to examine the tower's curious decorations. Both this main prang and the four minor ones that encircle it are covered in bits of broken porcelain, arranged to create an amazing array of polychromatic flowers. (Local people gained much merit by donating their crockery for the purpose.) Statues of mythical figures such as *yaksha* demons and half-bird, half-human *kinnari* support the different levels and, on the first terrace, the mondops at each cardinal point contain statues of the Buddha at the most important stages of his life: at birth (north), in meditation (east), preaching his first sermon (south) and entering Nirvana (west). The second platform surrounds the base of the prang proper, whose closed entranceways are guarded by four statues of the Hindu god Indra on his three-headed elephant Erawan. In the niches of the smaller prangs stand statues of Phra Pai, the god of the wind, on horseback.

WAT PRAYOON

Map 2, B6. Express boat to Tha Saphan Phut (Memorial Bridge), then walk across the bridge.

Downstream of Wat Arun, beside Memorial Bridge, **Wat Prayoon** is worth visiting for its unusual collection of miniature chedis and shrines, set on an artificial hill constructed on a whim of Rama III's, after he'd noticed the pleasing shapes made by dripping candle wax. Wedged in among the grottoes, caverns and ledges of this uneven mass are numerous shrines to departed devotees, forming a phenomenal gallery of different styles, from traditionally Thai chedis, bots or prangs to such obviously foreign designs as the tiny Wild West house complete with cactuses at the front door. Turtles fill the pond surrounding the mound – you can feed them with the banana and papaya sold nearby.

At the edge of the pond stands a memorial to the unfortunate few who lost their lives when one of the saluting cannons exploded at the temple's dedication ceremony in 1836.

About ten minutes' walk upstream from Wat Prayoon, the Catholic church of **Santa Cruz** sits at the heart of what used to be Thonburi's **Portuguese quarter**. The Portuguese came to Thailand both to trade and to proselytize, and by 1856 had established the largest of the European communities in Bangkok: four thousand Portuguese Christians lived in and around Thonburi at this time, about one percent of the total population. The Portuguese ghetto is a thing of the distant past, but this is nonetheless an interesting patch to stroll through, comprising narrow backstreets and tiny shophouses stocked with all manner of goods, from two-baht plastic toys to the essential bottles of chilli sauce.

ROYAL BARGE MUSEUM

Map 2, A3. Daily 8.30am–4.30pm; B30. Express boat to Tha Rot Fai (Bangkok Noi pier); or bus AC#3, AC#7, AC#9, AC#11, AC#32, #124 or #127.

Until about twenty years ago, the king would process down the Chao Phraya River to Wat Arun in a flotilla of royal barges at least once a year, on the occasion of Kathin, the annual donation of robes by the laity to the temple at the end of the rainy season. Fifty-one barges, filling the width of the river and stretching for almost a kilometre, drifted slowly to the measured beat of a drum and the hypnotic strains of ancient boating hymns, chanted by over two thousand oarsmen whose red, gold and blue uniforms complemented the black and gold craft.

The hundred-year-old boats are becoming quite frail, so such a procession is now a rare event – the last was in 1999, to mark the king's 72nd birthday. The three elegantly narrow vessels at the heart of the ceremony now spend their time moored in the **Royal Barge Museum** on the north bank of Khlong Bangkok Noi. Up to 50m long and intricately lacquered and gilded all over, they taper at the prow into magnificent mythical figures after a design first used by the kings of Ayutthaya. Rama I had the boats copied and, when those fell into disrepair, Rama V commissioned the exact reconstructions still in use today. The most important of the trio is *Sri Suphanahongse*, which bears the king and queen and is instantly recognizable by the five-metre-high prow representing a golden swan. In front of it floats *Anantanagaraj*, fronted by a magnificent seven-headed naga and bearing a Buddha image, while the royal children bring up the rear in *Anekchartphuchong*, which has a monkey god from the *Ramayana* at the bow.

The museum is a feature of most canal tours. To **get there** on your own, cross the Phra Pinklao Bridge on foot or by bus and take the first left (Soi Wat Dusitaram), which leads to the museum through a jumble of walkways and houses on stilts. Alternatively, take a ferry to Bangkok Noi station (Tha Rot Fai); from there follow the tracks until you reach the bridge over Khlong Bangkok Noi, cross it and follow the signs. Either way it's about a ten-minute walk.

ROYAL BARGE MUSEUM

Dusit

C onnected to Ratanakosin via the boulevards of Rajdamnoen Klang and Rajdamnoen Nok, the spacious, leafy area known as Dusit has been a royal district since the reign of Rama V (1860–1910). The first Thai monarch to visit Europe, Rama V returned with radical plans for the modernization of his capital, the fruits of which are most visible in Dusit: notably Vimanmek Palace and Wat Benjamabophit, the so-called Marble Temple. Today the peaceful Dusit area retains its European feel, and much of the country's decision-making goes on behind the high fences and impressive facades that line its leafy avenues: Government House is here, and the king lives on the eastern edge of the area, in the Chitrlada Palace.

VIMANMEK PALACE AND THE ROYAL ELEPHANT NATIONAL MUSEUM

Map 2, E1. Daily 9.30am–4pm; compulsory free guided tours every 30min, last tour 3.15pm; B50, or free if you have a Grand Palace ticket, which remains valid for one month. Note that the same dress rules apply here as to the Grand Palace (see p.70). Main entrance on Thanon Rajwithi; other ticket gates on Thanon Ratchasima and

Thanon U-Thong. Bus #56 (westbound) from Banglamphu; or
AC#10 and AC#16 from Victory Monument.

Vimanmek Palace was built by Rama V as a summer
retreat on the little east-coast island of Ko Si Chang, from
where it was transported bit by bit in 1901. Constructed
entirely of golden teak without a single nail, the L-shaped
"Celestial Residence" is encircled by verandas that look out
on to well-kept lawns, flower gardens and lotus ponds. The
ticket price also covers entry to half a dozen other small
museums in the palace grounds, including the Support
Museum and Elephant Museum described below, and all
visitors are treated to free performances of traditional Thai
dance daily at 10.30am & 2pm.

Not surprisingly, Vimanmek soon became Rama V's
favourite palace, and he and his enormous retinue of officials, concubines and children stayed here for lengthy periods between 1902 and 1906. All of Vimanmek's 81 rooms
were out of bounds to male visitors, except for the king's
own apartments, which were entered by a separate staircase.
On display inside is Rama V's collection of artefacts from all
over the world, including bencharong ceramics, European
furniture and bejewelled Thai betel-nut sets. Considered
progressive in his day, Rama V introduced many newfan-
gled ideas to Thailand: the country's first indoor bathroom
is here, as is the earliest typewriter with Thai characters,
and some of the first portrait paintings – portraiture had
until then been seen as a way of stealing part of the sitter's
soul.

- -

Dusit has no accommodation of its own, but
the guest houses of north Banglamphu, near the
Thewes express-boat stop, are fairly near (see p.158).
Restaurants in this area are listed on p.192.

- -

THE ROYAL WHITE ELEPHANTS

In Thailand the most revered of all elephants are the so-called white elephants. Actually tawny brown albinos, they are considered so sacred that they all, whether wild or captive, belong to the king; Buddhist mythology, which tells how the barren Queen Maya became pregnant with the future Buddha after dreaming that a white elephant had entered her womb. The thirteenth-century King Ramkhamhaeng adopted the beast as a symbol of the great and the divine, and ever since, a Thai king's greatness is measured by the number of white elephants he owns. The present king, Rama IX, has twelve, the largest collection to date.

Before an elephant can be granted official "white elephant" status, it has to pass a stringent assessment of its physical and behavioural characteristics. Key qualities include a paleness of seven crucial areas – eyes, nails, palate, hair, outer edges of the ears, tail and testicles – and an all-round genteel demeanour, manifested, for instance, in the way in which it cleans its food before eating, or in a tendency to sleep in a

Elsewhere in the Vimanmek grounds several small throne halls have been converted into tiny museums displaying royal portraits, antique clocks and other collectors' items. The most interesting of these is the **Support Museum Abhisek Dusit Throne Hall**, showcasing the exquisite handicrafts produced under Queen Sirikit's charity project, Support, which works to revitalise traditional Thai arts and crafts. Outstanding exhibits include a collection of handbags, baskets and pots woven from the *lipao* fern that grows wild in southern Thailand; jewellery and figurines inlaid with the iridescent wings of beetles; gold and silver nielloware; and lengths of intricately woven silk from the northeast.

kneeling position. The most recent addition to King Bhumibol's stables was first spotted in Lampang in 1992, but experts from the Royal Household had to spend a year watching its every move before it was finally given the all-clear. Tradition holds that an elaborate ceremony should take place every time a new white elephant is presented to the king: the animal is paraded with great pomp from its place of capture to Dusit, where it's anointed with holy water before an audience of the kingdom's most important priests and dignitaries, before being housed in the royal stables. Recently though, the king has decreed that as a cost-cutting measure there should be no more ceremonies for new acquisitions, and only one of the royal white elephants is now kept inside the royal palace – the others live in less luxurious rural accommodation.

The expression "white elephant" probably derives from the legend that the kings used to present enemies with one of these creatures, whose upkeep proved so expensive that the recipient went bust trying to keep it.

Just inside the eastern, Thanon U-Thong, entrance to the Vimanmek compound stand two whitewashed buildings that once served as the stables for the king's white elephants. Now that the sacred pachyderms have been relocated, the stables have been turned into the **Royal Elephant National Museum**. Inside you'll find some interesting pieces of elephant paraphernalia, including sacred ropes, mahouts' amulets and magic formulae, as well as photos of the all-important ceremony in which a white elephant is granted royal status.

- -
**Vimanmek is also served by the open-topped
Bangkok Sightseeing Bus (see p.55).**
- -

DUSIT ZOO (KHAO DIN)

Map 2, E2. Daily 8am–6pm; B30, children B5. Main entrance on Thanon Rajvithi, and another one on Thanon U-Thong. Bus #56 (westbound) from Banglamphu; or AC#10 and AC#16 from Victory Monument.

Just across Thanon U-Thong is **Dusit Zoo**, also known as Khao Din; once part of the Chitrlada Palace gardens, it is now a public park. All the usual suspects are here, including big cats, elephants, orang-utans, chimpanzees and a reptile house, but the enclosures are pretty basic and not especially heart-warming. However, it's a reasonable place for kids to let off steam, with plenty of shade, a full complement of English-language signs, a lake with pedalos and lots of foodstalls.

Dusit Zoo can be quite fun for kids; for other child-friendly sights and activities in Bangkok, see p.244.

WAT BENJAMABOPHIT

Map 2, E3. Daily 7am–5pm; B20. Bus AC#3 or AC#9.

Ten minutes' walk southeast from Vimanmek along Thanon Sri Ayutthaya, **Wat Benjamabophit** is the last major temple to have been built in Bangkok. It's an interesting fusion of classical Thai and nineteenth-century European design, with its Carrara marble walls – hence the touristic tag "The Marble Temple" – complemented by the bot's unusual stained-glass windows, Victorian in style but depicting figures from Thai mythology. Inside, a fine replica of the highly revered Phra Buddha Chinnarat image of Phitsanulok presides over the small room containing Rama V's ashes. The courtyard behind the bot houses a gallery of Buddha images from all over Asia, set up by Rama V as an overview of different representations of the Buddha.

Wat Benjamabophit is one of the best temples in Bangkok to see religious **festivals** and rituals. Whereas monks elsewhere tend to go out on the streets every morning in search of alms, at the Marble Temple the ritual is reversed, and merit-makers come to them. Between about 6 and 7.30am, the monks line up outside the temple gates on Thanon Nakhon Pathom, their bowls ready to receive donations of curry and rice, lotus buds, incense, even toilet paper and Coca-Cola. The demure row of saffron-robed monks is a sight that's well worth getting up early for. The evening candlelight processions around the bot during the Buddhist festivals of Maha Puja (in February) and Visakha Puja (in May) are among the most entrancing in the country (see p.33).

WAT BENJAMABOPHIT

Downtown Bangkok

Extending east from the rail line and south to Thanon Sathorn, the **downtown** area is central to the colossal expanse of Bangkok as a whole, but rather peripheral in a sightseer's perception of the city. This is where you'll find the main financial district, around Thanon Silom; Thailand's most prestigious centre of higher learning, Chulalongkorn University; and the green expanse of **Lumphini Park**. The chief shopping centres cluster around the corner of Rajdamri and Rama I roads, extending east towards Thanon Sukhumvit and west to Siam Square (not in fact a square, but a grid of small commercial streets on the south side of Thanon Rama I, between Phrayathai and Henri Dunant roads).

Scattered widely across the downtown area are just a few attractions for visitors, including the noisy and glittering **Erawan Shrine**, and three attractive museums housed in traditional teak buildings: the **Suan Pakkad Palace Museum**, **Jim Thompson's House** and the **Kamthieng House**. The infamous **Patpong** district hardly shines as a tourist sight, yet, lamentably, its sex bars provide Thailand's single biggest draw for foreign men.

If you're heading downtown from Banglamphu, allow at least an hour to get to any of the places mentioned here by **bus**. Depending on the time of day, it may be quicker to take an **express boat** downriver and then change onto the **Skytrain**. For other parts of the downtown area, it might be worth considering the regular **longtails** on Khlong Sen Seb, which runs parallel to Thanon Phetchaburi.

For details of accommodation downtown
see p.170, for restaurants see p.197.

SUAN PAKKAD PALACE MUSEUM

Map 2, H4. 352–4 Thanon Sri Ayutthaya. Daily 9am–4pm; B100. Ⓢ Phaya Thai; or bus AC#13, #38, #62 or #72.

In the northern part of downtown, the **Suan Pakkad Palace Museum** stands on what was once a cabbage patch (which gave it its name) but is now one of the finest gardens in Bangkok. Most of this private collection of beautiful Thai objects from all periods is displayed in six traditional wooden houses, which were transported to Bangkok from various parts of the country. You can either take a mediocre guided tour in English (free) or explore the loosely arranged collection yourself (a free handout is usually available and some of the exhibits are labelled).

The Marsi Gallery, attached to Suan Pakkad,
has recently opened to display some interesting
temporary exhibitions of contemporary art
(daily 9am–6pm; Ⓣ246 1775–6 for details).

The highlight is the renovated **Lacquer Pavilion**, across the reedy pond at the back of the grounds. Set on stilts, the pavilion is actually an amalgam of two eighteenth- or late seventeenth-century temple buildings, a *ho trai* (library) and a *ho khien* (writing room), one inside the other, which were found between Ayutthaya and Bang Pa-In. The interior walls are beautifully decorated with gilt on black lacquer: the upper panels depict the life of the Buddha while the lower ones show scenes from the *Ramayana* (see pp.74-75). Look out especially for the grisly details in the tableau on the back wall, showing the earth goddess drowning the evil forces of Mara. Underneath are depicted some European dandies on horseback, probably merchants, whose presence suggests that the work was executed before the fall of Ayutthaya in 1767.

The carefully observed details of daily life and nature are skilful and lively, especially considering the restraints which the **lacquering technique** places on the artist, who has no opportunity for corrections or touching up: the design has to be punched into a piece of paper, which is then laid on the panel of black lacquer (a kind of plant resin); a small bag of chalk dust is pressed on top so that the dust penetrates the minute holes in the paper, leaving a line of dots on the lacquer to mark the pattern; a gummy substance is then applied to the background areas which are to remain black, before the whole surface is covered in microscopically thin squares of gold leaf; thin sheets of blotting paper, sprinkled with water, are then laid over the panel, which when pulled off bring away the gummy substance and the unwanted pieces of gold leaf that are stuck to it, leaving the rest of the gold decoration in high relief against the black background.

The **Ban Chiang House** has a very good collection of elegant, whorled pottery and bronze jewellery, which the former owner of Suan Pakkad Palace, Princess Chumbot, excavated from tombs at Ban Chiang, the major Bronze Age settlement in the northeast. Scattered around the rest of the museum, you'll come across some attractive Thai and Khmer religious sculpture among an eclectic jumble of artefacts: fine ceramics as well as some intriguing kiln-wasters, failed pots which have melted together in the kiln to form weird, almost rubbery pieces of sculpture; an extensive collection of colourful papier-mâché *khon* masks;

beautiful betel-nut sets (see p.242) and elegant monks' ceremonial fans; and some rich teak carvings, including a 200-
year-old temple door showing episodes from *Sang Thong*, a
folk tale about a childless king and queen who discover a
handsome son in a conch shell.

To the north of Suan Pakkad, the Victory Monument
can be seen from way down Thanon Phrayathai. Erected
after the Indo-Chinese War of 1940–41, when Thailand
pinched back some territory in Laos and Cambodia while
the French were otherwise occupied in World War II,
it now commemorates all of Thailand's military glories.

JIM THOMPSON'S HOUSE

Map 6, B3. 6 Soi Kasemsan 2, Thanon Rama I. Daily from 9am,
viewing on frequent 45min guided tours in several languages, last
tour 4.30pm, café and shop open until 5.30pm; B100, under-25s
B50; ⓦwww.jimthompson.com. Ⓢ National Stadium; or bus AC#2,
AC#8, #15, #25, AC#29, #29 or #40.

Just northwest of Siam Square, **Jim Thompson's House** is
a kind of Ideal Home in elegant Thai style, and a peaceful
refuge from downtown chaos. The house was the residence
of the legendary American adventurer, entrepreneur, art
collector and all-round character whose mysterious disappearance in the jungles of Malaysia in 1967 has made him
even more of a legend among Thailand's farang community.
Apart from putting together this beautiful home,
Thompson's most concrete contribution was to turn traditional silk-weaving from a dying art into the highly successful international industry it is today.

The grand, rambling **house** is in fact a combination of
six teak houses, some from as far afield as Ayutthaya and
most over two hundred years old. Like all traditional houses,

THE LEGEND OF JIM THOMPSON

Thai silk-weavers, art dealers and conspiracy theorists all owe a debt to Jim Thompson, who even now, over thirty years after his disappearance, remains Thailand's most famous farang. An architect by trade, Thompson left his New York practice in 1940 to join the Office of Strategic Services (later to become the CIA), a tour of duty which was to see him involved in clandestine operations in North Africa, Europe and, in 1945, the Far East, where he was detailed to a unit preparing for the invasion of Thailand. When the mission was pre-empted by the Japanese surrender, he served for a year as OSS station chief in Bangkok, forming links that were later to provide grist for endless speculation.

After an unhappy and short-lived stint as part-owner of the *Oriental Hotel*, Thompson found his calling in the struggling silk-weavers of the area near the present Jim Thompson House, whose traditional product was unknown in the West and had been all but abandoned by Thais in favour of less costly imported textiles. Encouragement from society friends and an enthusiastic write-up in *Vogue* convinced him there was a foreign market for Thai silk, and by 1948 he had founded the Thai Silk Company Ltd. Success was assured when, two years later, the company was commissioned to make the costumes for the Broadway run of *The King and I*. Thompson's celebrated eye for colour combinations and his tireless promotion – in the early days, he could often be seen in the lobby of the *Oriental* with bolts of silk slung over his shoulder, waiting to pounce on any remotely curious tourist – quickly made his name synonymous with Thai silk.

Like a character in a Somerset Maugham novel, Thompson played the role of Western exile to the hilt. Though he spoke no Thai, he made it his personal mission to preserve traditional arts and architecture at a time when most Thais were more keen to emulate the West, assembling his famous Thai house and stuffing it with all manner of Oriental *objets d'art*. At the same time he held firmly to his farang roots and society connections: no foreign gathering in Bangkok was complete without Jim Thompson, and virtually every Western luminary passing through Bangkok – from Truman Capote to Ethel Merman – dined at his table.

If Thompson's life was the stuff of legend, his disappearance and presumed death only added to the mystique. On Easter Sunday, 1967, Thompson, while staying with friends in a cottage in Malaysia's Cameron Highlands, went out for a stroll and never came back. A massive search of the area, employing local guides, tracker dogs and even shamans, turned up no clues, provoking a rash of fascinating but entirely unsubstantiated theories. The grandfather of them all, advanced by a Dutch psychic, held that Thompson had been lured into an ambush by the disgraced former prime minister of Thailand, Pridi Panyonyong, and spirited off to Cambodia for indeterminate purposes; later versions, supposing that Thompson had remained a covert CIA operative all his life, proposed that he was abducted by Vietnamese communists and brainwashed to be displayed as a high-profile defector to communism. More recently, an amateur sleuth claims to have found evidence that Thompson met a more mundane fate, having been killed by a careless truck driver and hastily buried.

they were built in wall sections hung together without nails on a frame of wooden pillars, which made it easy to dismantle them, pile them onto a barge and float them to their new home. Although he had trained as an architect, Thompson had more difficulty in putting them back together again; in the end, he had to go back to Ayutthaya to hunt down a group of carpenters who still practised the old house-building methods. Thompson added a few unconventional touches of his own, incorporating the elaborately carved front wall of a Chinese pawnshop between the drawing room and the bedroom, and reversing the other walls in the drawing room so that their carvings faced into the room.

The impeccably tasteful **interior** has been left as it was during Thompson's life, even down to the cutlery on the dining table. Complementing the fine artefacts from throughout Southeast Asia is a stunning array of Thai arts and crafts, including one of the best collections of traditional Thai paintings in the world. Thompson picked up plenty of bargains from the Thieves' Quarter (Nakhon Kasem) in Chinatown, before collecting Thai art became fashionable and expensive. Other pieces were liberated from decay and destruction in upcountry temples, while many of the Buddha images were turned over by ploughs, especially around Ayutthaya. Some of the exhibits are very rare, such as a seventeenth-century Ayutthayan teak Buddha, but Thompson also bought pieces of little value and fakes, simply for their looks – a shopping strategy that's all the more sensible in the jungle of today's Thai antiques trade.

THE ERAWAN SHRINE

Map 6, H4. Ⓢ Chit Lom; or bus AC#4, AC#8, AC#11, AC#13, AC#15, #15, #25 or #40.

For a break from high culture, drop in on the **Erawan Shrine** (*Saan Phra Pom* in Thai), at the corner of Ploenchit and Rajdamri roads. Remarkable as much for its setting as anything else, this shrine to Brahma, the ancient Hindu creation god, and Erawan, his elephant, squeezes in on one of the busiest and noisiest corners of modern Bangkok, in the shadow of the *Grand Hyatt Erawan Hotel* – whose existence is the reason for the shrine. When a string of calamities held up the building of the original hotel in the 1950s, spirit doctors were called in, who instructed the owners to build a new home for the offended local spirits: the hotel was then finished without further mishap.

Be prepared for sensory overload here: the main structure shines with lurid glass of all colours and the overcrowded precinct around it is almost buried under scented garlands and incense candles. You might also catch a lacklustre group of traditional **dancers** performing here to the strains of a small classical orchestra – worshippers hire them to give thanks for a stroke of good fortune. To increase their future chances of such good fortune, visitors buy a bird or two from the flocks incarcerated in cages here; the bird–seller transfers the requested number of captives to a tiny hand-held cage, from which the customer duly liberates the animals, thereby accruing merit. People set on less abstract rewards will invest in a lottery ticket from one of the physically handicapped sellers: they're thought to be the luckiest you can buy.

BAN KAMTHIENG

Map 8, E6. 131 Soi Asoke (Soi 21), off Thanon Sukhumvit. Tues–Sat 9am–5pm; entry by donation until renovations are completed in 2002. Ⓢ Asok; or longtail boat along Khlong Sen Seb to Tha Saphan Asoke, then bus #38; or bus AC#1, AC#8, AC#11, AC #13, #38 or #40.

Another reconstructed traditional Thai residence, **Ban Kamthieng** was moved in the 1960s from Chiang Mai to Thanon Sukhumvit and set up as an ethnological museum by the Siam Society. Built on the banks of the River Ping in the mid-nineteenth century, it differs from both Suan Pakkad and Jim Thompson's House in being the home of a rural family in northern Thailand.

The ground-level display of farming tools and fish traps evokes the upcountry practice of fishing in flooded rice paddies to supplement the supply from the rivers. Upstairs, the main rooms of the house are much as they would have been 150 years ago – the raised floor is polished and smooth, sparsely furnished with only a couple of low tables and seating mats, and a betel-nut set to hand. The rectangular lintel above the door to the inner room is a *hum yon*, carved in floral patterns that represent testicles and designed to ward off evil spirits.

Next door to Kamthieng House, in the same compound, is the more recently acquired **Sangaroon House**, built here to house the folk-craft collection of Thai architect and lecturer Sangaroon Ratagasikorn. Upon his return to Thailand after studying in America under Frank Lloyd Wright, Sangaroon became fascinated by the efficient designs of rural utensils and began to collect them as teaching aids. Those on display include baskets, fishing pots and *takraw* balls, all of which fulfil his criteria of being functional, simple and beautiful, with no extraneous features.

THE QUEEN SAOVABHA MEMORIAL INSTITUTE

Map 7, K4. Displays Mon–Fri 10.30am & 2pm, Sat, Sun & holidays 10.30am; B70. Ⓢ Sala Daeng; or bus AC#2 or AC#7.

The **Queen Saovabha Memorial Institute** (*Sathan Saovabha*), often simply known as the **Snake Farm**, at the corner of Thanon Rama IV and Thanon Henri Dunant, is a bit of a circus act, but an entertaining, informative and worthy one at that. Run by the Thai Red Cross, it has a double function: to produce snake-bite serums, and to educate the public on the dangers of Thai snakes.

The latter mission involves putting on **displays** that begin with a slick half-hour slide show illustrating, among other things, how to apply a tourniquet and immobilize a bitten limb. Things warm up with a live demonstration of snake handling and feeding and venom extraction, which is well presented and safe, and gains a perverse fascination from the knowledge that the strongest venoms of the snakes on show can kill in only three minutes. The climax of the display comes when, having watched a python squeezing great chunks of chicken through its body, the audience is invited to handle a docile Burmese constrictor.

LUMPHINI PARK

Map 2, H8. Daily 5am–8pm. Ⓢ Sala Daeng or Ratchadamri; or bus AC#2, AC#4, AC#7, AC#15, #15 or #62.

If you're sick of cars and concrete, head for **Lumphini Park** (*Suan Lum*), at the east end of Thanon Silom, where the air is almost fresh and the traffic noise dies down to a low murmur. Named after the town in Nepal where the Buddha was born, the park is arranged around two lakes, where you can join the locals in feeding the turtles and fish with bread or take out a pedalo or a rowing boat (B40 per hour), and is landscaped with a wide variety of local trees and numerous pagodas and pavilions, usually occupied by Chinese chess players.

To recharge your batteries in Lumphini Park, make for the garden restaurant, *Pop*, in the northwest corner, or the pavement food stalls at the northern edge of the park.

In the early morning and at dusk, exercise freaks hit the outdoor gym on the southwest side of the park, or en masse do some jogging along the yellow-marked circuit or some balletic t'ai chi, stopping for the twice-daily broadcast of the king's anthem. The wide open spaces here are a popular area for gay cruising, and you might be offered dope, though the police patrol regularly. For all that, it's not at all an intimidating place.

PATPONG

Map 7, J5. Ⓢ Sala Daeng; or bus AC#2, AC#4, AC#15 or #15.

Concentrated into a small area between the eastern ends of Silom and Suriwong roads, the neon-lit go-go bars of the **Patpong** district loom like rides in a tawdry sexual Disneyland. In front of each bar, girls cajole passers-by with a lifeless sensuality while insistent touts proffer printed menus detailing the degradations on show. Inside, bikini-clad or topless women gyrate to Western music and play hostess to the (almost exclusively male) spectators; upstairs, live shows feature women who, to use Spalding Gray's phrase in *Swimming to Cambodia*, "do everything with their vaginas except have babies".

Patpong was no more than a sea of mud when the capital was founded on the marshy riverbank to the west, but by the 1960s it had grown into a flash district of nightclubs and dance halls for rich Thais, owned by a Chinese millionaire godfather who gave his name to the area. In 1969, an American entrepreneur turned an existing teahouse into a luxurious nightclub to satisfy the tastes of soldiers on R&R trips from Vietnam, and so Patpong's transformation into a Western sex reservation began. At first, the area was rough and violent, but over the years it has wised up to the desires of the affluent farang, and now markets itself as a packaged concept of Oriental decadence.

The centre of the skin trade lies along the interconnected sois of **Patpong 1 and 2**, where lines of go-go bars share their patch with respectable restaurants, a 24-hour supermarket and an overabundance of chemists. By night, it's a thumping theme park, whose blazing neon promises tend towards self-parody, with names like *French Kiss* and *Love Nest*. Budget travellers, purposeful safari-suited businessmen and noisy lager louts throng the streets, and even the most demure tourists – of both sexes – turn out to do some shopping at the night market down the middle of Patpong 1, where hawkers sell fake watches, bags and designer T-shirts. By day, a relaxed hangover descends on the place. Bar-girls hang out at food stalls and cafés in respectable dress, often recognizable only by their faces, pinched and strained from the continuous use of antibiotics and heroin in an attempt to ward off venereal disease and boredom. Farang men slump at the bars on Patpong 2, drinking and watching videos, unable to find anything else to do in the whole of Bangkok.

Beyond the west end of Thanon Silom, the old farang trading quarter between Thanon Charoen Krung (New Road) and the river is the only area in Bangkok where you could eke out an architectural walk, though it's hardly compelling. Incongruous churches and "colonial" buildings – the best of these the *Oriental Hotel*'s Authors' Wing, where nostalgic afternoon teas are served – are hemmed in by Chinatown (see p.105) to the north and the spice shops and *halal* canteens of the Muslim area on Charoen Krung.

The small dead-end alley to the east of Patpong 2, **Silom 4** (ie Soi 4, Thanon Silom), hosts Bangkok's hippest nightlife, its bars, clubs and pavements heaving at weekends with the capital's brightest and most overprivileged young things. A few gay venues still cling to Silom 4, but the focus of the scene has recently shifted to **Silom 2**. In between, **Soi Thaniya's** hostess bars and one of the city's swishest shopping centres, Thaniya Plaza, cater mostly to Japanese tourists, while **Soi 6** (Soi Tantawan) to the west of Patpong attracts a curious mix of Korean and hardcore gay visitors.

PATPONG

THE SEX INDUSTRY

Bangkok owes its reputation as the carnal capital of the world to a thriving sex industry fuelled by more than one thousand sex-related businesses. But contrary to the image fostered by the girlie bars of Patpong, the vast majority of Thailand's prostitutes of both sexes (estimated at anywhere between 200,000 and 700,000) work with Thai men, not foreigners.

Prostitution and polygamy have long been intrinsic to the Thai way of life. Until 1910, Thai kings had always kept a retinue of concubines, and the practice was aped by nobles and merchants keen to have lots of sons and heirs. Though the monarch is now monogamous, it is still acceptable practice for men of all classes to keep mistresses (known as *mia noi,* or minor wives), a tradition bolstered by the popular philosophy which maintains that an official wife (*mia luang*) should be treated like the temple's main Buddha image – respected and elevated upon the altar – whereas the minor wife is an amulet, to be taken along wherever you go. For those not wealthy enough to take on *mia noi,* prostitution is a far less costly and equally accepted option. Statistics indicate that at least two fifths of sexually active Thai men are thought to use the services of prostitutes twice a month on average.

The farang sex industry began during the Vietnam War, when the American military set up seven bases around Thailand and the country became a playground for GIs on R&R breaks. When the bases were evacuated in the mid-1970s, tourists moved in to fill the vacuum, and sex tourism has since grown to become an established part of the Thai economy. The two-million-plus foreign males who arrive here each year represent foreign-exchange earnings of B50 billion.

PATPONG

The majority of the women who work in the Patpong bars come from the poorest rural areas of north and northeast Thailand. **Economic refugees** in search of a better life, they're easily drawn into an industry where they can make in a single night what it takes a month to earn in the rice fields; a couple of lucrative years in the sex bars is often the most effective way of helping to pay off family debts.

Despite its ubiquity, prostitution has been **illegal** in Thailand since 1960, but sex-industry bosses easily get round the law by registering their establishments as entertainment venues and making payoffs to the police. Sex workers, on the other hand, have few legal rights and will often endure violence rather than face fines and long rehabilitation sentences. Life is made even more difficult by the fact that abortion is illegal in Thailand. In an attempt to redress some of the iniquities, an amendment to the **anti-prostitution law**, passed in April 1996, attempts to treat sex workers as victims rather than criminals and to punish owners and customers of any place of prostitution, but this has been met with some cynicism, owing to the number of influential police and politicians allegedly involved in the sex industry.

In recent years, the spectre of **AIDS** has put the problems of the sex industry into sharp focus: according to a joint study by Chulalongkorn University and the European Union, there are currently around one million HIV carriers in Thailand, and there have been over 270,000 AIDS-related deaths in the country since 1985. Since 1988, the government has successfully conducted an aggressive AIDS awareness campaign, a vital component of which has been to send health officials into brothels to administer blood tests and give out condoms.

PATPONG

Chatuchak and the outskirts

The amorphous clutter of Greater Bangkok doesn't harbour many attractions, but there are a handful of places on the outskirts of the city which make pleasant half-day outings. Nearly all the places described in this chapter can be reached fairly painlessly by some sort of city transport, either by ferry up the Chao Phraya River, or by city bus.

If you're in Bangkok on a Saturday or Sunday, it's well worth making the effort to visit the enormous **Chatuchak Weekend Market**, the perfect place to browse and to buy. The open-air **Prasart Museum** and **Muang Boran Ancient City** are both recommended for anyone who hasn't got the time to go upcountry and admire Thailand's temples and palaces in situ; both these cultural theme parks boast finely crafted replicas of traditional Thai buildings. Taking a boat ride up the Chao Phraya River makes a nice change to sitting in city-centre traffic, and the upstream town of **Nonthaburi** and the nearby island of **Ko Kred** provide the ideal excuse for doing just that.

CHATUCHAK WEEKEND MARKET

Sat & Sun 7am–6pm. ⓢ Saphan Kwai or Mo Chit; or bus AC#2, AC#3, AC#9, AC#10, AC#12, AC#29 or AC#39 (about an hour's ride north of Banglamphu or Sukhumvit).

With six thousand open-air stalls to peruse, and wares as diverse as Lao silk, Siamese kittens and designer lamps to choose from, the enormous **Chatuchak Weekend Market** is Bangkok's most enjoyable shopping experience. It occupies a huge patch of ground between the Northern Bus Terminal and Mo Chit Skytrain station, and is best reached by Skytrain if you're coming from downtown areas. The Mo Chit stop is the most convenient, but some people prefer to get off at Saphan Kwai and then walk through the amulet stalls that line the road up to the southern (handicraft) part of the market.

Though its primary customers are Bangkok residents in search of inexpensive clothes and home accessories, Chatuchak also has plenty of collector- and tourist-oriented **stalls**. Best buys include antique lacquerware, unusual sarongs, cotton clothing and crafts from the north, jeans, traditional musical instruments, silver jewellery and ceramics, particularly the five-coloured *bencharong*. The market is divided into 26 numbered **sections**, plus a dozen unnumbered ones, each of which is more or less dedicated to a certain range of goods, for example household items, plants, used books or handicrafts. If you have several hours to spare, it's fun just to browse at whim, but if you're looking for souvenirs, handicrafts or traditional textiles you should start with sections 22, 24, 25 and 26, which are all in a cluster at the southwest (Saphan Kwai) end of the market; the "Dream" section behind the TAT office is also full of interesting artefacts.

Nancy Chandler's Map of Bangkok has a fabulously detailed
and informatively annotated map of all the sections in the
market, but should be bought before you arrive.
Alternatively, drop in at the TAT office, located in the
Chatuchak market building on the southwest edge of the
market, across the car park, as they dish out smaller but
useful plans of the market for free.

The market also contains a large – and controversial –
wildlife section, and has long been a popular clearing-
house for protected and endangered species such as gib-
bons, palm cockatoos and Indian pied hornbills; many of
these are smuggled in from Laos and Cambodia and sold to
private animal collectors and foreign zoos, particularly in
eastern Europe. The illegal trade goes on beneath the
counter, but you're bound to come across fighting cocks
around the back (demonstrations are almost continuous),
miniature flying squirrels being fed milk through pipettes,
and iridescent red and blue Siamese fighting fish, kept in
individual jars and shielded from each other's aggressive
stares by sheets of cardboard.

There's no shortage of **food** stalls inside the market compound, particularly at the southern end, where you'll find
plenty of places serving inexpensive *phat thai* and Isaan
snacks. Close by these stalls is a classy little juice bar called
Viva where you can rest your feet while listening to the
manager's jazz tapes. The biggest restaurant here is *Toh Plue*,
behind TAT on the edge of the Dream section, which
makes a good rendezvous point. For vegetarian sustenance,
head for *Chamlong's* (also known as *Asoke*), an open-air,
cafeteria-style restaurant just outside the market on Thanon
Kamphaeng Phet (across Thanon Kamphaeng Phet 2), set
up by Bangkok's former governor as a service to the citi-
zenry (Sat & Sun 8am–noon). You can **change money**

(Sat & Sun 7am–7pm) in the market building at the south end of the market, across the car park from the stalls area, and there's an ATM here too.

THE PRASART MUSEUM

9 Soi 4A, Soi Krungthep Kreetha, Thanon Krungthep Kreetha. Tues–Sun 10am–3pm; B500; call ☎379 3601 to book the compulsory tour. Bus #93 from Thanon Si Phraya near River City, or from Thanon Phetchaburi or Thanon Phetchaburi Mai.

Located right out on the eastern edge of the city, and still surrounded by fields, the **Prasart Museum** is an unusual open-air exhibition of traditional Asian buildings, collected and reassembled by wealthy entrepreneur and art lover Khun Prasart. The museum is rarely visited by independent tourists, partly because of its intentionally limited opening hours and inflated admission price, and partly because it takes at least an hour and a half to get here by bus from Banglamphu or Silom, but it makes a pleasant day out and is worth the effort.

Set in a gorgeously lush tropical garden, the museum comprises about a dozen replicas of **traditional buildings**, including a golden teak palace inspired by the royal residence now housed at the National Museum, a Chinese temple and water garden, a Khmer shrine, a Sukhothai-era teak library set over a lotus pond, and a European-style mansion, fashionable with Bangkok royalty in the late nineteenth century. Some of these structures have been assembled from the ruins of buildings found all over Asia, but there's no attempt at purist authenticity – the aim is to give a flavour of architectural styles, not an exact reproduction. Many of the buildings, including the Thai wat and the Chinese temple, were constructed from scratch, using designs dreamed up by Khun Prasart and his team.

All the buildings are beautifully crafted, with great atten-

THE PRASART MUSEUM

tion paid to carvings and decorations, and many are filled with antique **artefacts**, including Burmese woodcarvings, prehistoric pottery from Ban Chiang and Lopburi-era statuettes. There are also some unusual pieces of royal memorabilia and an exquisite collection of *bencharong* ceramics. Khun Prasart also owns a ceramics workshop which produces reproductions of famous designs; they can be bought either at the museum, or at his showroom, the Prasart Collection, on the second floor of the Peninsular Plaza shopping centre on Thanon Rajdamri.

The easiest way to get to the museum is by ordinary **bus** #93, which you can pick up either on Thanon Si Phraya near River City and the GPO, or anywhere along its route on Phetchaburi and New Phetchaburi roads. The #93 terminates on Thanon Krungthep Kreetha, but you should get off a couple of stops before the terminus, at the first stop on Thanon Krungthep Kreetha, as soon as you see the sign for the Prasart Museum (about 1hr 15min bus ride from Si Phraya). Follow the sign down Soi Krungthep Kreetha, go past the golf course and, after about a 15-minute walk, turn off down Soi 4A.

MUANG BORAN ANCIENT CITY

Map 1, I7. Daily 8am–5pm; B50, kids B25. Bus AC#7, AC#8, AC#11 or #25 to Samut Prakan, then songthaew #36.

The brochure for **Muang Boran Ancient City** sells the place as a sort of cultural fast-food outlet – "a realistic journey into Thailand's past in only a few hours, saving you the many weeks of travel and considerable expense of touring Thailand yourself". The open-air museum, 33km southeast of the city centre, is a considerably more authentic experience than its own publicity makes out, showcasing past and present Thai artistry and offering an enjoyable introduction to the country's architecture.

Some of Muang Boran's ninety-odd buildings are **originals**, including the rare scripture library rescued from Samut Songkhram. Others are painstaking **reconstructions** from contemporary documents (the Ayutthaya-period Sanphet Prasat palace is a particularly fine example) or **scaled-down copies** of famous monuments such as the Grand Palace. A sizeable team of restorers and craftspeople maintains the buildings and helps keep some of the traditional techniques alive; if you come here during the week you can watch them at work.

NONTHABURI

Map 1, H5.

A trip to **Nonthaburi**, the first town beyond the northern boundary of Bangkok, is the easiest excursion you can make from the centre of the city and affords a perfect opportunity to recharge your batteries. The last stop upriver for **express boats**, Nonthaburi is 75 minutes from Sathorn Bridge on a "daily standard" boat, or 55 minutes if you catch a yellow-flag "special express".

The ride is half the fun in itself, weaving round huge, crawling rice barges and tiny canoes, and the slow pace of the boat gives you plenty of time to take in the sights on the way. On the north side of Banglamphu, you'll pass the royal boat house in front of the National Library on the east bank, where you can glimpse the minor ceremonial boats which escort the grand royal barges. Further out are dazzling Buddhist temples and drably painted mosques, catering for Bangkok's growing Muslim population, as well as a few remaining communities who still live in houses on stilts or houseboats – around Krungthon Bridge, for example, you'll see people living on the huge teak vessels used to carry rice, sand and charcoal.

DURIANS

The naturalist Alfred Russel Wallace, eulogizing the taste of the durian, compared it to "rich butter-like custard highly flavoured with almonds, but intermingled with wafts of flavour that call to mind cream cheese, onion sauce, brown sherry and other incongruities". He neglected to discuss the smell of the fruit's skin, which is so bad – somewhere between detergent and dogshit – that durians are barred from Thai hotels and aeroplanes. The different varieties bear strange names which do nothing to make them more appetizing: "frog", "golden pillow", "gibbon" and so on. However, the durian has fervent admirers, perhaps because it's such an acquired taste, and because it's considered a strong aphrodisiac. Aficionados discuss the varieties with as much subtlety as if they were vintage champagnes, and treat the durian as a social fruit, to be shared around despite a price tag of up to B3000 each.

Durian season is roughly April to June. The most famous durian orchards are around Nonthaburi, where the fruits are said to have an incomparably rich and nutty flavour due to the fine clay soil. If you don't smell them first, you can recognize durians by their sci-fi appearance: the shape and size of a rugby ball, but slightly deflated, they're covered in a thick, pale-green shell which is heavily armoured with short, sharp spikes (duri means "thorn" in Malay). By cutting along one of the faint seams with a good knife, you'll reveal a white pith in which are set a handful of yellow blobs with the texture of a bad soufflé: this is what you eat. The taste is best when the smell is at its highest, about three days after the fruit has dropped. Be careful when out walking: due to its great weight and sharp spikes, a falling durian can lead to serious injury, or even an ignominious death.

Disembarking at Nonthaburi, you immediately get the feeling of being out in the sticks, despite the noisy bus terminal that confronts you: the pier, on the east bank of the river, is overrun by a market that's famous for the quality of its fruit; the old Provincial Office across the road is covered in rickety wooden latticework; and the short promenade, its lampposts hung with models of the town's famous durian fruit, lends a seaside atmosphere.

To break up your trip with a slow, scenic drink or lunch, you'll find a floating seafood restaurant, *Rim Fung*, to your right at the end of the prom which, though a bit over-priced, is quiet and breezy.

If you're thirsty for more cruising on the water, take a longtail boat from Nonthaburi pier up Khlong Om (round trip 45min; B20): the canal, lined with some grand suburban mansions, traditional wooden houses, temples and durian plantations, leads almost out into open country.

Wat Chalerm Phra Kiat

Set in relaxing grounds about 1km north of Nonthaburi pier on the west bank of the river, elegant **Wat Chalerm Phra Kiat** injects a splash of urban refinement among a grove of breadfruit trees. From the express-boat pier, take the ferry straight across the Chao Phraya and then catch a motorbike taxi.

The beautifully proportioned temple, which has been lavishly restored, was built by Rama III in memory of his mother, whose family lived in the area. Entering the walls of the temple compound, you feel as if you're coming upon a stately folly in a secret garden, and a strong Chinese influ-

NONTHABURI

ence shows itself in the unusual ribbed roofs and elegantly curved gables, decorated with pastel ceramics. The restorers have done their best work inside: look out especially for the simple, delicate landscapes on the shutters.

Joe Louis Puppet Theatre

96/48 Muu 7, Soi Krungthep–Nonthaburi 12, Nonthaburi.

Several kilometres east of the express-boat pier, the **Joe Louis Puppet Theatre** is a unique attraction, which though pricey is well worth the trip for both adults and children. To get there from Nonthaburi pier, take bus #30 or #65 along Thanon Pracharat, the main road back towards the centre of Bangkok, and get off at the entrance to the soi; you'll then need to hire a motorbike taxi, samlor or songthaew as the theatre is difficult to find deep in the soi. Coming from central Bangkok, you might want to catch the Skytrain to Mo Chit, at the top end of the Sukhumvit line, and take a taxi from there.

The puppets in question are jointed stick puppets (*hun lakorn lek*), an art form which was developed under Rama IV in the mid-nineteenth century, but which had all but died out before the owner of the theatre, **Sakorn Yangkeowsod** (aka Joe Louis), came to its rescue in the 1980s. Each two-foot-tall puppet is manipulated by three puppeteers, who are accomplished *khon* dancers in their own right, complementing their charges' elegant and precise gestures with graceful movements in a harmonious ensemble.

Hour-long **shows** (B600; book in advance on ☏527 7737–8) are put on daily at the theatre at 10am, with an extra Saturday show at 8pm, but you should turn up an hour in advance for informative demonstrations of how the puppets and *khon* masks are made. The puppets perform mostly stories from the *Ramakien*, accompanied by commentary in English and traditional music of a high standard.

KO KRED

Map 1, H4.

About 7km north of Nonthaburi, the tiny island of **Ko Kred** lies in a particularly sharp bend in the Chao Phraya, cut off from the east bank by a waterway created to make the cargo route from Ayutthaya to the Gulf of Thailand just that little bit faster. Although it's slowly being discovered by day-trippers from Bangkok, this artificial island remains something of a time capsule: a little oasis of village life completely at odds with the metropolitan chaos downriver. Roughly ten square kilometres in all, Ko Kred has no roads, just a concrete path that circles its circumference, with a few arterial walk-ways branching off towards the interior. Villagers, the majority of whom are ethnic Mons, use a small fleet of motorbike taxis to cross their island, but as a sightseer you're much bet-ter off on foot: a round-island walk takes less than an hour and a half and it's practically impossible to get lost.

There are few sights as such on Ko Kred, but its lushness and comparative emptiness make it a perfect place in which to wander. You'll no doubt come across one of the island's potteries and kilns, which churn out the regionally famous earthenware flower-pots and small water-storage jars and employ a large percentage of the village workforce. Several shops dotted around the island sell Ko Kred terracotta, including what's styled as the Ancient Mon Pottery Centre near the island's northeast corner, which also displays delicate and venerable museum pieces and Mon-style Buddha shrines. The island's clay is also very rich in nutrients and therefore excellent for fruit-growing – banana trees, coconut palms, pomelo, papaya and durian trees all grow in abun-dance on Ko Kred, fed by an intricate network of irrigation channels that crisscrosses the interior. In among the orchards the Mons have built their wooden houses, mostly in tradi-tional style and raised high above the marshy ground on stilts.

KO KRED

A handful of attractive riverside wats complete the picture, most notably **Wat Paramaiyikawat** (aka Wat Poramai), at the main pier at the northeast tip of the island. This engagingly ramshackle eighteenth-century temple was restored by Rama V in honour of his grandmother, with a Buddha relic placed in its Mon-style chedi. Amongst an open-air scattering of Burmese-style alabaster Buddha images, the tall bot shelters some fascinating nineteenth-century murals, depicting scenes from temple life at ground level and the life of the Buddha above, all set in delicate imaginary landscapes.

On Sundays only, the Chao Phraya Express Boat Co (℡02/623 6001–3) runs **tours** to Ko Kred from central Bangkok (B220), heading upriver from Tha Prachan (Maharat) in Ratanakosin at 9am, taking in Wat Poramai and the Ancient Mon Pottery Centre, before circling the island, dropping in at Wat Chalerm Phra Kiat in Nonthaburi (see p.149) and arriving back at Tha Prachan at about 3pm. At other times, the main drawback of a day-trip to Ko Kred is the difficulty of **getting there**. Your best option is to take a Chao Phraya Express boat to Nonthaburi, then bus #32 to Pakkred pier – or, if you're feeling flush, a chartered longtail boat direct to Ko Kred (about B150). From Pakkred, the easiest way of getting across to the island is to hire a longtail boat, although shuttle boats cross at the river's narrowest point to Wat Poramai from Wat Sanam Nua, about 1km's walk or a short samlor or motorbike-taxi ride south of the Pakkred pier.

The only bright spot about the irksome journey to Ko Kred via Pakkred is the chance to eat at the excellent *Hong Seng* restaurant, just north of the pier; in a clean, airy wooden building on the river bank, delicious dishes such as *kung plaa* (river shrimp) with hot lemon grass salad are served up daily from 11am to 3pm.

KO KRED

LISTINGS

Accommodation

B earing in mind Bangkok's appalling traffic jams, you should think especially carefully about what you want to do in the city before deciding which part of town to stay in. For double rooms under B400, the widest choice lies with the **guest houses** of Banglamphu and the smaller, dingier travellers' ghetto that has grown up around Soi Ngam Duphli, off the south side of Thanon Rama IV.

ACCOMMODATION PRICES

Throughout this guide, guest houses and hotels have been categorized according to the price codes given below. These categories represent the minimum you can expect to pay in the high season (roughly July, Aug & Nov–Feb) for a double room. If travelling on your own, expect to pay anything between sixty and one hundred percent of the rates quoted for a double room.

The top-whack hotels will add seven percent tax and a ten-percent service charge to your bill – the price codes below are based on net rates after taxes have been added.

❶ under B150
❷ B150–250
❸ B250–400
❹ B400–600
❺ B600–900
❻ B900–1200
❼ B1200–1800
❽ B1800–3000
❾ B3000+

BOOKING A HOTEL ONLINE

Many hotels offer discounts to customers who book through their own website, but you can often get even bigger discounts (up to sixty percent off the published prices of selected mid-range and upmarket accommodation) if you use a commercial online hotel-booking service such as those listed below.

Accommodating Asia Ⓦ www.accomasia.com/thailand.htm

Asia Hotel Ⓦ www.asia-hotels.com.

Asia Ways Ⓦ www.asiaways.com.

Hotel Thailand Ⓗ hotelthailand.com.

Siam Net Ⓦ www.siam.net.

Stay In Thailand Ⓦ www.stayinthailand.com.

Thai Focus Ⓦ www.thaifocus.com.

Thailand Hotels Association Ⓦ www.thaihotels.org.

Thailand Hotels and Resorts Ⓦ www.hotels.siam.net.

Bangkok guest houses are tailored to the independent traveller's needs and range from cramped, no-frills crash pads to airier places with private bathrooms. Unless you pay a cash deposit in advance, bookings are rarely accepted by guest houses, but it's often useful to phone ahead and establish whether a place is full already – during peak season you may have difficulty getting a room after noon.

Moderate and **expensive** rooms are mainly concentrated downtown around Siam Square and in the area between Thanon Rama IV and Thanon Charoen Krung (New Road); along Thanon Sukhumvit, where the eastern suburbs start; and to a lesser extent in Chinatown. Air-conditioned rooms with hot-water bathrooms can be had for as little as B500 in these areas, but for that you're looking at a rather basic cubicle. You'll probably have to pay more like B1000 for smart furnishings and a swimming pool, or B3000 and over for a room in a five-star, international chain hotel.

Many of the expensive hotels listed in this guide offer special **deals for families**, usually allowing one or two under-12s to share their parents' room for free, so long as no extra bedding is required. It's also often possible to cram two adults and two children into the double rooms in inexpensive and mid-priced hotels (as opposed to guest houses), as beds in these places are usually big enough for two.

BANGLAMPHU

Nearly all backpackers head straight for **Banglamphu**, Bangkok's long-established travellers' ghetto, which is within easy reach of the Grand Palace and other major sights in Ratanakosin (a riverfront walkway from Phra Athit to Ratanakosin is in the offing). At its heart stands the legendary **Thanon Khao San**, crammed with guest houses, dodgy travel agents and restaurants serving yoghurt shakes and

GETTING TO AND FROM BANGLAMPHU

All the guest houses listed lie only a few minutes' walk from the express boat stops of Tha Banglamphu (map 3, B8) or Tha Thewes (map 3, E3). Public longtail boats also ply Khlong Sen Seb from the Tha Phanfa terminus near Democracy Monument (map 3, I14).

Useful bus routes in and out of Banglamphu include airport bus AB2, which makes several stops in Banglamphu; AC and ordinary #3, AC#12 and AC#32 from the Northern (Mo Chit) Bus Terminal; AC#7 and AC#11 from the Southern Bus Terminal; AC#11 from the Eastern Bus Terminal; #53 to Hualamphong train station and, in the opposite direction, to the Grand Palace, and #56 to Chinatown; AC#3, AC#9, AC#10, AC#12 and AC#39 for Chatuchak Weekend Market; and AC and ordinary #15 to Siam Square.

muesli, the sidewalks lined with ethnic clothes stalls, racks of bootleg music and software CDs, tattooists and hair-braiders. Accommodation on Khao San itself is noisy and poor value though, with few places offering windows in their rooms, so you may prefer to stay on one of the nearby streets.

Good alternative areas include **Soi Chana Songkhram**, which encircles the wat of the same name; **Phra Athit**, running alongside the Chao Phraya River and packed with trendy Thai café-bars and restaurants (it also has a useful express-boat stop); or the residential alleyways that parallel Thanon Khao San to the south, **Trok Mayom** and **Damnoen Klang Neua**. About ten minutes' walk north from Thanon Khao San, the **Thanon Samsen sois** offer a more authentically Thai atmosphere. A further fifteen minutes' walk in the same direction will take you to Thanon Sri Ayutthaya, behind the National Library and a seven-minute walk from the **Thewes** express-boat stop; this is the most attractive area in Banglamphu, where rooms are larger and guest houses smaller.

THANON KHAO SAN AND SOI DAMNOEN KLANG NEUA

Chart Guest house
Map 3, C11. 58–60 Thanon Khao San ☎ 282 0171.
Clean, comfortable enough hotel in the heart of backpacker land; the cheapest rooms share bathrooms and the priciest have air-con. Rooms in all categories are a little cramped, though they all have windows. ②–④

J & Joe House
Map 3, C12. 1 Trok Mayom ☎ 281 2949.
Simple, inexpensive rooms, all with shared bathrooms, in a traditional wooden house located among real Thai homes (very unusual for Banglamphu) in a narrow alley off Khao San. ②

Khao San Palace Hotel

Map 3, D11. 139 Thanon Khao San ⓣ 282 0578.

Clean and well-appointed smallish hotel, where all rooms are en suite, but only some have windows. The priciest options have air-con and TV. Avoid the rooms overlooking Khao San as they can be noisy at night. ③–④

Lek House

Map 3, D11. 125 Thanon Khao San ⓣ 281 8441.

Classic old-style Khao San guest house with small, basic rooms and shared facilities; less shabby than many others in the same price bracket. ②

Marco Polo Hostel

Map 3, D11. 108/7–10 Thanon Khao San ⓣ 281 1715.

Fairly grim windowless boxes in the heart of the ghetto, though all have air-con and private shower. ③

Nat II

Map 3, F12. 91–95 Soi Damnoen Klang Neua (aka Soi Post Office) ⓣ 282 0211.

Large, clean rooms, some with windows, in a fairly quiet location, though you may be woken by the 5am prayer calls at the neighbourhood mosque. There are only a couple of other guest houses on this road, so it has a friendly, neighbourhood feel to it, even though Khao San is less than 200m away. ②

Royal Hotel

Map 3, C13. 2 Thanon Rajdamnoen Klang ⓣ 222 9111, ⓕ 224 2083.

Used mostly for conferences, this hotel is conveniently located just five minutes' stroll from Sanam Luang (it's a further 10min or so to the Grand Palace), but getting to Thanon Khao San entails a life-endangering leap across

THANON KHAO SAN AND SOI DAMNOEN KLANG NEUA

Almost every alternate building on Thanon Khao San and on the west arm of Soi Ram Bhuttri offers internet access, as do many of the guest houses; intense competition keeps the rates very low.

---

two very busy main roads. Though all rooms have air-con and the facilities are perfectly adequate, the place lacks atmosphere and isn't exactly plush for the price – the grim facade is enough to put anyone off. **⑦**

Sawasdee Bangkok Inn

Map 3, D12. On a tiny soi connecting Thanon Khao San with the parallel Trok Mayom ⓣ 280 1251, ⓕ 281 7818, ⓦ www.sawasdee-hotels.com. Easily spotted because of its mauve-painted facade, this popular and efficiently run mini-hotel has a good atmosphere and a range of comfortable rooms, though the cheapest are a bit cramped and have no bathroom. Priciest options here include air-con and TV, which makes them good value. You can get Thai massage therapy and lessons on the premises, and there's an attractive garden eating area. **③—④**

7 Holder Guest house

Map 3, E12. 216/2–3 Soi Damnoen Klang Neua ⓣ 281 3682.
Clean and modern place round the back of Thanon Khao San, though none of the simply furnished rooms have bathrooms and only some have windows. Fan and air-con available. **②—③**

Siam Oriental

Map 3, D12. 190 Thanon Khao San ⓣ 629 0311, ⓕ 629 0310.
Guest house right in the middle of Thanon Khao San, offering smallish rooms, all with attached bathrooms and some with windows; some have air-con too. **③**

Smile Guest House

Map 3, D13. 151–161 Trok Sa-ke, off the southern arm of Thanon Tanao ⓣ 02/622 1590, ⓕ 622 0730.
Located less than five minutes' walk from Khao San, across Rajdamnoen Klang, this is a fairly good-value place that's

There are numerous money exchange places on Thanon Khao San, including two branches of national banks with ATMs.

quiet and out of the tourist ghetto. All rooms have air-conditioning and decent tiled bathrooms, and there's internet access downstairs. ❸

Sweety

Map 3, F12. Soi Damnoen Klang Neua ☎ 280 2191, ℱ 280 2192, ℮ sweetygh@hotmail.com. Popular place that's one of the least expensive in Banglamphu; it's nicely located away from the fray but convenient for Khao San. Rooms are very small but all have windows, and beds with thick mattresses; some have private bathrooms. ❶–❷

Vieng Thai Hotel

Map 3, D11. Soi Ram Bhuttri ☎ 280 5392, ℱ 281 8153. The best of the options in Banglamphu's upper price bracket: convenient for the shops and restaurants of Thanon Khao San and Banglamphu, and geared towards tourists not business people. All rooms here have air-con, TV, hot water and mini-bar, and there's a sizeable swimming pool. ❼

SOI CHANA SONGKHRAM AND PHRA ATHIT

Baan Sabai

Map 3, B10. 12 Soi Rongmai ☎ 02/629 1599. Welcome newcomer to the Banglamphu guest-house scene, located in a quiet soi overlooking the Wat Chana Songkhram compound. Built round a courtyard, this large, hotel-style guest house has a range of clean, comfortable, decent-sized en-suite rooms (some with air-con), and is host to the pleasant *Bangkok Times* restaurant downstairs. ❸–❹

Chai's House

Map 3, B11. 49/4–8 Soi Rongmai, between Soi Chana Songkhram and Thanon Chao Fa ☎ 281 4901, ℱ 281 8686. Quietish place, away from most other guest houses, with large, clean, simple rooms, all with shared bathrooms. The rate is per person, which makes singles better value than doubles. ❷

Merry V

Map 3, B9. 35 Soi Chana Songkhram ⓣ 282 9267.
Large, efficiently run and scrupulously clean guest house offering some of the cheapest accommodation in Banglamphu. Rooms are basic and slightly cramped, and they all share bathrooms. Good noticeboard in the downstairs restaurant. ❷

My House

Map 3, C9. 37 Soi Chana Songkhram ⓣ 282 9263.
Popular place offering a range of simple but exceptionally clean rooms. The cheapest share bathrooms, the most expensive have private bathrooms and air-con. ❷–❹

New Siam Guest House

Map 3, B9. 21 Soi Chana Songkhram ⓣ 282 4554, ⓕ 281 7461.
Efficiently run place offering comfortably furnished hotel-style rooms, all with fans and windows, and plenty of clothes hooks. The cheapest rooms share bathrooms, the priciest are ensuite and have air-con. ❸–❺

Peachy Guest House

Map 3, B10. 10 Thanon Phra Athit ⓣ 281 6471.
Popular, cheap and cheerful place set round a small courtyard, with clean if spartan rooms, most with shared bathrooms but some with air-con. Also has B80 dorm beds. Popular with long-stay guests. ❷–❸

Pra Arthit Mansion

Map 3, B10. 22 Thanon Phra Athit ⓣ 280 0744, ⓕ 280 0742, ⓔ praarthit@bkk.a-net.net.th.
Recommended mid-range place offering very good, comfortable rooms with air-con, TV, hot water and mini-bar. The fifth-floor rooms have the

The excellent Bangkok Information Centre is on Thanon Phra Athit (map 3, A10), and there's a 24-hour tourist information and assistance booth in front of the police station on the west corner of Thanon Khao San (map 3, C11).

best views of Banglamphu's rooftops. No restaurant, lobby or other hotel facilities, but staff are friendly and the location is quiet and convenient. ❺

SAMSEN AND THEWES

Backpackers Lodge

Map 3, G2. Soi 14, 85 Thanon Sri Ayutthaya ⓣ 282 3231. Quiet, family-run place in the peaceful Thewes quarter of north Banglamphu. Just a handful of simple rooms, all with shared bathroom, and a communal area downstairs. The cheapest accommodation in this area. ❷

Bangkok International Youth Hostel

Map 3, I4. 25/2 Thanon Phitsanulok ⓣ 282 0950, ⓕ 628 7416, ⓦ www.tyha.org. Mostly patronized by travelling Thai students: only open to YHA members and nothing special considering the competition. The double rooms have bathrooms, and

some have air-con; there are dorm beds for B70. ❷–❸

New World Lodge Hotel

Map 3, E9. Samsen Soi 2 ⓣ 281 5596, ⓕ 282 5614, ⓦ www.new-lodge.com. Good-value, large, unadorned rooms, each with a desk, phone, shower and either fan or air-con. All rooms have balconies, and some have khlong views. The cheapest rooms, simply furnished and sharing bathrooms, are in the less appealing guest-house wing. ❷–❺

Shanti Lodge

Map 3, G2. Soi 16, Thanon Sri Ayutthaya ⓣ 281 2497. Quiet, attractively furnished and comfortable rooms make this deservedly the most popular place in the Thewes area. Facilities range from rooms with shared bathrooms to en-suite ones with air-con. The vegetarian restaurant downstairs is recommended. ❸–❺

Tavee Guest House

Map 3, G2. Soi 14, 83 Thanon Sri Ayutthaya ⓣ 282 5983.

Good-sized rooms; quiet and friendly and one of the cheaper places in the Thewes quarter. Offers rooms with shared bathroom plus some en-suite ones with air-con, as well as B80 dorm beds. ❷–❹

Thai Hotel

Map 3, H10. 78 Thanon Pracha Thipatai ⓣ 282 2831, ⓕ 280 1299.

Comfortable enough, but a little overpriced, considering its slightly inconvenient location. All rooms have air-con and there's a decent-sized pool here too. ❼

Villa

Map 3, D8. 230 Samsen Soi 1 ⓣ 281 7009.

Banglamphu's most therapeutic guest house, a lovely old Thai house and garden with just ten large rooms, each idiosyncratically furnished in simple, semi-traditional style; bathrooms are shared. Fills up quickly, but it's worth going on the waiting list if you're staying a long time. Rooms priced according to their size. ❸–❹

Vimol Guest House

Map 3, F9. 358 Samsen Soi 4 ⓣ 281 4615.

Old-style, family-run guest house in a quiet but interesting neighbourhood that has just a couple of other tourist places. The simple, cramped rooms have shared bathrooms and a welcoming atmosphere. ❶

CHINATOWN AND HUALAMPHONG STATION AREA

Not far from the Ratanakosin sights, **Chinatown (Sampeng)** is one of the most vibrant and typically Asian parts of Bangkok. Staying here, or in one of the sois around the nearby **Hualamphong Station**, can be noisy, but there's always plenty to look at, and some travellers base themselves here to get away from the travellers' scene in Banglamphu.

Bangkok Center

Map 5, I6. 328 Thanon Rama IV ⊤238 4848, ⒡236 1862, ⒲www.bangkokcentrehotel.com. Handily placed (just across the road from the train station) upper-mid-range option with efficient service. Rooms are smartly furnished, and all have air-con and TV; there's a pool, restaurant and internet access on the premises. ❻

Chinatown Hotel

Map 5, F5. 526 Thanon Yaowarat ⊤225 0204, ⒡226 1295, ⒲www.chinatown.co.th. Classy Chinese hotel in the heart of the gold-trading district. Comfortably furnished rooms, all with air-con and TV. Kids under 12 can share their parents' rooms for free. ❺–❻

FF Guest House

Map 5, I6. 338/10 Trok La-O, off Thanon Rama IV ⊤233 4168. The closest budget accommodation to the station, but very basic indeed and a bit of a last resort. To get there from the station, cross Thanon Rama IV and walk left for 200m, and then right down Trok La-O to the end of the alley. ❷

Krung Kasem Sri Krung Hotel

Map 5, H5. 1860 Thanon Krung Kasem ⊤225 0132, ⒡225 4705. Rather shabby Chinese hotel just 50m across the khlong from the station. All rooms have air-con and TV, but could do with an overhaul. ❹

New Empire Hotel

Map 5, G5. 572 Thanon Yaowarat ⊤234 6990, ⒡234 6997, ⒠newempirehotel@ hotmail.com. Medium-sized hotel right in the thick of the Chinatown bustle, offering fairly run-of-the-mill rooms with shower and air-con. ❹

River View Guest House

Map 2, D7. 768 Soi Panurangsri, Thanon Songvad ⊤235 8501, ⒡237 5428. Large but unattractive rooms, with fan and cold water at the lower end of the range, air-con, hot water, TVs and fridges at the top. Great views over the bend in the river,

CHINATOWN AND HUALAMPHONG STATION AREA

GETTING TO AND FROM CHINATOWN AND HUALAMPHONG

Useful bus routes for Chinatown include airport bus AB4 and both AC and ordinary #29, which all run from the airport to Hualamphong Station; AC#7, #25 and #53, which all go to Ratanakosin (for Wat Po and the Grand Palace); the east-bound #25 and #40 buses both go to Siam Square, where you can change onto the Skytrain system. For full details see pp.56–58.

especially from the top-floor restaurant, and handy for Chinatown, Hualamphong Station and the GPO. To find it through a maze of crumbling Chinese buildings, head north for 400m from River City shopping centre (on the express-boat line) along Soi Wanit 2, before following signs to the guest house to the left. ④–⑤

TT2 Guest House

Map 2, E7. 516 Soi Sawang, off Thanon Maha Nakorn ☎ 236 2946, ℻ 236 3054, ⓔ ttguesthouse@hotmail.com. The best budget place in the station area, though significantly more expensive than *FF*. Clean, friendly and well run with good bulletin boards and traveller-orientated facilities, including left luggage

at B7 a day and a small library. All rooms share bathrooms, and there are B100 beds in a three-person dorm. Roughly a 15min walk from either the station or the Si Phraya express-boat stop; to get here from the station, cross Thanon Rama IV, then walk left for 250m and right down Thanon Maha Nakorn as far as the *Full Moon* restaurant (opposite Trok Fraser & Neave), where you turn left and then first right. ③

White Orchid Hotel

Map 5, F4. 409–421 Thanon Yaowarat ☎ 226 0026, ℻ 225 6403. One of the plushest hotels in Chinatown, right at the hub of the gold-trading quarter. All rooms have air-con and TV, and there's a *dim sum* restaurant on the premises. ⑥

DOWNTOWN: AROUND SIAM SQUARE AND THANON PLOENCHIT

Siam Square – not really a square, but a grid of shops and restaurants between Phrayathai and Henri Dunant roads – and nearby **Thanon Ploenchit** are as central as Bangkok gets, handy for all kinds of shopping, nightlife, the Skytrain and Hualamphong station. There's no budget accommodation here, but alongside the expensive hotels a few scaled-up guest houses have sprung up. Concentrated in their own "ghetto" on **Soi Kasemsan 1**, which runs north off Thanon Rama I just west of Thanon Phrayathai (it's also

DOWNTOWN: AROUND SIAM SQUARE AND THANON PLOENCHIT

GETTING TO AND FROM SIAM SQUARE AND THANON PLOENCHIT

This area is well served by the Skytrain, with Central Station, the junction of the Silom and Sukhumvit lines, hard by Siam Square, while the National Stadium station (Silom Line) puts you right on the doorstep of the Soi Kasemsan 1 accommodation. Airport bus AB1 crosses the western end of Thanon Ploenchit in front of the Erawan Shrine on its way down Thanon Rajdamri, while AB4 runs west along Thanon Ploenchit and Thanon Rama I to Siam Square, before heading south down Thanon Phrayathai. Dozens of other buses of all kinds run through the area, most passing the focal junction by the Erawan Shrine. Probably the most useful for travellers are those which stop near Soi Kasemsan 1, including AC#8 and ordinary #15, which both run west to Ratanakosin, and AC and ordinary #29 (Airport–Hualamphong Station). Soi Kasemsan 1 is five minutes' walk from the Khlong Sen Seb longtail boat stop at Thanon Phrayathai, and adventurous guests at the *Hilton* are very handily placed for the stop at Thanon Witthayu.

the next soi along from Jim Thompson's House; see p.131), these offer an informal guest-house atmosphere, with hotel comforts – air-conditioning and en-suite hot-water bathrooms – at moderate prices.

MODERATE

A-One Inn

Map 6, C4. 25/13 Soi Kasemsan 1, Thanon Rama I ℡ 215 3029, ℻ 216 4771.
The original upscale guest house, and still justifiably popular, with helpful staff. Bedrooms come in a variety of sizes, including family rooms (but no singles), and the broad range of facilities includes a reliable left-luggage room, a tour service, satellite TV and a sociable café. ❹

The Bed & Breakfast

Map 6, C3. 36/42 Soi Kasemsan 1, Thanon Rama I ℡ 215 3004, ℻ 215 2493.
Bright, clean, family-run and friendly, though the rooms – carpeted and with en-suite telephones – are a bit cramped. As the name suggests, a simple breakfast is included. ❹

Wendy House

Map 6, C4. 36/2 Soi Kasemsan 1, Thanon Rama I ℡ 216 2436–7, ℻ 612 3487.
As cramped as the name suggests, with no frills in the service, but clean and comfortable enough. TV in every room, and a small restaurant on the ground floor. ❹

White Lodge

Map 6, C4. 36/8 Soi Kasemsan 1, Thanon Rama I ℡ 216 8867 or 215 3041, ℻ 216 8228.
Well-maintained, shining white cubicles and a welcoming, if slightly eccentric, family-style atmosphere, with very good continental breakfasts at *Sorn's* next door. ❹

EXPENSIVE

Hilton International

Map 6, K2. Nai Lert Park, 2 Thanon Wireless ℡ 253 0123,

Ⓕ 253 6509, Ⓦ www.hilton.com. The main distinguishing feature of this member of the international luxury chain is its eight acres of beautiful gardens, into which are set a verdant landscaped swimming pool, jogging track, tennis courts and popular health club, and which are overlooked by many of the spacious, balconied bedrooms. Good deli-café and French and Chinese restaurants. Ⓨ

Jim's Lodge
Map 6, L7. 125/7 Soi Ruam Rudee, Thanon Ploenchit Ⓣ 255 3100–3, Ⓕ 253 8492, Ⓔ anant@asiaaccess.net.th. In a relatively peaceful residential area, handy for the British and American embassies. Luxurious international standards on a small scale and at bargain prices; no swimming pool, but there's a roof garden with outdoor jacuzzi. Ⓥ

Le Royal Meridien and Le Meridien President
Map 6, I4. 971 Thanon Ploenchit Ⓣ 656 0444, Ⓕ 656 0555, Ⓦ www.lemeridien-bangkok.com. Very handily placed for the

Erawan Shrine and shopping, the thirty-year-old landmark of the *President* has recently been rejuvenated with the building of the towering *Royal Meridien* next door, aimed primarily at business travellers. Room rates compare very favourably with those of other five-star hotels in Bangkok. Ⓨ

Regent
Map 6, H6. 155 Thanon Rajdamri Ⓣ 251 6127, Ⓕ 254 5390, Ⓦ www.rih.com. The stately home of Bangkok's top hotels, offering a choice between large, well-endowed rooms and resort-style "cabanas" with private patios in the landscaped gardens. Afternoon tea is served under extravagant Thai murals in the grand lobby, and facilities include a health club and spa, and the highly acclaimed *Spice Market* Thai restaurant. Ⓨ

Siam Orchid Inn
Map 6, I3. 109 Soi Rajdamri, Thanon Rajdamri Ⓣ 251 4417, Ⓕ 255 3144, Ⓔ siam_orchidinn@hotmail.com. Very handily located behind

the Narayana Phand souvenir centre; a friendly, cosy place with an ornately decorated lobby, a tasty restaurant, and air-con, hot water, cable TV, mini-bars and phones in the comfortable bedrooms. The room rate (at the lower end of this price code) includes breakfast. ❼

DOWNTOWN: SOUTH OF THANON RAMA IV

South of Thanon Rama IV, the left bank of the river contains a full cross-section of places to stay. At the eastern edge there's **Soi Ngam Duphli**, a ghetto of budget guest houses which is often choked with traffic escaping the jams on Thanon Rama IV. Though the neighbourhood is generally on the slide, the best guest houses, tucked away on quiet **Soi Saphan Khu**, can just about compare with Banglamphu's finest.

DOWNTOWN: SOUTH OF THANON RAMA IV

GETTING TO AND FROM THE SOUTHERN DOWNTOWN AREA

The Silom Line of the Skytrain runs through this area, flying over Thanon Silom, before veering down Soi Chong Nonsi then along Thanon Sathorn to the river. The big advantage of staying at the western edge of this area is that you'll be handily placed for Chao Phraya express boats, with useful stops at Wat Muang Kae (*Newrotel*), the *Oriental Hotel* and Sathorn (*Shangri-La*). Indeed, if you're staying anywhere in this area and travelling by public transport to Ratanakosin, you're best off catching a bus to the nearest express-boat stop, or the Skytrain to Saphan Taksin station, and finishing your journey on the water. The most useful bus for Soi Ngam Duphli is likely to be AC#7, which among other things would allow you to check out alternative accommodation in Banglamphu if necessary, while countless buses run along Thanon Silom, including airport bus AB1.

Some medium-range places are scattered between Thanon Rama IV and the river, ranging from the notorious (the *Malaysia*) to the sedate (the *Bangkok Christian Guest House*). The area also lays claim to the capital's biggest selection of top hotels, which are among the most opulent in the world. It's also good for eating and shopping, with a generous sprinkling of embassies for visa-hunters.

INEXPENSIVE

ETC Guest House
Map 7a. 5/3 Soi Ngam Duphli
ⓣ 287 1477 or 286 9424,
ⓕ 287 1478,
ⓔ ETC@mozart.inet.co.th.
Above a branch of the recommended Banglamphu travel agent of the same name, and very handy for Thanon Rama IV, though consequently noisy. Friendly, helpful and very clean, catering mainly to Japanese travellers. Rooms can be dingy, and come with shared or en-suite hot-water bathrooms; breakfast is included. ❷–❸

Freddy's 2 Guest House
Map 7a. 27/40 Soi Sri Bamphen
ⓣ 286 7826, ⓕ 213 2097.
Popular, clean, well-organized guest house with a variety of rooms and plenty of comfortable common areas, including a café and beer garden at the rear. Rather noisy. Especially good rates for singles (B100). ❷

Lee 3 Guest House
Map 7a. 13 Soi Saphan Khu
ⓣ 679 7045, ⓕ 286 3042.
The best of the Lee family guest houses spread around this and the adjoining sois. Decent and quiet, with reasonably-sized rooms, though stuffy. ❷

Lee 4 Guest House
Map 7a. 9 Soi Saphan Khu
ⓣ 286 7874 or 679 8116.
Simple, secure, airy rooms, most with en-suite cold-water bathrooms, in a dour modern tower at the entrance to the alley; service also dour. ❷

DOWNTOWN: SOUTH OF THANON RAMA IV

Madam Guest House

Map 7a. 11 Soi Saphan Khu
ⓣ286 9289, ⓕ213 2087.
Cleanish, often cramped, but
characterful rooms, with or
without their own
bathrooms, in a warren-like,
balconied wooden house next
door to *Lee 3*. Friendly, but
sometimes a bit raucous at
night. ❷

Sala Thai Daily Mansion

Map 7a. 15 Soi Saphan Khu
ⓣ287 1436.
The pick of the Soi Ngam
Duphli area, at the end of a
quiet, shaded alley. A clean
and efficiently run place, with
bright, modern rooms
(priced according to size)
with wall fans; a roof terrace
makes it all the more pleasant.
❷–❸

TTO Guest House

Map 7a. 2/35 Soi Sri Bamphen
ⓣ286 6783, ⓕ679 7994.
Rough, poorly designed but
spacious rooms, all with
fridge and phone, some with
air-con and hot water, in a
friendly establishment down a
quiet alley off the south side
of Soi Sri Bamphen. ❸

MODERATE

Bangkok Christian Guest House

Map 7, K7. 123 Soi 2,
Saladaeng, off the eastern end
of Thanon Silom ⓣ234 1852,
ⓕ237 1742,
ⓔbcgh@loxinfo.co.th.
Well-run, orderly missionary
house whose plain air-con
rooms with hot-water
bathrooms surround a quiet
lawn. Breakfast included. ❼

Charlie House

Map 7a. 1034/36–37 Soi
Saphan Khu ⓣ679 8330–1,
ⓕ679 7308,
ⓔCHARLIE_H_TH@yahoo.com.
Decent mid-range alternative
to the crash pads of Soi
Ngam Duphli; has a bright,
air-chilled lobby restaurant,
serving good, reasonably
priced food, and small,
carpeted bedrooms with
minimal floral decor, hot-
water bathrooms, air-con
and TV, close to Thanon
Rama IV. Cheap internet
access. No smoking. ❹

La Residence

Map 7, G5. 173/8–9 Thanon Suriwong, above *All Gaengs* restaurant ☏266 5400–1, ☏237 9322, ✉residenc@loxinfo.co.th. Small, intimate hotel; the cutesy rooms stretch to mini-bars and cable and satellite TV. ❼

Malaysia Hotel

Map 7a. 54 Soi Ngam Duphli ☏679 7127–36, ☏287 1457, ✉malaysia@ksc15.th.com. Once a travellers' legend, famous for its compendious noticeboard, now something of a sleaze pit with a notorious 24-hour coffeeshop and massage parlour. The accommodation itself is reasonable value though: rooms are large and have air-con and hot-water bathrooms; some have fridge, TV and video too. There's a swimming pool (B50 per day for non-guests) and reasonably priced internet access. ❺

Newrotel

Map 7, C5. 1216/1 Thanon Charoen Krung, between the GPO and the *Oriental Hotel* ☏630 6995, ☏237 1102, ✉newrotel@idn.co.th. Smart, clean, kitschly decorated and good value, with air-con, hot-water bathrooms, fridges and cable TV, the price including American or Chinese breakfast. ❼

Niagara

Map 7, G7. 26 Soi Suksa Witthaya ☏233 5783, ☏233 6563. No facilities other than a coffee shop at this hotel off the south side of Thanon Silom, but the clean bedrooms, with air con, hot-water bathrooms, satellite TV and telephones, are a snip. ❹

EXPENSIVE

Dusit Thani Hotel

Map 7, L6. 946 Thanon Rama IV ☏236 0450-9, ☏236 6400, ⓦwww.dusit.com. Centrally placed top-class establishment on the corner of Thanon Silom, geared for both business and leisure, with very high standards of service. Many of the elegant rooms enjoy views of Lumphini Park and the sleek downtown high-rises. The hotel is famous for its restaurants, including the top-floor *Tiara*, which has probably the most spectacular vistas in Bangkok. ❾

Montien Hotel

Map 7, J4. 54 Thanon Suriwong ☎ 233 7060–9, ℻ 236 5219, ⓦ www.montien.com. Grand, airy and solicitous luxury hotel on the corner of Thanon Rama IV, with a strongly Thai character. It's very handily placed for business and nightlife, and famous for the astrologers who dispense predictions to guests in the lobby. ❾

Oriental Hotel 02 659 9000

Map 7, B5. 48 Oriental Ave, off Thanon Charoen Krung (New Rd) ☎ 236 0400, ℻ 236 1937, ⓦ www.mandarin-oriental.com. One of the world's best; effortlessly stylish riverside hotel, with immaculate service (1200 staff to around 400 rooms, and a neat little trick with matchsticks so they can make up your room while you're out). It's long outgrown the original premises, an atmospheric,

colonial-style wooden building, now dubbed the Authors' Wing – indeed, there can't be many famous scribes who haven't stayed here, with suites named after a motley crew descending from Joseph Conrad through Graham Greene to Barbara Cartland. ❾

Peninsula Bangkok

Map 7, A6. 333 Thanon Charoennakorn, Klongsan ☎ 861 2888, ℻ 861 1112, ⓦ www.peninsula.com. On the Thonburi side of the Chao Phraya, this superb top-class hotel self-consciously aims to rival the *Oriental* across the river, with flawless service and a stylish modernity that makes its competitor look a little dated. The hotel operates a shuttle boat across to a pier and reception area by the *Shangri-La Hotel*. ❾

Pinnacle

Map 7a. 17 Soi Ngam Duphli ☎ 287 0111–31, ℻ 287 3420, ⓦ www.pinnaclehotels.com. Bland but reliable international-standard place, close to Thanon Rama IV, with rooftop jacuzzi and fitness centre; rates, which are at the lower end of this price code, include breakfast. **7**

Shangri-La

Map 7, B7. 89 Soi Wat Suan Plu, Thanon Charoen Krung (New Rd) ⓣ 236 7777, ⓕ 236 8579, ⓦ www.shangri-la.com. Grandiose establishment voted – for what it's worth – top hotel in the world by *Condé Nast Traveler* readers in 1996. It boasts the longest river frontage of any hotel in Bangkok, and makes the most of it, with gardens, restaurants – including the award-winning *Salathip* for Thai cuisine – and two pools by the Chao Phraya; the two accommodation wings are linked by free tuk-tuk if you can't be bothered to walk. A list of facilities as long as your arm leaves nothing to chance; good deals offered to families with children. **9**

Sukhothai

Map 7, L9. 13/3 Thanon Sathorn Thai ⓣ 287 0222, ⓕ 287 4980, ⓦ www.hotel sukhothaibangkok.com. The most elegant of Bangkok's top hotels, its decor inspired by the walled city of Sukhothai. Low-rise accommodation coolly furnished in silks, teak and granite, amid gardens set well back from the main road. Excellent Italian and Thai restaurants. **9**

Swiss Lodge

Map 7, J7. 3 Thanon Convent ⓣ 233 5345, ⓕ 236 9425, ⓦ www.swisslodge.com. Swish, friendly, good-value, solar-powered boutique hotel, just off Thanon Silom and ideally placed for business and nightlife. The imaginatively named theme restaurant *Café Swiss* serves fondue, raclette and all your other Swiss favourites, while the tiny terrace swimming pool confirms the national stereotypes of neatness and clever design. **8**

YMCA Collins International House

Map 7, L8. 27 Thanon Sathorn Thai ⓣ 287 1900, ⓕ 287 1996, ⓦ www.ymcabangkok.com. First-class facilities, including swimming pool and cable TV, with no frills. **7**

THANON SUKHUMVIT

Packed with high-rise hotels and office blocks, mid-priced foreign-food restaurants, souvenir shops, tailors, bookstores and stall after stall selling fake designer gear, **Thanon Sukhumvit** is a lively place that attracts a high proportion of single male tourists to its enclaves of girlie bars on Soi Nana Tai, Soi Cowboy and the Clinton Entertainment Plaza. But for the most part it's not a seedy area, and is home to many expats and middle-class Thais. Staying here gives you a huge choice of restaurants, bars and shops, on

GETTING TO AND FROM THANON SUKHUMVIT

The Skytrain (see p.62) has stops all the way along Sukhumvit, making journeys to places such as Siam Square and Chatuchak Weekend Market a fast and hassle-free undertaking. Useful buses for getting from Sukhumvit to Ratanakosin include AC#8 and #25 – both of which run via Siam Square, so you could also take the Skytrain to Siam Square and then change on to the bus; #25 and #40 go to Hualamphong Station and Chinatown, and AC#13 goes to Chatuchak Weekend Market. Full details of bus routes are given on pp.56–58. Airport bus AB3 has stops all the way along Thanon Sukhumvit.

A much faster way of getting across town is to hop on one of the longtail boats that ply Khlong Sen Seb; the canal service begins at Phanfa near Democracy Monument in the west of the city, runs parallel with part of Thanon Sukhumvit and has stops at the northern ends of Soi Nana Neua (Soi 3) and Soi Asoke (Soi 21), from where you can either walk down to Thanon Sukhumvit itself, hop on a bus, or take a motorbike taxi; see p.66 for details.

Sukhumvit and the adjacent Ploenchit roads, but you're a long way from the main Ratanakosin sights, and the sheer volume of traffic on Sukhumvit means that travelling by bus across town can take an age. Although this is not the place to come if you're on a tight budget, it's a reasonable area for mid-range hotels; the four- and five-star hotels on Sukhumvit tend to be more orientated towards business travellers than tourists, but what they lack in glamour they more than make up for in facilities. The best accommodation here is between sois 1 and 21. Advance reservations are accepted at all places listed below and are recommended during high season.

INEXPENSIVE

The Atlanta

Map 8, A6. Far southern end of Soi 2 ⓣ 252 1650, ⓕ 656 8123, ⓦ www.theatlantahotel.bizland .com.

Classic old-style hotel with lots of colonial-era character, welcoming staff, and some of the cheapest accommodation on Sukhumvit. Rooms are simple and a bit scruffy, but all have attached bathrooms; some have air-con and hot water. There are two swimming pools, as well as internet access and a left-luggage facility. The hotel restaurant is recommended, serving an extensive Thai menu which includes lots of vegetarian dishes; classic movies set in Asia are shown in the restaurant every night. ④–⑤

Miami Hotel

Map 8, C10. Soi 13 ⓣ 253 5611, ⓕ 253 1266, ⓔ miamihtl@asiaaccess.net.th.
Very popular, long-established budget hotel built around a swimming pool. Large, spartan and slightly shabby rooms; the cheapest have shared bathrooms, the priciest come with air-con. ③–⑤

Sukhumvit 11

Map 8, A8. Behind the 7-11 store at 1/3 Soi 11 ⓣ 253 5927, ⓕ 253 5929, ⓦ www.suk11.com.

THANON SUKHUMVIT

One of the few backpacker-oriented guest houses in this area, with B175 beds in five-person air-con dorms as well as air-con doubles with shared bathroom. Friendly place with informative noticeboards, left luggage and lockers, and a very nice roof terrace/balcony seating area. ❹

SV Guest House

Map 8, D5. Soi 19 ⓣ 253 1747, ⓕ 255 7174.
Some of the least expensive beds in the area; the rooms, some of which have air-con, are clean and well maintained, and all share bathrooms. ❸

Thai House Inn

Map 8, B5. Down a soi beside the *Amari Boulevard* at 1/1 Soi 7 ⓣ 255 4698, ⓕ 253 1780, ⓔ thaihouseinn@hotmail.com.
Simple, guest-house-style rooms, but reasonably priced for such a central Sukhumvit location. All rooms have air-con, TV and fridge, and there's a Thai-food canteen in the lobby. ❹

MODERATE

Bangkok Inn

Map 8, B9. Soi 11/1 ⓣ 254 4834, ⓕ 254 3545, ⓦ www.bangkokinn.cjb.net.
A cosy, friendly, German-run place with clean, smart rooms, all boasting air-con, shower, fridge and TV. Central and good value. ❺

City Lodge

Map 8, A10. Soi 9 ⓣ 253 7705, ⓕ 255 4667, ⓦ www.amari.com.
Map 8, E6. Soi 19 ⓣ 254 4783, ⓕ 255 7340, same website.
Part of the Amari group, these two small, unashamedly mid-range hotels have comfortably equipped rooms with air-con, phone and TV. Both are very centrally located, though the Soi 9 branch suffers from having half its rooms literally overlooking the Nana Skytrain platform. Advance booking advised. ❼

THANON SUKHUMVIT

Federal Hotel

Map 8, C3. 27 Soi 11 ⓣ 253 0175, ⓕ 253 5332, ⓔ federalhotel@hotmail.com.
Efficiently-run, mid-sized hotel at the far end of Soi 11, so there's a feeling of space and a relatively uncluttered skyline; many rooms look out on the appealing poolside seating area. All rooms have air-con, TV and fridge; the upstairs ones are in better condition and worth paying a little extra for. ❺–❻

Grand Inn

Map 8, B4. Soi 3 ⓣ 254 9021, ⓕ 254 9020.
Small, very central hotel offering sizeable, reasonably priced air-con rooms with TV and fridge. Good value. ❺–❻

Premier Travelodge

Map 8, C5. Soi 8 ⓣ 251 3031, ⓕ 253 3195.
Well-equipped, centrally located small hotel offering good-value rooms with shower, bathtub, air-con, fridge and TV. ❺

White Inn

Map 8, B6. Soi 4 ⓣ 251 1662, ⓕ 254 8865.
At the far, quiet end of the soi; slightly quaint establishment which cultivates the ambience of an Alpine lodge. Just eighteen fairly good, comfortable air-con rooms, most with a balcony overlooking the small swimming pool. ❺

EXPENSIVE

Amari Boulevard Hotel

Map 8, C4. Soi 5 ⓣ 255 2930, ⓕ 255 2950, ⓦ www.amari.com.
Medium-sized, unpretentious and friendly upmarket tourist hotel. Rooms are comfortably furnished and all enjoy fine views of the Bangkok skyline; the deluxe ones have private garden patios as well. There's an attractive rooftop swimming pool and garden terrace which becomes the Thai-food restaurant *Season* in the evenings. ❾

THANON SUKHUMVIT

Ambassador Hotel

Map 8, C9. Between sois 11 and 13 ⓣ 254 0444, ⓕ 254 7503. Sprawling hotel complex on Sukhumvit that's popular with Asian package tourists and has an excellent range of facilities, including over a dozen restaurants. Rooms are a bit faded, though reasonable value. ⑧

Grand Pacific Hotel

Map 8, D6. Above Robinsons Department Store between sois 17 and 19 ⓣ 651 1000, ⓕ 255 2441, ⓦ www.grandpacifichotel .com.
Conveniently located four-star hotel with smart, well-maintained rooms and good high-rise views. Facilities include three restaurants, a swimming pool, a gym and a business centre. Good value for its class. ⑨

Imperial Queen's Park

Map 8, G9. Soi 22 ⓣ 261 9000, ⓕ 261 9530.
Enormous and very swish high-rise hotel, whose large, comfortable rooms are nicely decorated with Thai-style furnishings. Facilities include two swimming pools and six restaurants. ⑨

JW Marriott Hotel

Map 8, B4. Between sois 2 and 4 ⓣ 656 7700, ⓕ 656 7711, ⓦ www.marriotthotels.com.
Deluxe hotel offering comfortable rooms with sophisticated phone systems and data ports geared towards business travellers. Facilities include three restaurants, a swimming pool, spa and fitness centre. ⑨

Landmark Hotel

Map 8, C5. Between sois 6 and 8 ⓣ 254 0404, ⓕ 253 4259, ⓦ www.landmarkbangkok.com.
One of the most luxurious hotels on Sukhumvit, orientated towards the business traveller. Several good restaurants, and shops, in the adjacent Landmark Plaza, plus a fitness club and rooftop pool on the premises. ⑨

Sheraton Grande Sukhumvit

Map 8, D6. Between sois 12 and 14 ⓣ 653 0333, ⓕ 653 0400, ⓦ www.luxurycollection.com.
Deluxe accommodation in

stylishly understated rooms, all of which offer fine views of the cityscape (the honeymoon suites have their own rooftop plungepools). Facilities include a gorgeous free-form swimming pool and tropical garden on the ninth floor, a spa with a range of treatment plans, and the trendy *Basil* Thai restaurant. Children under 17 stay for free if sharing adults' room. ❾

Eating

Bangkok boasts an astonishing fifty thousand **places to eat** – that's almost one for every hundred citizens – ranging from grubby streetside noodle shops to the most elegant of restaurants. Despite this glut, an awful lot of tourists venture no further than the front doorstep of their guest house, preferring the dining-room's ersatz Thai or Western dishes to the more adventurous fare to be found in even the most touristy accommodation areas.

Thai restaurants of all types are found all over the city. The best **gourmet Thai** restaurants operate from the downtown districts around Sukhumvit and Silom roads, proffering wonderful royal, traditional and regional cuisines that definitely merit an occasional splurge – though even here, you'd have to push the boat out to spend more than B500 per person. Over in Banglamphu, Thanon Phra Athit has become famous for its dozen or so trendy little restaurant-bars, each with distinctive decor and a contemporary Thai menu that's angled at young Thai diners. At the other end of the scale there are the **night markets** and **street stalls**, where you can generally get a lip-smacking feast for around B80. These are so numerous in Bangkok that we can only flag the most promising areas – but wherever you're staying, you'll hardly have to walk a block in any direction before encountering something appealing.

Of the non-Thai cuisines, Chinatown naturally rates as the most authentic district for pure **Chinese** food; likewise neighbouring Pahurat, the capital's Indian enclave, is best for unadulterated **Indian** dishes. The place to head for Western, **travellers' food** – from herbal teas and hamburgers to muesli – as well as a hearty range of veggie options is Thanon Khao San, packed with small, inexpensive tourist restaurants; standards vary, but there are some definite gems among the blander establishments.

Fast food comes in two forms: the mainly Thai version, which stews canteen-style in large tin trays on the upper floor **food courts** of department stores all over the city, and the old Western favourites like *McDonald's* and *Kentucky Fried Chicken* that mainly congregate around Thanon Sukhumvit, Siam Square and Thanon Ploenchit – an area that also has its share of decent Thai and foreign restaurants.

Downtown Bangkok has a good quota of coffee shops, including several branches of *Black Canyon* and *Starbucks*, the latter expensive but usually graced with armchairs and free newspapers.

Few Thais are **vegetarian**, but in the capital it's fairly easy to find specially concocted Thai and Western veggie dishes, usually at tourist-oriented eateries. Even at the plainest street stall, it's rarely impossible to persuade the cook to rustle up a vegetable-only fried rice or noodle dish. If you're vegan you'll need to stress that you don't want egg when you order, as eggs get used a lot; cheese and other dairy produce, however, don't feature at all in Thai cuisine.

Hygiene is a consideration when eating anywhere in Bangkok, but being too cautious means you'll end up spending a lot of money and missing out on some real treats

A FOOD AND DRINK GLOSSARY

Note: This glossary includes phonetic guidance to assist you with menu selection; a guide to the Thai language appears in Contexts (p.337).

Noodles

Ba mìi (kràwp)	Egg noodles (crisp fried)
Kwáy tĩāw (sên yaì/ sên lék)	White rice noodles (wide/thin)
Kwáy tĩāw/ ba mìi haêng	Rice noodles/egg noodles fried with egg, small pieces of meat and a few vegetables
Kwáy tĩāw/ba mìi nám (mũu)	Rice noodle/egg noodle soup, made with chicken broth (and pork balls)
Kwáy tĩāw/ba mìi rât nâ (mũu)	Rice noodles/egg noodles fried in gravy-like sauce with vegetables (and pork slices)
Phàt siyú	Wide or thin noodles fried with soy sauce, egg and meat
Phàt thai	Thin noodles fried with egg, beansprouts and tofu, topped with ground peanuts

Rice

Khâo	Rice
Khâo man kài	Slices of chicken served over rice
Khâo mũu daeng	Red pork with rice
Khâo nâ kài/pèt	Chicken/duck served with sauce over rice
Khâo niãw	Sticky rice
Khâo pàt	Fried rice
Khâo rât kaeng	Curry over rice
Khâo tôm	Rice soup

Curries and soups

Kaeng karii	Mild, Indian-style curry
Kaeng khĭaw wan	Green curry
Kaeng mátsàman	Rich Muslim-style curry, usually with beef and potatoes
Kaeng phánaeng	Thick, savoury curry
Kaeng phèt	Hot, red curry
Kaeng sôm	Fish and vegetable curry
Tôm khàa kài	Chicken coconut soup
Tôm yam kûng	Hot and sour prawn soup
Kaeng jèut	Mild soup with vegetables and usually pork

Other dishes

Hâwy thâwt	Omelette stuffed with mussels
Kài pàt bai kraprao	Chicken fried with basil leaves
Kài pàt nàw mái	Chicken with bamboo shoots
Kài pàt mét mámûang	Chicken with cashew nuts
Kài pàt khĭng	Chicken with ginger
Kài yâang	Grilled chicken
Khài yát sài	Omelette with pork and vegetables
Khānom jiin nám yaa	Noodles topped with fish curry
Kûng chúp paêng thâwt	Prawns fried in batter
Lâap	Spicy ground meat
Mũu prîaw wăan	Sweet and sour pork
Néua phàt krathiam phrík thai	Beef fried with garlic and pepper
Néua phàt nám man hŏy	Beef in oyster sauce
Pàt phàk bûng fai daeng	Morning glory fried in garlic and bean sauce
Pàt phàk lăi yàng	Stir-fried vegetables
Pàw pía	Spring rolls

Plaa nêung páe sá	Whole fish steamed with vegetables and ginger
Plaa rât phrík	Whole fish cooked with chillies
Plaa thâwt	Fried whole fish
Sàté	Satay
Sôm tam	Spicy papaya salad
Thâwt man plaa	Fish cake
Yam néua	Spicy grilled beef salad

Fruit (*phŏnlamáï*)

Fàràng	Guava (year-round)
Khanŭn	Jackfruit (year-round)
Klûay	Banana (year-round)
Lamyai	Longan (July–Oct)
Línjìì	Lychee (April–May)
Mámûang	Mango (March–June)
Ngáw	Rambutan (May–Sept)
Málákaw	Papaya (year-round)
Mákhăam	Tamarind (Dec–Jan)
Mánao	Lemon/lime (year-round)
Mangkùt	Mangosteen (April–Sept)
Mapráo	Coconut (year-round)
Sàppàròt	Pineapple (year-round)
Sôm	Orange (year-round)
Sôm oh	Pomelo (Oct–Dec)
Taeng moh	Watermelon (year-round)
Thúrian	Durian (April–June)

Sweets (*khanŏm*)

Khanŏm beuang	Small crispy pancake folded over with coconut cream and strands of sweet egg
Khâo lăam	Sticky rice, coconut cream and black beans cooked and served in bamboo tubes

Khâo niãw daeng	Sticky red rice mixed with coconut cream
Khâo niãw thúrian/ mámûang	Sticky rice mixed with coconut cream, and durian/mango
Klûay khàek	Fried banana
Lûk taan chêum	Sweet palm kernels served in syrup
Sãngkhayaa	Coconut custard
Tàkôh	Jelly (jello) topped with coconut cream

Drinks (*khreûang deùm*)

Bia	Beer
Chaa ráwn/yen	Hot/iced tea
Kaafae ráwn/yen	Hot/iced coffee
Kâew	Glass
Khúat	Bottle
Mâekhõng	Thai brand-name rice (or anglicized whisky "Mekhong")
Nám klûay	Banana shake
Nám mánao/sôm	Fresh, bottled or fizzy lemon/orange juice
Nám plào	Drinking water (boiled or filtered)
Nám sõdaa	Soda water
Nám tan	Sugar
Nám yen	Cold water
Nom jeùd	Milk
Ohlíang	Iced coffee
Sohdaa	Soda water
Thûay	Cup

Ordering

Can I see the menu?	*Khãw duù menu?*
I would like . . .	*Khãw . . .*
With/without	*Sai/mâi sai*
I am vegetarian	*Phõm* (male)/*diichãn* (female) *kin jeh*
Can I have the bill please?	*Khãw check bin?*

– you can be pretty sure that any noodle stall or curry shop that's permanently packed with customers is a safe bet. Thais don't drink water straight from the tap, and nor should you: plastic bottles of drinking water (*nam plao*) are sold everywhere for around B10, as well as the full multinational panoply of soft drinks.

HOW TO EAT THAI FOOD

Thai food is eaten with a fork (left hand) and a spoon (right hand); there is no need for a knife as food is served in bite-sized chunks, which are forked onto the spoon and fed into the mouth. Chopsticks are provided for noodle dishes, and the sticky rice (*khao niaw*) available in northeastern Thai restaurants is always eaten with the fingers of the right hand, rolled into small balls and dipped into chilli sauces. Never eat with the fingers of your left hand, which is used for washing after going to the toilet.

Instead of being divided into courses, a Thai meal – even the soup – is served all at once, and shared communally, so that complementary taste combinations can be enjoyed. The more people, the more taste and texture sensations; if there are only two of you, it's best to order at least three dishes, plus your own individual plates of steamed rice, while three diners would order at least four dishes and so on. Only put a serving of one dish on your rice plate at each time, and then only one or two spoonfuls.

Bland food is anathema to Thais, and restaurant tables usually come decked out with a condiment set featuring chopped chillies in watery fish sauce, sugar, and dried and ground red chillies – and often extra ground peanuts and a bottle of chilli ketchup as well. If you do bite into a chilli, the way to combat the searing heat is to take a mouthful of plain rice – swigging water just exacerbates the sensation.

In the more expensive restaurants you may have to pay a **service charge** (usually ten percent) and seven percent government **tax**. In the listings below, telephone numbers are given for the more popular or out-of-the-way places, where bookings may be advisable.

As soft-drink bottles are returnable, don't be surprised if a shopkeeper or stallholder pours the contents into a small plastic bag, perhaps with some crushed ice, deftly fastens the bag with an elastic band and inserts a straw, rather than charging you extra for taking away the bottle.

BANGLAMPHU AND DEMOCRACY AREA

Banglamphu is a great area for eating. **Khao San** is stacked full of guest-house restaurants serving cheap travellers' fare, and there are also some good veggie places here. Down on riverside **Thanon Phra Athit**, the pavement heaves with arty little café-restaurants serving reasonably priced modern Thai food to students from nearby Thammasat University, while out on the Banglamphu **fringes** there are a few recommended trendy Thai places, plus some traditional options too.

AROUND KHAO SAN

Coffee Corner
Map 3, D12. West end of Trok Mayom/Damnoen Klang Neua.
Daily 10am–10pm.
Makeshift, inexpensive alleyway café serving ten different blends of freshly brewed coffee, plus espressos and cappuccinos.

Himalayan Kitchen
Map 3, C11. 1 Thanon Khao San.
Daily 11am–11pm.
First-floor restaurant with good bird's-eye views of Khao San action. Both the food and the

decor draw their inspiration from Nepal, with religious *thanka* paintings on the wall and mid-priced thalis (veg and non-veg) on the menu.

La Casa
Map 3, D12. Thanon Khao San. Daily 11am–11pm.
Stylish and fairly pricey Italian place that's the sister operation of the *Chiang Mai* restaurant. All the standard pizza and pasta formulae are here, plus there are some innovative pasta salads, including a recommended Greek-style one. If you're feeling particularly adventurous you can round off with fettucine doused in chocolate sauce and ice-cream.

May Kaidee
Map 3, E12. 123–125 Thanon Tanao, though actually on the parallel soi to the east; easiest access is to take first left on Soi Damnoen Klang Neua (Soi Post Office).
Daily until about 9pm.
Simple, soi-side food stall plus tables serving the best vegetarian fare in Banglamphu. Try the tasty green curry with coconut, the curry-fried tofu with vegetables or the sticky black-rice pudding.

Night markets
Map 3, E11 and D10. In front of 7/11 at the Thanon Tani/Soi Ram Bhuttri intersection, and at the Soi Ram Bhuttri/Thanon Chakrabongse intersection.
Daily from around 5.30pm until the early hours.
Small knots of hot-food stalls serving very cheap night-market fare including *phat thai*, *kway tiaw nam*, satay, fresh fruit juices and cold beer.

Prakorb House
Map 3, C11. Thanon Khao San. Daily 9am–10pm.
Archetypal travellers' haven, with only a few tables, and an emphasis on wholesome ingredients. Inexpensive herbal teas, mango shakes, delicious pumpkin curry, and lots more besides.

Royal India
Map 3, D11. Opposite Boots on Thanon Khao San.
Daily 11am–11pm.
Excellent, reasonably priced

Indian food at this very popular branch of the Pahurat original. Dishes taste authentic and are served in copious quantities. Service is not exactly speedy, but you can fill in the gaps by watching the movies that play every night in the dining area.

Sarah

Map 3, C11. Off Thanon Chakrabongse, between the Shell petrol station and the police station.
Mon–Thurs & Sun 11am–11pm, Fri until 4pm.
Inexpensive Israeli restaurant, serving hearty platefuls of workaday falafels, hummus, salads and dips. It's next to a guest house patronized mainly by Israeli travellers, so the food is reasonably authentic, and a good option for vegetarians.

Sorn Daeng

Map 3, G13. Southeast corner of Democracy Monument.
Daily 10am–10pm.
The main customers at this large air-con restaurant are local office workers, so the menu offers a good range of

standard, fairly inexpensive Thai fare. The southern curries are recommended, particularly the rich sweet beef *kaeng matsaman*.

PHRA ATHIT AREA

Hemlock

Map 3, B9. 56 Thanon Phra Athit ⓣ282 7507. Next door but one from *Pra Athit Mansion*; the sign is visible from the road but not from the pavement.
Mon–Sat 5pm–midnight.
Small, stylish, highly recommended air-con restaurant that's very popular with students and young Thai couples. Offers a long and interesting mid-priced menu of unusual Thai dishes, including banana flower salad (*yam hua plii*), coconut and mushroom curry, grand lotus rice and various *larb* and fish dishes. The traditional *miang* starters (shiny green wild tea leaves filled with chopped vegetables, fish and meat) are also very tasty, and there's a good vegetarian selection. Worth reserving a table on Friday and Saturday nights.

Joy Luck Club

Map 3, C8. Opposite the fort at the point where Thanon Phra Athit turns into Thanon Phra Sumen.

Daily 11am–11pm.

Despite its name, the only thing that's noticeably Chinese about this cute little art-house café–restaurant are the red lanterns hanging outside. Inside are just half a dozen tables (each designed with a glassed-in display of artefacts), modern art on the walls and occasional live music at night. The Thai food is delicious and reasonably priced, and there's a big veggie menu, including various green and *matsaman* curries, plus lots of cocktails.

Krua Nopparat

Map 3, C8. 130–132 Thanon Phra Athit.

Daily 10.30am–9.30pm.

The decor in this unassuming air-con restaurant is noticeably plain compared to all the arty joints on this road, but the Thai food is good – try the eggplant wingbean salad and the battered crab – and the prices very inexpensive.

Tonpo

Map 3, B8. Thanon Phra Athit, next to Tha Banglamphu.

Daily 10am–10pm.

Sizeable seafood menu and a relatively scenic riverside location; a good place for a beer and a (mid-priced) snack at the end of a long day's sightseeing.

Tuk

Map 3, C9. Corner of Soi Ram Bhuttri and Soi Chana Songkhram.

Daily 7am–11pm.

The perfect breakfast place, with lots of inexpensive options, ranging from American and European to Israeli and Chinese, plus wholemeal bread and good yoghurt.

SAMSEN, THEWES AND THE FRINGES

Bangkok Bar

Map 3, H13. 591 Thanon Phra Sumen.

Daily 6pm–2am.

Housed in an elegant 150-year-old canalside house, complete with high ceilings,

SAMSEN, THEWES AND THE FRINGES

wooden floors and fine fretwork, this place is well worth trying both for its setting and for its good-value upmarket Thai cuisine. There's a gallery upstairs to entertain you while you're waiting for food. Recommendations include seafood with young coconut, fish-head curry and deep-fried pillows of tofu.

Dachanee

Map 3, H10. 18/2 Thanon Pracha Thipatai, near *Thai Hotel*.
Daily 10am–10pm.
Popular with local office workers, this air-con restaurant serves up moderately priced standard Thai fare such as fiery *tom yam* as well as tasty extras like tofu- and beansprout-stuffed *khanom buang* (crispy Vietnamese-style pancakes).

Dragon Eyes

Map 3, F6. Samsen/Wisut Kasat junction.

Mon–Sat 6pm–midnight.
Small, mid-priced restaurant serving stylish renditions of standard Thai dishes – try the *khao pat* with added fruit and nuts, or the chilli-fried chicken with cashews (*kai pat met mamuang himapaan*) – as well as more unusual fare. Popular with young Thai couples and has a lively atmosphere; there's a huge selection of bar drinks as well, and, as you'd expect from a place managed by a *Bangkok Post* music critic, a fine range of music.

Isaan restaurants

Map 2, D3. Behind the Rajdamnoen Boxing Stadium on Thanon Rajdamnoen Nok.
Daily 11am–midnight.
There's at least five restaurants in a row here, all of them serving inexpensive northeastern fare to hungry boxing fans: take your pick for hearty plates of *kai yaang* and *khao niaw*.

For advice on getting to this area on public transport see p.157, and for a more detailed breakdown of useful bus routes see pp.56–58.

SAMSEN, THEWES AND THE FRINGES

Kainit

Map 2, C4. Thanon Titong, next to Wat Suthat.

Daily 11am–11pm.

Rather formal Italian restaurant that's mainly patronized by expats, but also works fine as a lunchtime treat after visiting Wat Suthat. The pizza and pastas are tasty but expensive.

Kaloang

Map 3, F2. Beside the river at the far western end of Thanon Sri Ayutthaya.

Daily 11am–11pm.

Flamboyant service and excellent seafood attracts a predominantly Thai clientele to this pricey open-air restaurant located beside the Chao Phraya River. Try the fried rolled shrimps served with a sweet dip, the roast squid cooked in a piquant sauce, or the steamed butter fish.

Na Pralan

Map 4, C5. Almost opposite the Gate of Glorious Victory, Thanon Na Phra Lan.

Mon–Sat 10am–10pm.

Technically in Ratanakosin but very close to Banglamphu, this small café, only a couple of doors up the street from the Silpakorn University Art College, is ideally placed for refreshment before or after a tour of the Grand Palace. Popular with students, it occupies a quaint old shophouse with battered, arty decor and air con. The mid-priced menu is well thought out and has some unusual twists, offering tasty daily specials – mostly one-dish meals with rice – and a range of Thai desserts, coffees, teas and beers.

Silver Spoon

Map 3, F3. 2/1 Thanon Krung Kasem, beside Tha Thewes.

Daily 11am–10.30pm.

Popular place for seafood – and riverine breezes, with decent Chao Phraya views and a huge mid-priced menu including baked cottonfish in mango sauce, steamed snakehead fish with chillies, and *tom yam kung*.

Tang Teh

Map 3, F6. 269–271 Thanon Wisut Kasat, corner of Thanon Samsen.
Daily noon–2.30pm & 6–11pm.
Quality Thai restaurant, with contemporary art on the walls and high-class food on the menu. The fried catfish with cashews and chilli sauce is recommended, as are the superb fishcakes and the steamed sea bass with Chinese plum sauce. There's also a fairly interesting veggie menu, and tasty home-made ice cream, all at moderate prices.

CHINATOWN AND PAHURAT

Chong Tee

Map 5, H6. 84 Soi Sukon 1, Thanon Traimit, between Hualamphong station and Wat Traimit.
This typical, long-standing, no-frills Chinese restaurant is known for its delicious and inexpensive pork satay and sweet toast.

Hua Seng Hong

Map 5, E4. 371 Thanon Yaowarat.
Not too hygienic, but the food is good and reasonably priced. Sit outside on the jostling pavement for delicious egg noodle soup with pork, duck or *wonton*, or good-value shark's fin soup. Inside the air-con restaurant, the main thrust is fish and seafood (try the asparagus with scallop), but also on offer are pricey Chinese specialities like goose feet, smoked whole baby pig and bird's nest.

Maturot

Map 5, F4. Soi Phadungdao (aka Soi Texas), Thanon Yaowarat.
Evenings only, until late.

For advice on getting to this area on public transport see p.166, and for a more detailed breakdown of useful bus routes see pp.56–58.

CHINATOWN AND PAHURAT

YELLOW-FLAG HEAVEN FOR VEGGIES

Every autumn, for nine days during the ninth lunar month (October or November), Thailand's Chinese community goes on a meat-free diet in order to mark the onset of the Vegetarian Festival (Ngan Kin Jeh), a sort of Taoist version of Lent. Nearly every restaurant and foodstall in Chinatown turns vegetarian for the period, flying small yellow flags to show that they are upholding the tradition. For vegetarian tourists this is a great time to be in town – just look for the yellow flag and you can be sure all dishes will be one hundred percent vegan. Soya substitutes are a popular feature on the vegetarian Chinese menu, so don't be surprised to find pink prawn-shaped objects floating in your noodle soup or unappetizingly realistic slices of fake duck. Many hotel restaurants also get in on the act during the Vegetarian Festival, running special veggie promotions for a week or two.

In a soi famous for its seafood stalls, the fresh, meaty prawns served up here, accompanied by *phak bung fai daeng* (fried morning glory) and *tom yam kung*, stand out. Inexpensive to moderate.

Royal India
Map 5, B3. Just off Thanon Chakraphet.
Daily 11am–11pm.
Serves the same excellent and highly authentic curries as its Banglamphu branch, but attracts an almost exclusively Indian clientele. Prices are very reasonable and portions large.

White Orchid Hotel
Map 5, F4. 409–421 Thanon Yaowarat.
Dim sum 11am–2pm & 5–10pm.
Recommended for its fairly pricey *dim sum*, with bamboo baskets of prawn dumplings, spicy spare ribs, stuffed beancurd and the like, served in three different portion sizes. All-you-can-eat lunchtime buffets are also worth considering.

You Sue Vegetarian

Map 5, I6. 75m east of Hualamphong Station at 241 Thanon Rama IV; directly across the road from the sign for the *Bangkok Centre Hotel*. Daily 6am–10pm.

Cheap and cheerful Chinese vegetarian café. Standard curries and Chinese and one-pot dishes are made with high-protein meat substitutes. Not worth making a special outing for, but handy for the station.

Every evening, the stall just outside *Hua Seng Hong* on Thanon Yaowarat sells cheap and delicious *bua loy nga dam nam khing*, soft rice dumplings stuffed with bittersweet black sesame in ginger soup.

DOWNTOWN: AROUND SIAM SQUARE AND THANON PLOENCHIT

Bali

Map 6, L5. 15/3 Soi Ruam Rudee ☎ 250 0711. Mon 5–10pm, Tues–Sun 11am–10pm.

Top-notch, authentic Indonesian food and homely, efficient service in a cosy old house with garden tables just off Thanon Ploenchit . Prices per dish are mostly moderate, or blow out on a seven-course *rijstaffel* for B250.

Café Botanica

Map 6, H4. 1st Floor, Gaysorn Plaza, Thanon Ploenchit ☎ 656 1305–6. Daily 10am–9.30pm.

A haven for footsore shoppers but worth a detour in its own right: excellent, moderately priced Thai and Western food, with an especially good choice of Thai salads and noodles, in a sophisticated, open-plan setting.

Inter

Map 6, E5. 432/1–2 Soi 9,
Siam Square ⓣ 251 4689.
Daily 10am–10pm.
Honest, efficient Thai
restaurant that's popular with
students and shoppers, serving
good, cheap one-dish meals
and more expensive curries in
a no-frills, fluorescent-lit
canteen atmosphere.

Kirin Restaurant

Map 6, D5. 226/1 Soi 2, Siam
Square ⓣ 251 2326–9.
Daily 11am–2pm & 6–10pm.
Swankiest, best and most
expensive of many Chinese
restaurants in the area; for a
blow-out, order the delicious
ped pak king, duck cooked
with vegetables and ginger.

Ma Be Ba

Map 6, J8. 93 Soi Lang Suan
ⓣ 254 9595.
Daily 11am–2.30pm &
5.30pm–1am (last food orders
11.30pm).
Lively, spacious and

extravagantly decorated Italian
restaurant dishing up excellent
pizzas and daily pasta specials,
usually seafood, from a huge
open kitchen; expensive.

Mah Boon Krong Food Centre

Map 6, C5. 6th Floor, MBK
shopping centre, corner of
Rama I and Phrayathai roads,
opposite Siam Square.
Daily 10am–10pm.
Increase your knowledge of
Thai food: ingredients, names
and pictures of inexpensive
dishes (including some
vegetarian ones, and a wide
range of desserts) from all
over the country are displayed
at the various stalls. A beer
terrace affords good views of
the cityscape.

Sarah Jane's

Map 6, K8. Ground Floor,
Sindhorn Tower 1, 130–132
Thanon Witthayu ⓣ 650 9992–3.
Daily 11am–10pm.
Long-standing, moderately

For advice on getting to this area on public
transport see p.167, and for a more detailed
breakdown of useful bus routes see pp.56–58.

---

priced restaurant, popular with Bangkok residents from Isaan (the northeast of Thailand), serving excellent, simple northeastern food. It's run by an American – and offers a smaller range of Italian dishes – but the *kai yaang* and *som tam* are supremely authentic nonetheless; try also the *neua nam tok* (barbecued beef salad) and the *yam pla dook foo* (finely chopped catfish, deep fried until crispy, with a mango topping). The premises are slick but unfussy, and can be slightly tricky to find at night towards the rear of a modern office block.

Sorn's

Map 6, C4. 36/8 Soi Kasemsan 1, Thanon Rama I ⒯ 215 5163.
Daily 6.30am–10pm.
In a quiet lane of superior guest houses, this is a laid-back, open-air hangout strewn with plants and vines, with an atmosphere like a beachside guest-house restaurant. A photographer and long-time resident of the US, Sorn serves up delicious, moderately priced versions of standard Thai dishes – the *tom*

khaa kai is especially good – as well as Western meals, varied breakfasts, good coffee and a full-service bar with reasonably priced wine.

Whole Earth

Map 6, J7. 93/3 Soi Lang Suan ⒯ 252 5574.
Daily 11.30am–2pm & 5.30–11pm.
The best veggie restaurant in Bangkok, serving interesting, moderately priced Thai and Indian-style food, plus some dishes for carnivores and delicious fresh fruit smoothies; relaxing atmosphere and good service. In the upstairs room (not always open), you can eat sprawled on cushions at low tables.

Zen

Map 6, H4. 6th Floor, World Trade Centre, corner of Ploenchit and Rajdamri roads ⒯ 255 6462.
Map 6, E4. 4th Floor, Siam Centre, Thanon Rama I ⒯ 658 1183–4.
Daily 10am–10pm.
Fairly expensive but good-value Japanese restaurant with wacky wooden design,

modern but nodding to traditional Japanese themes, and seductive booths. Among a huge range of dishes, the complete meal sets (with pictures to help you choose) are delicious and filling, and the soups particularly good.

DOWNTOWN: SOUTH OF THANON RAMA IV

Akane Japanese Noodle

Map 7, J6. Central Department Store, Thanon Silom (plus branches around town, including in the World Trade Centre, corner of Rajdamri and Rama I). Daily 11am–10pm.

Deliciously authentic *soba*, *udon*, *ramen* and *sushi* dishes, some surprisingly moderately priced, in unpretentious café-style surroundings; handy after shopping or before hitting Silom's nightlife.

All Gaengs

Map 7, G5. 173/8–9 Thanon Suriwong ⓣ 233 3301. Mon–Fri 11.30am–2pm & 6.30–10pm, Sat & Sun 6.30–10pm.

Large moderately priced menu of tasty curries (*kaeng*, sometimes spelt *gaeng*) and spicy Thai salads (*yam*) served in cool, modern, air-con surroundings underneath *La Residence* hotel – a good place to fire yourself up for the nightclubs over on Thanon Silom.

Angelini's

Map 7, B7. *Shangri-La Hotel*, 89 Soi Wat Suan Plu, Thanon Charoen Krung (New Rd) ⓣ 236 7777. Daily 11am–late.

One of the capital's best Italians, pricey but not too extravagant. The setting is lively and relaxed, with open-plan kitchen and big picture windows onto the pool and river, though the music can be obtrusive. Whether you're vegetarian or not, it's worth plumping for the pumpkin ravioli with truffle butter sauce; otherwise, there are some unusual main courses as well as old favourites like *ossobuco*, or you can invent your own wood-oven-baked pizza.

A NIGHT ON THE RIVER

The Chao Phraya River looks fabulous at night, when most of the noisy longtails have stopped terrorizing the ferries, and the riverside temples and other grand monuments – including the Grand Palace and Wat Arun – are elegantly illuminated. Joining one of the nightly dinner cruises in a converted traditional rice barge along the river is a great way to appreciate it all. Call ahead to reserve a table and check departure details – some places offer free transport from hotels, and some cruises may not run during the rainy season (May–Oct).

Maeyanang

Run by the *Oriental Hotel* ☏ 236 0400. Departs Si Phraya pier (map 7, C3) at 7pm, returning at 9.30pm. Thai and international buffet. B1600.

Manohra

Run by the *Marriott Royal Garden Riverside Hotel*, south of Taksin Bridge in Thonburi (map 7, A7) ☏ 476 0021. Departs at 7.30pm, returning 10pm. Eight-course Thai set meal. B1200.

Pearl of Siam

☏ 292 1649. Departs Si Phraya pier (map 7, C3) at 7.30pm, returning at 9.30pm. Thai and international buffet. B1100.

Shangri-La Horizon

☏ 236 7777. Departs *Shangri-La Hotel* pier (map 7, B7) at 7.30pm, returning at 10pm. International buffet. B1200.

Thai Wan Fa

☏ 237 0077. Departs Si Phraya pier (map 7, C3) at 7pm, returning at 9pm. Thai or seafood set menu. B700 or B750.

For advice on getting to this area on public transport see p.170, and for a more detailed breakdown of useful bus routes see pp.56–58.

DOWNTOWN: SOUTH OF THANON RAMA IV

Aoi

Map 7, I6. 132/10–11 Soi 6, Thanon Silom ⊤ 235 2321–2 (plus a branch in Emporium on Thanon Sukhumvit ⊤ 02/664 8590).

Daily 11.30am–2pm & 6–11pm. The best place in town for a Japanese blowout, justifiably popular with the expat community. Excellent authentic food and elegant decor. Lunch sets available and a sushi bar.

Ban Chiang

Map 7, D7. 14 Soi Srivieng, Thanon Surasak ⊤ 236 7045. Daily 11.30am–2pm & 5.30–10.30pm. Fine central and northeastern Thai cuisine – try the *kaeng liang*, a delicious broth chock full of vegetables and shrimps – at moderate to expensive prices. The restaurant can be difficult to find, off the western end of Thanon Silom down towards Thanon Sathorn, but rewards persistence with an elegant, surprisingly quiet setting in an old wooden house with garden tables.

Bussaracum

Map 7, F8. 139 Sethiwan Building, Thanon Pan ⊤ 266 6312–8.

Daily 11am–2pm & 5–10pm. Superb royal Thai cuisine, offering recipes created for the court which until recently were kept secret from the common folk. Only top-quality ingredients are used, and great care is taken over the look of individual dishes, which are often decorated with carved fruit and vegetables. Expensive, but well worth it.

Chai Karr

Map 7, D6. 312/3 Thanon Silom ⊤ 233 2549. Daily 11.30am–9pm. Small restaurant, fifteen minutes' walk west of the main Silom action, opposite the *Holiday Inn*. Traditional wooden decor is the setting for a wide variety of moderately priced Thai and Chinese dishes, followed by liqueur coffees and coconut ice cream.

Charuvan

Map 7, J6. 70–2 Thanon Silom, near the entrance to Soi 4.
Daily 9am–9pm.
Clean basic restaurant, lackadaisical verging on rude, with a walled-in air-con room. Specializing in inexpensive and tasty duck on rice (the beer's a bargain too), it's popular with both Soi 4 clubbers and Patpong barflies.

Deen

Map 7, E6. 786 Thanon Silom.
Mon–Sat 11am–9.30pm.
Small, neat, well-lit café with air con (no smoking), almost opposite Silom Village (no English sign). It draws most of its clientele from the Islamic south of Thailand, serving fairly cheap Thai and Chinese standard dishes with a southern twist, as well as spicy Indian-style curries and southern Thai specialities such as *grupuk* (crispy fish) and *roti* (Muslim pancakes).

Harmonique

Map 7, C4. 22 Soi 34, Thanon Charoen Krung (New Rd) ⓣ 237 8175.
Daily 10am–10pm.

Relaxing, welcoming restaurant, on the lane between Wat Muang Kae express-boat pier and the GPO, that's well worth a trip. Tables are scattered throughout several converted houses decorated with antiques, and a quiet, leafy courtyard; the moderately priced Thai food is varied and excellent – among the seafood specialities, try the crab curry.

Himali Cha-Cha

Map 7, C5. 1229/11 Thanon Charoen Krung (New Rd) ⓣ 235 1569.
Daily 11am–3.30pm & 6–10.30pm.
Fine, moderately priced north Indian restaurant a short way down an alley to the south of GPO, founded by a character who was chef to numerous Indian ambassadors, and now run by his son. Homely atmosphere, attentive service and a good vegetarian selection.

Laicram

Map 7, K6. 2nd Floor, Thaniya Plaza, Soi Thaniya.
Daily 10.30am–3pm & 5–10pm.

DOWNTOWN: SOUTH OF THANON RAMA IV

Proficient, moderately expensive restaurant tucked away in a shopping centre off the eastern end of Thanon Silom. On offer are plenty of unusual specialities from around Thailand on a huge menu, plus loads of veggie dishes and traditional desserts.

Le Bouchon
Map 7, J5. 37/17 Patpong 2, near Thanon Suriwong ⓣ234 9109.
Daily 11am–11.30pm.
Cosy, welcoming bar-bistro that's much frequented by the city's French expats, offering pricey French home cooking on a regularly changing menu; the lamb with rosemary sauce is strongly recommended, as is booking.

Mango Tree
Map 7, I6. 37 Soi Tantawan, Thanon Suriwong ⓣ236 2820.
Daily 10am–2pm & 6–10pm.
Excellent authentic Thai food in a surprisingly peaceful haven between Suriwong and Silom, where you can eat indoors or out in the garden to the live strains of a traditional Thai ensemble.

Moderate to expensive, but highly rated by Bangkokians, so definitely worth booking.

Mei Jiang
Map 7, A6. *Peninsula Hotel*, 333 Thanon Charoennakorn, Klongsan ⓣ861 2888.
Daily 11.30am–2pm & 6.30–10pm.
Probably Bangkok's best Chinese restaurant, with beautiful views of the hotel gardens and the river night and day. It's designed like an elegant teak box, without the gaudiness of many Chinese restaurants, and staff are very attentive and graceful. Specialities include duck smoked with tea and excellent lunchtime *dim sum* – a bargain at around B65 a dish.

Ranger
Map 7a. Mahamek Driving Range ⓣ679 8964. South end of Soi Ngam Duphli, by Ministry of Aviation compound.
Daily 6am–10pm.
Unusual location by a golf driving range, but the setting for this moderately priced restaurant is pastoral cute, on stilted, tree-shaded platforms

above a quiet, lotus-filled pond. Specialities include *yam hua pree*, gooey and delicious banana flower salad with dried shrimp and peanuts; some veggie dishes are available and the service is friendly and attentive.

Ratree Seafood

Map 7, K6. Soi 1, Thanon Silom.

Daily, evenings only.

Famous street stall with twenty or so tables, surrounded by many similar competitors, at the eastern end of Thanon Silom opposite Thaniya Plaza. Temptingly displayed, brightly lit on ice, is all manner of reasonably priced fresh seafood (the specialities are *poo chak ka chan* – oily, orange, medium-sized sea crab – and barbecued fish) and there's noodle soup too.

Sui Heng

Map 7, A9. Mouth of Soi 65, Thanon Charoen Krung (New Rd).

Daily, evenings only, until late.

In a good area for stall-grazing, south of Taksin Bridge, a legendary Chinese street vendor who has been selling one dish for over seventy years: *khao man kai*, tender boiled chicken breast served with delicious broth and rice cooked in stock.

Thaichine

Map 7, D8. 233 Thanon Sathorn ⓣ 212 6401.

Daily 10am–11pm.

In a grand, century-old building that was formerly the Thai-Chinese Chamber of Commerce, this is an elegant, comfortable restaurant, where the eclectic Asian decor matches the menu's delicious combination of moderately priced Thai, Vietnamese and Chinese dishes.

Tongue Thai

Map 7, C5. 18–20 Soi 38, Thanon Charoen Krung ⓣ 630 9918–9.

Daily 11am–10.30pm.

In front of the Oriental Place shopping mall. Very high standards of food and cleanliness, with charming, unpretentious service, in an elegantly decorated 100-year-old shophouse. Veggies are amply catered for with delicious dishes such as tofu in black bean sauce and deep-fried banana flower and corn cakes, while carnivores should try the fantastic beef curry (*panaeng neua*). Expensive.

THANON SUKHUMVIT

Ambassador Hotel Seafood Centre

Map 8, C9. Inside the *Ambassador Hotel* complex, between sois 11 and 13. Daily 11am–10pm.

Cavernous hall of a restaurant that spills over into a covered courtyard with over a dozen stalls serving all manner of moderately priced fish and seafood dishes, including soups and barbecued fish.

Baan Kanitha

Map 8, F4. Soi 23. Daily 11am–2pm & 6–11pm.

The big attraction at this long-running favourite haunt of Sukhumvit expats is the setting in a traditional Thai house. The food is upmarket Thai and expensive, and includes lots of fiery salads (*yam*), and a good range of *tom yam* soups, green curries and seafood curries.

Basil

Map 8, D6. Inside the *Sheraton Grande Hotel*, between sois 12 and 14. Daily 11.30am–2pm & 6–10pm.

Mouthwateringly fine traditional Thai food with a modern twist is the order of the day at this trendy, relatively informal restaurant in the super-deluxe five-star *Sheraton*. Recommendations include the grilled river prawns with chilli and the *matsaman* curry (both served with red and green rice), and the surprisingly delicious durian cheesecake. Vegetarian menu on request.

Cabbages and Condoms

Map 8, D7. Soi 12. Daily 11am–10pm.

Run by the Population and Community Development Association of Thailand (PDA): diners are treated to authentic, mid-priced Thai food in the Condom Room, and relaxed scoffing of barbecued seafood in the beer garden. Try the *plaa samlii* (fried cottonfish with mango and chilli) or the *kai haw bai toey* (marinated chicken baked in pandanus leaves). All proceeds go to the PDA, and there's an adjacent shop selling all kinds of double-entendre T-shirts, keyrings and of course condoms.

De Meglio

Map 8, C4. Soi 11.
Daily 11.30am–2.30pm & 5.30–11pm.
Upmarket Italian restaurant presided over by a chef who was trained by Anton Mosiman. Many of the antipastos are unusual Thai-Italian hybrids, and both the linguini with clams and the crab cannelloni with fennel salad are recommended. Authentic wood-fired pizzas are a house speciality.

Emporium Food Court

Map 8, G8 & H8. 5th Floor, Emporium Shopping Centre, between sois 22 and 24.
Ⓢ Phrom Phong.
Typical food court of twenty stalls selling very cheap but reasonable quality Thai standards including fishball soup, fried chicken and satay. Buy coupons at the entrance booth and find a window table for pleasant views over Queen Sirikit park. For something more upmarket, there are a dozen small restaurant concessions on the same floor as the food court, ranging from Italian to Japanese.

Haus München

Map 8, D5. Soi 15.
Daily 10am–1am.
Large but moderately priced helpings of authentic German and Austrian classics, from pigs' knuckles to *bratwurst*, served in a restaurant that's modelled on a Bavarian

For advice on getting to this area on public transport see p.176, and for a more detailed breakdown of useful bus routes see pp.56–58.

THANON SUKHUMVIT

lodge. There's usually some recent German newspapers to peruse here too.

Lemongrass

Map 8, H9. Soi 24, ☏ 258 8637. Daily 11am–2pm & 6–11pm. Scrumptious Thai nouvelle cuisine served in the elegant surroundings of a converted traditional house; the minced chicken with ginger is a particular winner. A vegetarian menu is available on request. Prices range from moderate to expensive. Advance reservations recommended.

Mrs Balbir's

Map 8, B9. Soi 11/1. Daily noon–11pm. Deservedly popular veg and non-veg Indian restaurant run by TV cook Mrs Balbir. Specialities include the spicy dry chicken and lamb curries (*masala kerai*) and the daily all-you-can-eat veggie buffet, which is recommended at B150 per person. Indian cookery courses are held here every week – see p.249 for details.

Nipa

Map 8, C5. Third floor of Landmark Plaza, between sois 4 and 6. Daily 11.30am–2.30pm & 5.30–11pm; last orders at 10.15pm. Tasteful traditional Thai-style place with a classy, fairly pricey menu that features an adventurous range of dishes, including spicy fish curry, several *matsaman* and green curries, excellent *som tam* and mouthwatering braised spare ribs. Also offers a sizeable vegetarian selection. Regular cookery classes are held here – see p.249 for details.

Suda Restaurant

Map 8, E6. Soi 14. Daily 11am–midnight. Unpretentious locals' hangout, patronized by office workers at lunch-time, but open till midnight. Standard, reasonably priced *kap khao* (dishes served with rice) and noodle dishes, plus some fish: fried tuna with cashews and chilli recommended.

THANON SUKHUMVIT

Thong U Rai

Map 8, F5. 22/4–5 Soi 23.
Daily 10.30am–midnight.
Highly recommended
bohemian place decked out
with paintings and antique
curios; serves mid-priced
Thai food including
especially good minced
chicken marinated in limes.

Whole Earth

Map 8, H10. Ten minutes' walk
down Soi 26 at no.71.
Daily 11.30am–2pm &
5.30–11pm.
Vegetarian restaurant serving
mid-priced meat-free Thai
and Indian food plus a few
dishes for carnivores. The
mushroom and tofu *larb*
served over baked rice is
worth the walk, especially if
you can get one of the low
tables on the first floor where
there's more atmosphere than
in the ground floor restaurant.

Yong Lee

Map 8, C10. Corner of Soi 15.
Mon–Sat 11.30am–9.30pm.
One of the few
unpretentious, up-country
style rice-and-noodle shops
on Sukhumvit. Run by a
Chinese family; rates are
inexpensive, considering the
competition.

THANON SUKHUMVIT

Nightlife

For many of Bangkok's visitors, nightfall in the city is the signal to hit the **sex bars**, the neon sumps that disfigure three distinct parts of town: along Thanon Sukhumvit's Soi Cowboy (between sois 21 and 23) and Nana Plaza (Soi 4), and, most notoriously, in the two small sois off the east end of Thanon Silom known as Patpong 1 and 2. But within spitting distance of the beer bellies flopped onto Patpong's bars lies **Silom 4**, Bangkok's most happening after-dark haunt, pulling in the cream of Thai youth and tempting an increasing number of travellers to stuff their party gear into their rucksacks: Soi 4, the next alley off Thanon Silom to the east of Patpong 2, started out as a purely gay area but now offers a range of styles in gay, mixed and straight pubs, dance bars and clubs.

Details of Bangkok's gay nightlife are given on p.222.

For convenient drinking, we've split the most recommended of the **bars and clubs** into four central areas. In **Banglamphu**, there are two main centres for night-time entertainment. The bars and clubs on and around Thanon Khao San are aimed at young Western travellers, with pool tables, cheap beer and either a programme of back-to-back video showings or a DJ with a good loud set of turntables;

Pag. :   1
- - - - - - - - - - - - *

Amount
- - - - - - *
45,00

some of these places also attract crowds of young Thai drinkers. A couple of blocks further west, Thanon Phra Athit is more of a Thai scene, though again there are always some farang drinkers in the mix. Here, the style-conscious little restaurant-bars have their tables spill over on to the pavement, and the live music is likely to be a lone piano player or guitarist.

Downtown bars, which tend to attract both farang and Thai drinkers, are concentrated on adjoining **Soi Lang Suan** and **Soi Sarasin**, and in studenty **Siam Square**, as well as around the east end of **Thanon Silom**. Lang Suan and Sarasin have their fair share of live-music bars, but the Western covers and bland jazz on offer are often less than inspiring; the better live-music venues are listed below. If, among all the choice of nightlife around Silom, you do end up in one of Patpong's sex bars, be prepared to shell out up to B600 for a small beer. Though many Patpong bars trumpet the fact that they have no cover charge, almost every customer gets ripped off in some way, and stories of menacing bouncers are legion. **Thanon Sukhumvit** watering holes tend to be either British-style pubs, bar-beers (open-sided drinking halls with huge circular bars) packed full of hostesses, or full-on girlie bars.

Local whisky is a lot better value than beer, and Thais think nothing of consuming a bottle a night, heavily diluted with soda water or coke and ice. The most widely available brand is Mekhong; distilled from rice, it's quite palatable once you've stopped expecting it to taste like Scotch.

During the cool season (Nov–Feb), an evening out at one of the seasonal **beer gardens** is a pleasant way of soaking up the urban atmosphere (and the traffic fumes). You'll find them in hotel forecourts or sprawled in front of shopping centres – the huge beer garden that sets up in front of the World Trade Centre on Thanon Rajdamri is extremely popular, and recommended; beer is served in pitchers here and bar snacks are available too.

BANGLAMPHU, RATANAKOSIN AND HUALAMPHONG

About Café

Map 5, H5. Five minutes' walk from Hualamphong Station at 418 Thanon Maitri Chit. Mon–Sat 10am–midnight.

Arty café-bar that's popular with trendy young Thais. There's a gallery space upstairs and exhibits usually spill over into the ground floor eating and drinking area, where tables and sofas are scattered about in an informal and welcoming fashion.

Austin

Map 3, C11. Just off Thanon Khao San, in the scrum behind *D&D Guest House*. Daily 6pm–2am.

Named in honour of the car (hence the neon silhouette), this homely three-floored bar plays loud music and is hugely popular with students from nearby Thammasat University, though it has yet to attract much of a farang crowd. The favoured drink is a jug of Sang Som rum over ice, mixed with soda and lemon and served with straws to share with your mates. Also on offer are lots of cocktails and fairly pricey beer.

Banana Bar

Map 3, D12. Trok Mayom/Damnoen Klang Neua. Daily from about 6pm.

Half a dozen tiny cubbyhole bars open up on this alley every night, each with just a handful of alleyside chairs and tables, loud music on the tape player, and a trendy bartender.

Bangkok Bar

Map 3, C10. West end of Soi Ram Bhuttri. Daily 6pm–2am.

Not to be confused with the restaurant of the same name on Thanon Phra Sumen, this small, narrow dance bar is fronted by a different DJ every night and draws capacity crowds of drinkers and clubbers.

Bayon

Map 3, D12. Thanon Khao San.
Daily 9pm–2am.
Sizeable but not terribly exciting upstairs dance floor playing disco and rave classics, and serving mid-priced drinks to a mixed crowd of Thais and farangs till the small hours.

Boh

Map 4, B8. Tha Thien, Thanon Maharat.
Daily 7pm–midnight.
Not quite in Banglamphu, but within easy striking distance in Ratanakosin. When the Chao Phraya express boats stop running around 7pm, this bar takes over the pier with its great sunset views across the river. Beer and Thai whisky with accompanying spicy snacks and loud Thai pop music – very popular with Silpakorn and Thammasat university students.

Comme

Map 3, C9. Opposite *Tonpo* riverside restaurant at the northern end of Thanon Phra Athit.
Daily 6pm–2am.
One of the most sophisticated bar-restaurants on this trendy road, where you can choose between the air-con section and the open-fronted streetside. Serves decent Thai food and well-priced drinks.

Dog Days

Map 3, B9. 100/2–6 Thanon Phra Athit.
Tues–Sun 5pm–midnight.
Quirky little bar-restaurant with a canine theme, a cosy atmosphere, and mid-priced food and drink.

Grand Guest House

Map 3, D12. Middle of Thanon Khao San.
Daily 24hr.
Cavernous place lacking in character but popular because

NIGHTLIFE: BANGLAMPHU, RATANAKOSIN AND HUALAMPHONG

For advice on getting to Banglamphu on public transport see p.157; for Hualamphong see p.166. For a more detailed breakdown of useful bus routes see pp.56–58.

it stays open round the clock. Videos are shown nonstop, usually movies in the day and MTV in the early hours.

Gulliver's Traveller's Tavern

Map 3, C11. Corner of Thanon Khao San and Thanon Chakrabongse.
Daily 11am–2am.
Backpacker-oriented air-con sports pub with two pool tables, sixteen TV screens, masses of sports memorabilia and reasonably priced beer.

Hole in the Wall Bar

Map 3, D11. Thanon Khao San.
Daily from about 6pm.
Small, low-key drinking-spot at the heart of the backpackers' ghetto. The dim lighting, more varied than average CD selection and competitively priced beer make this a popular place.

Spicy

Map 3, E13. Thanon Tanao.
Daily 6pm–2am.
Fashionably modern, neon-lit youthful hangout, mainly patronized by students from the nearby university. Best for beer, whisky and snacks, but serves main dishes too.

Susie Pub

Map 3, D11. Next to *Marco Polo Guest House* off Thanon Khao San.
Daily 11am–2am.
Big, dark, phenomenally popular pub that's usually standing-room-only after 9pm. Has a pool table, decent music, resident DJs and cheapish beer. Packed with farangs and young Thais.

SIAM SQUARE, THANON PLOENCHIT AND NORTHERN DOWNTOWN

- -

Ad Makers

Map 6, J5. 51/51 Soi Langsuan ☎ 652 0168.
Daily 5.30pm–2am.
Friendly, spacious bar with Wild West-style wooden decor, featuring nightly bands playing "songs for life" – Thai folk music blended with Western progressive and folk rock; cheap drinks.

Brown Sugar

Map 6, I9. 231/19–20 Soi Sarasin ⓣ 250 0103. Mon–Sat 11am–2am, Sun 5pm–1am.
Lively joint, one of the capital's top jazz venues, that manages to be both chic and homely. House jazz band Mon–Sat from 9.30pm, Sunday jam from 9.30pm.

Concept CM²

Map 6, F5. *Novotel*, Soi 6, Siam Square ⓣ 255 6888. Daily 7pm–2am; admission price depends on what's on.
More theme park than nightclub, with live bands and various, barely distinct entertainment zones, including karaoke and an Italian restaurant. Drinks are pricey.

Dallas Pub

Map 6, F5. Soi 6, Siam Square ⓣ 255 3276. Daily 7pm–2am.
In complete contrast to the sophisticated *CM²* nightclub opposite, a typical dark, noisy hangout in the "songs for life" tradition. Lots of fun: singalongs to decent live bands, dancing round the tables, and friendly, casual staff.

Fou Bar

Map 6, E5. 264/4–6 Soi 3, Siam Square. Daily 11am–2am.
Smart, modernist but easy-going hangout for students and 20-somethings, with reasonably priced drinks, a good choice of accompanying snacks and some interesting Thai-Italian crossovers for main dishes. Hard to find above a juice bar/internet café by Siam Square's Centrepoint.

Hard Rock Café

Map 6, E5. Soi 11, Siam Square ⓣ 254 0830. Daily 11am–2am.
Genuine outlet of the famous international chain – yes, you

For advice on getting to this area see p.167. For a more detailed breakdown of useful bus routes see pp.56–58.

NIGHTLIFE: SIAM SQUARE, THANON PLOENCHIT AND NORTHERN DOWNTOWN

can buy the T-shirt. Big sounds including live bands Mon–Sat from around 10.30pm, brash enthusiasm, bank-breaking prices.

Saxophone

Map 2, H3. 3/8 Victory Monument (southeast corner), Thanon Phrayathai ⓣ 246 5472. Daily 6pm–3am.

Lively, spacious venue that hosts nightly jazz, blues, folk and rock bands and attracts a good mix of Thais and farangs; decent food, relaxed drinking atmosphere and, all things considered, reasonable prices.

SOUTHERN DOWNTOWN: SOUTH OF THANON RAMA IV

- - - - - - - - - - - - - - - - - -

The Barbican

Map 7, K5. 9/4–5 Soi Thaniya, east end of Thanon Silom ⓣ 234 3590. Daily 11am–1am. Stylishly modern fortress-like

decor to match the name: dark woods, metal and undressed stone. With Guinness on tap and the financial pages posted above the urinals, you could almost be in a smart City of London pub – until you look out of the windows onto the soi's incongruous Japanese hostess bars. Good food, DJ sessions and happy hours Mon–Fri 5–7pm.

Deeper

Map 7, J6. Soi 4, Thanon Silom.

Long-running hardcore dance club, done out in metal and black to give an underground feel. Closed after a police raid at the time of writing, but unlikely to remain so.

Hyper

Map 7, J6. Soi 4, Thanon Silom. Daily 9pm–2.30am. Long-standing Soi 4 people-watching haunt, with laid-

- -

For advice on getting to this area see p.170; a more detailed breakdown of useful bus routes appears on pp.56–58.

- -

back dance music and a fun crowd.

Lucifer

Map 7, J6. 76/1–3 Patpong 1.
Daily midnight–4am.
Popular rave club in the dark heart of Patpong, largely untouched by the sleaze around it. Done out with mosaics and stalactites like a satanic grotto, with balconies to look down on the dance-floor action. *Radio City*, the interconnected bar downstairs, is only slightly less raucous, with jumping live bands and tables out on the sweaty pavement.

Shenanigans

Map 7, J6. 1/5 Thanon Convent, off the east end of Thanon Silom ☎266 7160.
Daily 11am–2am.
Blarney Bangkok-style: a warm, relaxing Irish pub,

tastefully done out in wood, iron and familiar knick-knacks and packed with expats, especially on Friday night. Guinness and Kilkenny Bitter on tap (happy hour 4–7.30pm), very expensive Irish food such as Belfast chaps (fried potatoes) and good veggie options (Mon–Thurs set lunches are better value), as well as a fast-moving rota of house bands.

Tapas Bar

Map 7, J6. Soi 4, Thanon Silom.
Daily 9pm–2am.
Cramped, vaguely Spanish-orientated bar (but no tapas), whose outside tables are probably the best spot for checking out the comings and goings on the soi; inside, there's house and garage downstairs, chilled-out ambient and funk upstairs.

SOUTHERN DOWNTOWN: SOUTH OF THANON RAMA IV

Maison du Vin on the second floor of the Thaniya Plaza, Thanon Silom (map 7, K6), sell a better-than-passable Chateau de Loei red and white wine, made by an eccentric Frenchman from grapes grown on the slopes of Phu Reua in northeast Thailand.

THANON SUKHUMVIT

- -

Cheap Charlies

Map 8, A8. Soi 11.
Daily from 3pm.
Hugely popular, long-running pavement bar where it's standing room only, but at a bargain B50 for a bottle of beer it's worth standing.

Imageries by the Glass

Map 8, H9. 2, Soi 24.
Mon–Sat 6pm–1.30am.
Usually packed out with Thai couples who come to hear the nightly live music from the roster of different vocalists including rock-, pop- and folk-singers. Pricey drinks.

Jools Bar and Restaurant

Map 8, B5. Soi 4, a short walk from the Soi Nana go-go strip.
Easy-going British-run pub, popular with expat drinkers (photos of regular customers plaster the walls). The cosy downstairs bar is mainly standing room only, and traditional British food is served at tables upstairs.

La Lunar

Map 8, H10. Near *Four Wings Hotel* on Soi 26, Thanon Sukhumvit.
Daily 6.30pm–2am. B500 including two drinks.
Swanky, well-designed place, whose various levels encompass a balconied disco with plenty of room to dance, a sushi bar and a pub with live bands. You need to dress up a bit to get in.

Manet Club, Renoir Club, Van Gogh Club

Map 8, H6 & H7. Soi 33.
Daily 4pm–midnight.
Three-in-a-row small, very similar, not-at-all-Parisian bars, of interest mainly for their air-conditioning and happy hours, which run daily from 4–9pm.

Old Dutch

Map 8, E6. Soi 23, at the mouth of the Soi Cowboy strip.
Daily 8.30am–2am.
Cool, dark, peaceful oasis at the edge of Sukhumvit's frenetic sleaze. The reasonably priced menu and a large stock of current US and European newspapers make

this a good daytime or early evening watering hole.

Q Bar

Map 8, C3. Far end of Soi 11. Daily 6pm–2am; arrive before 11pm if you want a seat. Very dark, very trendy, New York-style bar occupying two floors and a terrace. Appeals to a mixed crowd of fashionable people, particularly on Friday and Saturday nights when the DJs fill the dance floor and there's a B300 cover charge that includes two free drinks.

For advice on getting to this area see p.176; a more detailed breakdown of useful bus routes appears on pp.56–58.

Gay Bangkok

Bangkok's **gay scene** is mainly focused on mainstream venues like karaoke bars, restaurants, massage parlours, gyms, saunas and escort agencies. Most of the action happens on Silom 4 (near Patpong), on the more exclusive Silom 2 (towards Thanon Rama IV), and at the rougher, mostly Thai bars of Thanon Sutthisarn near the Chatuchak Weekend Market. The scene is heavily male, and there are hardly any lesbian-only venues, though quite a few gay bars are mixed. As with the straight scene, the majority of gay bars feature go-go dancers and live sex shows. Those listed here do not.

Recently the gay community of Bangkok has hosted a flamboyant Gay Pride festival in November; check upcoming dates on the websites listed on p.221.

Buddhist tolerance and a national abhorrence for confrontation and victimization combine to make Thai society relatively unfussed about homosexuality, if not exactly positive about same-sex relationships. There is no mention of homosexuality at all in Thai **law**, which means that the age of consent for gay sex is sixteen, the same as for heterosexuals. Although excessively physical displays of affection are frowned upon for both heterosexuals and homosexuals,

FURTHER INFORMATION

Anjaree, PO Box 322, Rajdamnoen PO, Bangkok 10200 Ⓣ & Ⓕ477 1776, Ⓔanjaree@loxinfo.com. Lesbian group that fights for homosexual rights; can provide some info on lesbian life in the city.

Dragon Castle's Gay Asia Ⓦdragoncastle.net. Justifiably bills itself as "Gay Thailand's leading website". Carries informed advice on all aspects of the gay scene, solid tips on potential dangers and pitfalls, plus plenty of listings and links.

Dreaded Ned's Ⓦwww.dreadedned.com. Information on almost every gay venue in the country, plus some interesting background on gay Thailand and a book list.

Gay Media's Gay Guide to Thailand Ⓦwww.gay-media.com. Exhaustive listings of Bangkok's gay-friendly hotels, bars, clubs and saunas.

Metro Ⓦwww.bkkmetro.com. Bangkok's monthly English-language listings magazine publishes extensive listings of gay venues and events.

Pink Ink Ⓦwww.khsnet.com/pinkink. Thailand's first gay and lesbian newsletter in English, featuring listings, gossip columns and news clippings, plus personal ads. Available free from major gay venues in Bangkok.

Utopia, Ⓦwww.utopia-asia.com.116/1 Soi 23, Thanon Sukhumvit Ⓣ259 9619. Bangkok's gay and lesbian centre (see p.223) maintains a useful website listing clubs, events and accommodation for gays and lesbians, and has useful links to other sites in Asia and the rest of the world.

Western gay couples should get no hassle about being seen together in public – it's much more acceptable, and common, in fact, for friends of the same sex (gay or not) to walk hand-in-hand, than for heterosexual couples to do so.

If you're in Bangkok for the first time, you might be interested in the **gay friends** service offered by the Utopia gay and lesbian centre (see opposite). These gay, English-speaking Bangkok residents are called Thai Friends and are keen to show tourists the sights of Bangkok. It's a strictly non-sexual arrangement and can be organized through the Utopia centre or via their website.

GAY BARS AND CLUBS

The Balcony

Map 7, J6. Soi 4, Thanon Silom Ⓢ Sala Daeng. Daily 6pm–3am. Unpretentious, fun place with a large, popular terrace, cheap drinks and decent Thai, Indian and Western food; karaoke and regular talent nights.

Dick's Café

Map 7, J5. 894/7–8 Soi Pratuchai, Thanon Suriwong Ⓢ Sala Daeng. Daily noon–4am. Stylish day-and-night café on a quiet soi opposite the prominent Wall Street Tower; ideal for cheap drinking, pastries or just chilling out.

Disco Disco

Map 7, K6. Soi 2, Thanon Silom Ⓢ Sala Daeng. Daily 9pm–2am.

Small, well-designed bar/disco, with reasonably priced drinks and good dance music for a fun young crowd.

DJ Station

Map 7, K6. Soi 2, Thanon Silom Ⓢ Sala Daeng. Daily 10pm–2.30am; B100 including one drink (B200 including two drinks Fri & Sat). Highly fashionable but unpretentious disco which gets packed at weekends, attracting a mix of Thais and foreigners. A cabaret show is staged every day at midnight.

Freeman Dance Arena

Map 7, K6. 60/18–21 Thanon Silom (in the soi beside 7-11 store, between Soi Thaniya and Thanon Rama IV) Ⓢ Sala Daeng. Daily 10pm–2.30am; B100 including one drink (B200 including two drinks Fri & Sat). Busy, compact disco playing poppy dance music; regular cabaret shows and chill-out tables out on the soi.

The Icon

Map 7, J6. 90–96 Soi 4, Thanon Silom Ⓢ Sala Daeng. Daily except Tues 9.30pm–3am; B200 including two drinks. Nightclub with good sounds and sound system, and a large dance floor; singing impersonators at 10.30pm, male dance cabaret at 11.45pm.

JJ Park

Map 7, K6. 8/3 Soi 2, Thanon Silom Ⓢ Sala Daeng. Daily 3pm–2.30am. Classy, Thai-oriented bar-restaurant, for relaxed socializing rather than raving, with live Thai music, comedy shows and good food.

Sphinx

Map 7, J6. 98–104 Soi 4, Thanon Silom Ⓢ Sala Daeng. Daily 6pm–3am. Chic decor, terrace seating and good food attract a sophisticated crowd to this ground-floor bar and restaurant; karaoke and live music upstairs.

Telephone Bar

Map 7, J6. 114/11–13 Soi 4, Thanon Silom Ⓢ Sala Daeng. Daily 8pm–2am. This cruisey, long-standing eating and drinking venue has good Thai cuisine and a terrace on the alley. It's best known, however, for its telephones: each table inside has a phone with a clearly displayed number so you can call up other customers.

Utopia

Map 8, F2. 116/1 Soi 23 (Soi Sawadee), Thanon Sukhumvit ⓣ 259 9619, ⓦ www.utopia-asia.com. Ⓢ Asok. Daily noon–midnight. Bangkok's first gay and lesbian community venue comprises a shop for books, magazines, fashion and gifts; gallery; cosy café and bar with weekly women-only nights (currently Fri).

Vega

Map 8, H7. Soi 39, Thanon Sukhumvit. Ⓢ Phrom Phong. Trendy lesbian-run bar-restaurant . The live music, karaoke and dance floor attract a mixed, fashionable crowd.

GAY BARS AND CLUBS

Entertainment

Traditional **Thai dancing** is the most accessible of the capital's performing arts, and can be seen at the National Theatre and a number of tourist-oriented restaurants. **Thai boxing** can be equally theatrical and is well worth watching: the live experience at either of Bangkok's two main national stadiums far outshines the TV coverage.

For information on the fascinating
Joe Louis Puppet Theatre, see p.150.

CINEMAS

Central Bangkok has over forty **cinemas**, many of which show recent American and European releases with their original dialogue and Thai subtitles. Most cinemas screen shows four times a day: programmes are detailed every day in the *Nation* and *Bangkok Post*, and listings and reviews appear in the monthly listings magazine, *Bangkok Metro*; cinema locations are printed on *Nancy Chandler's Map of Bangkok*. Seats cost from B60 to B120, depending on the plushness of the cinema; at all cinemas, you'll be expected to stand for the king's anthem, which is played before every performance.

There are four massive movie theatres in Siam Square, and nearly every major downtown shopping plaza has two or three screens on its top floor. Western films are also occasionally shown at the Japan Cultural Centre, Goethe Institut and Alliance Française: check the English-language press for details. And if it's been a while since you've caught up on the new releases, check out the dozens of video-showing restaurants along Banglamphu's Thanon Khao San, where recent blockbusters are screened back-to-back every day and night of the year, all for the price of a banana smoothie or a cheese sandwich.

CULTURE SHOWS

Many tourist restaurants feature nightly culture shows – usually a hotchpotch of Thai dancing and classical music, with a martial arts demonstration thrown in. In some cases there's a set fee for dinner and show, in others the performance is free but the à la carte prices are slightly inflated. In Banglamphu, all tour agents offer a dinner show package including transport for around B600 per person.

Baan Thai
Soi 32, Thanon Sukhumvit,
ⓣ258 5403.
Nightly at 8.45pm; B550.
Ⓢ Thong Lo.
Housed in a traditional teak home, this is a pleasant setting for the nightly performances of traditional Thai dance. Audiences are served a set meal during the show.

Silom Village
Map 7, E6. Thanon Silom,
ⓣ234 4581.
Nightly at 7.30pm; B450.
The outdoor restaurant inside this complex of tourist shops stages a nightly fifty-minute cultural show to accompany the set menu.

SHRINE DANCING

Thai dancing is performed for its original **ritual purpose**, usually several times a day, at the Lak Muang Shrine behind the Grand Palace (map 4, E5) and the Erawan Shrine on the corner of Thanon Ploenchit (map 6, H4). Both shrines have resident troupes of dancers who are hired by worshippers to perform *lakhon chatri*, a sort of *khon* dance-drama, to thank benevolent spirits for answered prayers. The dancers are always dressed up in full gear and accompanied by musicians, but the length, number of dancers and complexity of the dance depends on the amount of money paid by the suppli-cant: a price list is posted near the dance area. The musicians at the Erawan Shrine are particularly highly rated, though the almost comic apathy of the dancers there doesn't do them justice.

THAI BOXING

The violence of the average **Thai boxing** match may be off-putting to some, but spending a couple of hours at one of Bangkok's two main stadiums can be immensely enter-taining, not least for the enthusiasm of the spectators and the ritualistic aspects of the fights.

Bouts, advertised in the English-language newspapers, are held in the capital every night of the week at the **Rajdamnoen Stadium**, next to the TAT office on

---

Jitti's Gym off Thanon Chakrabongse in Banglamphu
(map 3, C11) holds open *muay Thai* classes every afternoon
(3–6pm; B300; ☎ 282 7854). Or contact the Muay Thai
Institute at 336/932 Prachathipat, Thanyaburi, Pathum Thani,
Bangkok 12130 (☎ 992 0096, ⓦ www.tat.or.th/do/learn.htm)
about training courses for foreigners ($160 for 40hr).

TRADITIONAL DANCE-DRAMA

Drama pretty much equals dance in Thai theatre, and many of the traditional dance-dramas are based on the Hindu epic the *Ramayana* (in Thai, *Ramakien*), a classic adventure tale of good versus evil which is taught in all the schools (see pp.74–75 for an outline of the story).

The most spectacular form of traditional Thai theatre is khon, a stylized drama performed in masks and elaborate costumes by a troupe of highly trained classical dancers. There's little room for individual interpretation in these dances, as all the movements follow a strict choreography that's been passed down through generations: each graceful, angular gesture depicts a precise event, action or emotion which will be familiar to educated *khon* audiences. The dancers don't speak, and the story is chanted and sung by a chorus who stand at the side of the stage, accompanied by a classical *phipat* orchestra.

A typical *khon* performance features several of the best-known Ramayana episodes, in which the main characters are recognized by their masks, headdresses and heavily brocaded costumes. Gods and humans don't wear masks, but it's generally easy enough to distinguish the hero Rama and heroine Sita from the action – they always wear tall gilded headdresses and often appear in a threesome with Rama's brother Lakshaman. Monkey masks are always open-mouthed, almost laughing, and come in several colours: the monkey army chief Hanuman always wears white, and his two right-hand men – Nilanol, the god of fire and Nilapat, the god of death – wear red and black respectively. In contrast, the demons have grim mouths, clamped shut or snarling out of usually green faces: Totsagan, king of the demons, wears a green face in battle and a gold one during peace, but always sports a two-tier headdress carved with two rows of faces.

RITUALS OF THE RING

Thai boxing (*muay Thai*) enjoys a following similar to football in Europe: every province has a stadium and whenever a fight is shown on TV you can be sure that large noisy crowds will gather round the sets in streetside restaurants and noodle shops.

There's a strong spiritual and ritualistic dimension to *muay Thai*, adding grace to an otherwise brutal sport. Each boxer enters the ring to the wailing music of a three-piece *phipat* orchestra, often flamboyantly attired in a lurid silk robe over the statutory red or blue boxer shorts. The fighter then bows, first in the direction of his birthplace and then to the north, south, east and west, honouring both his teachers and the spirit of the ring. Next he performs a slow dance, claiming the audience's attention and demonstrating his prowess as a performer.

Any part of the body except the head may be used as an offensive weapon in *muay Thai*, and all parts except the groin are fair targets. Kicks to the head are the blows which cause most knockouts. As the action hots up, so the orchestra speeds up its tempo and the betting in the audience becomes more frenetic. It can be a gruesome business, but it was far bloodier before modern boxing gloves were made compulsory in the 1930s – combatants used to wrap their fists with hemp impregnated with a face-lacerating dosage of ground glass.

Thanon Rajdamnoen Nok (map 2, D3; Mon, Wed & Thurs 6pm & 9pm, Sun 5pm), and at Lumphini Stadium on Thanon Rama IV (map 2, I8; Tues & Fri 6.30pm, Sat 5pm & 8.30pm). Tickets go on sale one hour before and, unless the boxers are big stars, start at B220, rising to B1000 for a ringside seat; tickets for the Sunday bouts at Rajdamnoen cost from B50. You might have to queue for a few minutes, but there's no need to get there early unless

THAI BOXING

there's a really important fight on. Sessions usually feature ten bouts, each consisting of five three-minute rounds (with two-minute rests in between each round), so if you're not a big fan it may be worth turning up an hour late, as the better fights tend to happen later in the billing. It's more fun if you buy one of the less expensive standing tickets, enabling you to witness the wild gesticulations of the betting aficionados at close range.

THEATRE

National Theatre
Map 4, E2. Next to the National Museum on the northwest corner of Sanam Luang; programme details on ☏224 1342 (Mon–Fri 8.30am–4.30pm). Express boat to Tha Banglamphu.

The usual programme at Bangkok's main venue for traditional dance and theatre comprises *khon* (classical) and *likay* (folk) theatre, and the occasional *nang thalung* (shadow-puppet play). As these can be quite long and esoteric performances, tourists often prefer the special medley shows, performed by students from the attached College of the Performing Arts, where the evening is broken up into bite-sized portions of dance, drama and music, often brought in from different parts of the country. From November through May, these take place almost every Saturday, and there are also similar shows throughout the year on the last Friday of every month. Tickets start at around B100; programme details can be checked by calling the theatre or TAT.

Consult the monthly listings magazine *Bangkok Metro* for details of current theatre and cinema programmes.

THEATRE

Sala Chalermkrung Theatre

Map 5, B1. 66 Thanon Charoen Krung (New Rd), on the intersection with Thanon Triphet in Pahurat, next to Old Siam Plaza; details of the current programme on ☏225 8757. For transport see p.112. This renovated historical theatre shows contemporary Thai drama and comedy most of the week, but occasionally stages traditional, tourist-friendly dance-dramas.

Thailand Cultural Centre

In the eastern part of the city on Thanon Ratchadapisek ☏645 2955. Buses AC#15 or AC#34.

The city's major venue for showcasing contemporary Thai drama and comedy is inconveniently located on the fringes of Bangkok. As well as innovative drama, it also puts on regular kids' theatre shows.

THEATRE

Shopping

Bangkok has a good reputation for **shopping**, particularly for silk, gems, fashions and English-language books. Antiques and handicrafts are good buys too, and some shops stock curiosities from the most remote regions of the country.

Downtown Bangkok is full of smart, multi-storeyed **shopping plazas** with names like Siam Centre, the Emporium and the Amarin Plaza, which is where you'll find the majority of the city's fashion stores, as well as those selling designer goods, and bookshops. The plazas tend to be pleasantly air-conditioned and thronging with trendy young Thais, but don't hold much interest for tourists unless you happen to be looking for a new outfit.

You're more likely to find useful items in one of the city's numerous **department stores**, most of which are also scattered about the downtown areas. The Central department stores (on Silom and Ploenchit roads) are probably the city's best, but Robinson's, on Sukhumvit Soi 19, on Thanon Rajdamri and at the Silom/Rama IV junction) are also good. Should you need to buy a crucial piece of **children's gear**, you'll find everything from bottles, dummies, slings and mosquito nets to English-language kids' books, clothes and games in the children's department store Buy Buy Kiddo on Sukhumvit Soi 12. The British chain of **pharmacies**, Boots the Chemist, has lots of branches across the city, including on Thanon Khao San, in the Times Square plaza between Sukhumvit sois 12 and 14, and in the Emporium on Sukhumvit.

Most of the department stores and tourist-oriented shops listed here keep late hours, opening at 10 or 11am every day including Sunday, and closing at about 9pm.

For travellers, spectating, not shopping, is apt to be the main draw of Bangkok's neighbourhood **markets** – notably the bazaars of Chinatown (see p.105) and the blooms and scents of Pak Khlong Talat, the flower and vegetable market just west of Memorial Bridge (see p.113). The massive Chatuchak Weekend Market is an exception, being both a tourist attraction and a marvellous shopping experience – see p.143 for details. If you're planning on some serious market exploration, get hold of the idiosyncratic *Nancy Chandler's Map of Bangkok*, which includes special sections on the main shopping areas.

With the chief exception of Chatuchak, most markets operate daily from dawn till early afternoon; early morning is often the best time to go to beat the heat and crowds. The Patpong **night market** (map 7, J5), which also spills out on to Thanon Silom, is *the* place to stock up on fake designer goods, from pseudo-Rolex watches to Tommy Hilfiger shirts; the stalls open at about 5pm until late into the evening.

ANTIQUES AND PAINTINGS

Bangkok is the entrepôt for the finest Thai, Burmese and Cambodian **antiques**, but the market has long been sewn up, so don't expect to happen upon any undiscovered treasure. Even experts admit that they sometimes find it hard to tell real antiques from fakes, so the best policy is just to buy on the grounds of attractiveness. The River City shopping complex, off Thanon Charoen Krung (New Rd; map 7, C3), devotes its third and fourth floors to a bewildering array of pricey treasures and holds an auction on the first Saturday of every month (viewing during the preceding week). The other main area for antiques is the stretch of Charoen Krung that runs between the GPO and the bottom of Thanon Silom (map 7, C5 & C6). Here you'll find a good selection of reputable individual businesses specializing in wood carvings, bronze statues and stone sculptures culled from all parts of Thailand and neighbouring countries as well.

- -

To export antiques or religious artefacts – especially Buddha images – from Thailand, you need to have a licence granted by the Fine Arts Department; apply through Bangkok's National Museum on Thanon Na Phra That (⊕226 1661 or 281 0433). Applications take at least a week to process and need to be accompanied by two postcard-sized photos of the object, taken face-on, and photocopies of the applicant's passport. Some antique shops will organize this for you.

- -

Street-corner stalls all over the city sell poor quality mass-produced traditional Thai **paintings**, but for a huge selection of better quality Thai art, visit Sombat Permpoon Gallery on Soi 1, Thanon Sukhumvit (map 8, A3), which carries thousands of canvases, framed and unframed, spanning the range from classical Ayutthayan-era-style village scenes to twenty-first-century abstracts. The gallery does have works by famous Thai artists like Thawan Duchanee, but prices for the more affordable works by less well-known painters start at B1500.

ANTIQUES AND PAINTINGS

●

233

BOOKS

English-language **bookstores** in Bangkok are always well stocked with everything to do with Thailand, and most carry fiction classics and popular paperbacks as well. The capital's few **secondhand** bookstores are surprisingly poor value, but you might turn up something worthwhile – or earn a few baht by selling your own cast-offs – in the shops and stalls along Thanon Khao San.

Aporia

Map 3, E12. Thanon Tanao, Banglamphu. For transport details see p.157.

Run by knowledgeable book-loving staff, Banglamphu's main outlet for new books keeps a good stock of titles on Thai and Southeast Asian culture and has a decent selection of travelogues, plus some English-language fiction. Also sells secondhand books.

Asia Books

Map 8, D6 Thanon Sukhumvit between sois 15 and 19 Ⓢ Asok; **Map 8, B5** Landmark Plaza between sois 4 and 6 Ⓢ Nana; **Map 8, D6** in Times Square between sois 12 and 14 Ⓢ Asok; **Map 8, G8** in Emporium between Sois 22 and 24 Ⓢ Phrom Phong; **Map 6, H5** in Peninsula Plaza on Thanon Rajdamri Ⓢ Chit Lom or longtail to Tha Pratunam; **Map 6, D4** in Siam Discovery Centre on Thanon Rama I Ⓢ Central Station; and **Map 7, K6** in Thaniya Plaza near Patpong off Thanon Silom Ⓢ Sala Dieng. English-language bookstore that's especially recommended for its books on Asia – everything from guidebooks to cookery books, novels to art (the Sukhumvit Soi 15–19 branch has the best Asian selection). Also keeps bestselling novels, and coffee-table books.

Books Kinokuniya

Map 8, H8. Third floor of the Emporium shopping centre, between sois 22 and 24 on Thanon Sukhumvit. Ⓢ Phrom Phong.

Huge English-language bookstore, with a broad range

of books ranging from bestsellers to travel literature and from classics to sci-fi; not so hot on books about Asia though.

Central department stores

Map 6, J4 Thanon Ploenchit Ⓢ Chit Lom and Map 7, E6 Thanon Silom Ⓢ Surasak; and at several other less convenient locations.

Reasonably good books department, which stocks paperback fiction, maps and reference books in English.

DK (Duang Kamol) Books

Map 6, C5 Third floor, MBK shopping centre Ⓢ Central Station; **Map 6, D5** 244–6 Soi 2, Siam Square Ⓢ Central Station; and **Map 8, C5** 180/1 Thanon Sukhumvit between sois 8 & 10 Ⓢ Nana.

One of Thailand's biggest bookseller chains, DK is especially good for maps and books on Thailand.

Shaman Books

Map 3, C11 & D12. Two branches on Thanon Khao San, Banglamphu. For transport details see p.157.

The best stocked and most efficient secondhand bookshop in the city, where all books are displayed alphabetically as well as being logged on to the computer – which means you can locate your choice in seconds. Lots of books on Asia (travel, fiction, politics and history) as well as a decent range of novels and general interest books. Don't expect bargains though.

CLOTHES AND THAI SILK

Noted for its thickness and sheen, **Thai silk** became internationally recognized only about forty years ago after the efforts of Jim Thompson (see p.132). Much of it comes from the northeast, but you'll find the lion's share of outlets and tailoring facilities in the capital. Prices start at about B350 per metre for two-ply silk (suitable for thin shirts and skirts), or B500 for four-ply (for suits).

COUNTERFEIT CULTURE

Faking it is big business in Bangkok, a city whose copyright regulations carry about as much weight as its anti-prostitution laws. Forged designer clothes and accessories are the biggest sellers; street vendors along Patpong, Silom, Sukhumvit and Khao San roads will flog you a whole range of inexpensive lookalikes, including Tommy Hilfiger shirts, D&G jeans, Calvin Klein wallets, Prada bags and Hermes scarves.

Along Patpong, after dark, plausible would-be Rolex, Cartier and Tag watches from Hong Kong and Taiwan go for about B500 – and are fairly reliable considering the price. If your budget won't stretch to a phony Rolex Oyster, there's plenty of opportunities for smaller expenditure at the stalls concentrated on Thanon Khao San, where pirated music CDs and software and games CD-ROMs are sold at a fraction of the normal price. Quality of the music CDs is usually fairly high but the choice is often less than brilliant, with a concentration on mainstream pop and rock albums. Finally, several stallholders along Thanon Khao San even make up passable international student and press cards – though travel agencies and other organizations in Bangkok aren't so easily fooled.

Bangkok can be a great place to have **tailored clothes** made: materials don't cost much, and work is often completed in just 24 hours. On the other hand, you may find yourself palmed off with artificial silk and a suit that falls apart in a week. Inexpensive silk and tailoring shops crowd Silom, Sukhumvit and Khao San roads, but many people opt for hotel tailors, preferring to pay more for the security of an established business. Be wary of places offering ridiculous deals – when you see a dozen garments advertised for a total price of less than $200, you know something's fishy – and look carefully at the quality of samples before making any decision. If you're staying in Banglamphu, keep an eye on guest-house noticeboards for cautionary tales from other travellers.

Thanon Khao San is lined with stalls selling low-priced **ready-mades**: the tie-dyed shirts, baggy cotton trousers, embroidered blouses and ethnic-style outfits are all aimed at backpackers and New Age hippies; the stalls of Banglamphu Market, around the edges of the abandoned New World department store (map 3, D10), have the best range of inexpensive Thai fashions in this area. For the best and latest fashions however, you should check out the shops in the Siam Centre and the Siam Discovery Centre, both across from Siam Square, and the high-fashion outlets at the upmarket Emporium on Sukhumvit.

Shoes and leather goods are good buys in Bangkok, being generally hand-made from high-quality leather and quite a bargain: check out the "booteries" along Thanon Sukhumvit.

Ambassador Fashions

Map 8, B9. 1/10–11 Soi Chaiyot, off Sukhumvit Soi 11, ☎253 2993. Ⓢ Nana. Long-established and reputable tailor, well versed in making both men's and women's wear. Clothes can be made within 24 hours if necessary. Call for free pick-up in Bangkok.

Emporium

Map 8, H8. Between sois 22 and 24 on Thanon Sukhumvit. Ⓢ Phrom Phong. Enormous and rather glamorous shopping plaza, with a good range of fashion outlets, from exclusive designer wear to trendy high-street gear. Brand names include Versace, Chanel and Louis Vuitton.

Jim Thompson's Thai Silk Company

Map 7, K5 9 Thanon Suriwong Ⓢ Sala Daeng; **Map 6, G4** World Trade Center Ⓢ Chit Lom or longtail to Tha Pratunam; **Map 6, J4** Central department store on Thanon Ploenchit Ⓢ Chit Lom;

CLOTHES AND THAI SILK

Map 8, G8 Emporium on Thanon Sukhumvit Ⓢ Phrom Phong; and at many hotels around the city.

A good place to start looking for traditional Thai fabric, or at least to get an idea of what's out there. Stocks silk and cotton by the yard and ready-made items from dresses to cushion covers, which are well designed and of good quality, but pricey. Also has a home furnishings section and a good tailoring service.

Khanitha

Map 7, J5 & B5. Branches at 111/3–5 Thanon Suriwong and the *Oriental* hotel. Express boat to Tha Oriental.

Specializing in women's suits, evening wear, and dressing gowns, tailored from the finest Thai silk.

Mah Boon Krong (MBK)

Map 6, C5. At the Rama I/Phrayathai intersection. Ⓢ Central Station.

Labyrinthine shopping centre which houses hundreds of small, mostly fairly inexpensive outlets, including plenty of high-street fashion shops.

Narry's

Map 8, B9. 155/22 Sukhumvit Soi 11/1, Ⓣ 254 9184, Ⓦ www.narry.com. Ⓢ Nana.

Good-value, award-winning tailor of men's and women's clothes. Finished items ready within 24 hours if necessary. Call for free pick-up in Bangkok.

Peninsula Plaza

Map 6, H5. Thanon Rajdamri. Ⓢ Chit Lom or longtail to Tha Pratunam.

Considered to be the most upmarket shopping plaza in the city, so come here for (genuine) Louis Vuitton and the like.

Siam Centre

Map 6, E4. Across the road from Siam Square. Ⓢ Central Station.

Particularly good for big name designer fashions as well as lesser-known labels; Kookaï, Greyhound and Soda Pop are typical outlets.

Siam Discovery Centre

Map 6, D4. Across the road from Siam Square. Ⓢ Central Station.

Flash designer gear, including plenty of name brands like D&G, Morgan, Max Mara and YSL.

Siam Square.
Map 6, D4–F5. Ⓢ Central Station.
It's worth poking around the alleys, especially near what's styled as "Centerpoint" between sois 3 and 4 – there are all manner of inexpensive boutiques here, some little more than booths, selling colourful street gear to the capital's fashionable students and teenagers.

GEMS AND JEWELLERY

Bangkok boasts the country's best **gem and jewellery** shops, and some of the finest lapidaries in the world, making this *the* place to buy cut and uncut stones such as rubies, blue sapphires and diamonds. The most exclusive gem outlets are scattered along Thanon Silom – try Mr Ho's at no. 987 – but many tourists prefer to buy from hotel shops, like Kim's inside the *Oriental*, where reliability is assured. Other recommended outlets include Johnny's Gems at 199 Thanon Fuang Nakhon, near Wat Rajabophit in Ratanakosin (map 4, G8); Merlin et Delauney at 1 Soi Pradit, off Thanon Suriwong; and Uthai Gems, at 28/7 Soi Ruam Rudee, off Thanon Ploenchit. For cheap and cheerful silver earrings, bracelets and necklaces, you can't beat the traveller-oriented jewellery shops along Thanon Khao San in Banglamphu.

While it's unusual for established jewellers to fob off tourists with glass and paste, a common sales technique is to charge a lot more than what the gem is worth based on its carat weight. Get the stone tested on the spot, and ask for a written guarantee and receipt. Be extremely wary of touts and the shops they recommend, and unless you're an experienced gem trader, don't even consider buying gems in bulk to sell at a supposedly vast profit elsewhere: many a

GEMS AND JEWELLERY

gullible traveller has invested thousands of baht on a handful of worthless multi-coloured stones. If you want independent professional advice or precious stones certification, contact the Asian Institute of Gemological Sciences, located inside the Jewelry Trade Center Building, 919/298 Thanon Silom ☎ 267 4315–9.

HANDICRAFTS AND TEXTILES

Many of the shopping plazas have at least one classy handicraft outlet, and competition keeps most prices in the city at upcountry levels. Handicraft sellers in Banglamphu tend to tout a limited range compared to the shops downtown, but several places on Thanon Khao San sell reasonably priced triangular pillows (*mawn khwaan*) in traditional fabrics, which make fantastic souvenirs but are heavy to post home; some places sell unstuffed versions, which are simple to post but a pain to fill when you return! Khao San is also a good place to pick up Thai shoulder bags woven to all specifications and designs, with travellers' needs in mind. The cheapest place to buy traditional textiles – including sarongs, triangular pillows and farmers' shirts – is **Chatuchak Weekend Market** (see p.143), and you might be able to nose out some interesting handicrafts here too.

Come Thai

Map 6, H4. Second floor of the Amarin Plaza (the Sogo building) on Thanon Ploenchit; currently has no English sign, but easily spotted by its carved wooden doorframe. Ⓢ Chit Lom or longtail to Tha Pratunam. Impressive range of unusual handwoven silk and cotton fabrics, much of it made up into traditional-style clothes such as Chinese mandarin shirts and short fitted jackets.

Kealang

Map 6, H4. Second floor of the Amarin Plaza (the Sogo building) on Thanon Ploenchit. Ⓢ Chit Lom or longtail to Tha Pratunam.

Stocks a huge variety of traditional style five-coloured *bencharong* pots and vases, as well as other multicoloured Thai-Chinese ceramics.

Khomapastr

Map 7, C3. First floor of River City shopping complex. Express boat to Tha Si Phraya. Unusual choice of attractive patterned fabrics, in lengths or made up into quirky cushion covers, attractive shirts and *mawn khwaan*.

Krishna's

Map 8, A10. Between sois 9 and 11, Thanon Sukhumvit. Ⓢ Nana.

The four-storey building is crammed full of artefacts from all over Asia. Though mass-produced metallic statuettes and Balinese masks seem to dominate, there are enough interesting curios (such as Nepalese jewellery and Japanese *netsuke* ornaments) to reward a thorough browse.

The Legend

Map 6, H4 Second floor of Amarin Plaza (the Sogo building) on Thanon Ploenchit Ⓢ Chit Lom or longtail to Tha Pratunam; and **Map 7, K6** third floor of Thaniya Plaza on Thanon Silom Ⓢ Sala Daeng. Stocks a small selection of well-made Thai handicrafts, from wood and wickerware to fabrics and ceramics, at reasonable prices.

Narayana Phand

Map 6, H4. 127 Thanon Rajdamri. Ⓢ Chit Lom or longtail to Tha Pratunam. This government souvenir centre was set up to ensure the preservation of traditional crafts and to maintain standards of quality, and makes a reasonable one-stop shop for last-minute presents. It offers a huge assortment of very reasonably priced goods from all over the country, including *khon* masks and shadow puppets, musical instruments and kites, nielloware and celadon, and hill-tribe crafts. Unfortunately the layout is not very appealing and the

HANDICRAFTS AND TEXTILES

place feels like a warehouse – in marked contrast to the much more inspiring Thai Crafts Museum in the Gaysorn Plaza next door (see p.243).

Prayer Textile Gallery

Map 6, D4. 197 Thanon Phrayathai, on the corner of Thanon Rama I. Ⓢ Central Station.

Traditional fabrics from the north and the northeast, as well as from Laos and Cambodia. The selection is good, but prices for these textiles are getting surprisingly high, particularly those now classified as antiques.

Rasi Sayam

Map 8, F5. A ten-minute hike down Sukhumvit Soi 23, opposite *Le Dalat Vietnamese* restaurant. Ⓢ Asok or longtail to Tha Asoke.

Mon–Sat 9am–5.30pm.

Very classy handicraft shop, specializing in eclectic and fairly pricey decorative and folk arts such as tiny betel-nut sets woven from *lipao* fern, sticky-rice lunch

baskets, coconut wood bowls, and *mut mee* textiles.

Silom Village

Map 7, E6. 286/1 Thanon Silom, just west of Soi Decho. Ⓢ Chong Nonsi.

A complex of wooden houses that attempts to create a relaxing, upcountry atmosphere as a backdrop for its pricey fabrics and occasionally unusual souvenirs, such as grainy *sa* paper made from mulberry bark.

Sukhumvit Square

Map 8, C5. Between sois 8 and 10, Thanon Sukhumvit. Ⓢ Nana.

Most stalls open evenings only, from around 5pm.

This open-air night-bazaar-style plaza doesn't really get going till nightfall, when it's well worth dropping by to check out the range of quality handicrafts, artefacts, antiques, textiles and clothing sold in the fifty little shops here.

Tamnan Mingmuang

Map 7, K6. Third floor, Thaniya Plaza, Soi Thaniya, east end of Thanon Silom. Ⓢ Sala Daeng.

HANDICRAFTS AND TEXTILES

Subsidiary of The Legend opposite, which aims to foster and popularize crafts from all over the country. Among the unusual items on offer are trays and boxes for tobacco and betel nut made from *yan lipao* (intricately woven fern vines), and bambooware sticky-rice containers, baskets and lamp shades.

Thai Celadon

Map 8, E7. Sukhumvit Soi 16. Ⓢ Asok.

Classic celadon stoneware made without commercial dyes or clays and glazed with the archetypal blues and greens that were invented by the Chinese to emulate the colour of precious jade. Mainly dinner sets, vases and lamps, plus some figurines.

Thai Craft Museum

Map 6, H4. Second and third floors of Gaysorn Plaza. Ⓢ Chit Lom or longtail to Tha Pratunam.

Most of the top two floors of Gaysorn Plaza shopping centre are taken over by this collection of three hundred different outlets selling classy, high-quality crafts, textiles, jewellery, art, clothes and souvenirs, much of which is commissioned from villages around the country. You won't find absolute bargains here, but you get what you pay for. The best one-stop souvenir shop in the capital.

Via

Map 3, E12. 55 Thanon Tanao, Banglamphu. For transport details see p.157.

A specialist outlet for miniature reproduction traditional Thai boats. The scale models are all made from teak with fine attention to detail, and cover a dozen different styles of boat, including rice barges, royal boats and longtails. Prices from B2000.

HANDICRAFTS AND TEXTILES

Kids' Bangkok

Thais are very tolerant of children so you can take them almost anywhere without restriction, and they always help break the ice with strangers. Aside from the usual **precautions**, watch out for crazy traffic, rabid dogs, cats and monkeys (see p.27), and fiery hot chillis (see p.188).

Disposable nappies (diapers) are sold at chemists, supermarkets, department stores and convenience stores across the city, as is international brand formula and baby food. A fold-up **buggy** could be useful, but don't expect smooth pavements and plentiful ramps. For details of Bangkok's well-stocked children's department store, Buy Buy Kiddo, see p.231.

Some hotels offer discounts for children's accommodation (see p.157 for details), and most of the theme parks and amusement centres listed below knock off at least a few baht, though Bangkok buses and boats do not.

The main drawback with Bangkok's kid-centred activities is that most of them are located a long way from the city centre. A number of adult-oriented **attractions** also go down well with kids, including Muang Boran Ancient City (see p.146), riding the pedalo boats in Lumphini Park (see p.137), taking longtail boat trips on the Thonburi canals (see p.116), the Snake Farm (see p.136), the Joe Louis puppet shows (see p.150), and the ice-skating rink inside the World Trade Centre on Thanon Rajaprarop (map 6, H4). If you're here in the right season, the annual spring kite festival is also fun (see p.85).

THEME PARKS AND AMUSEMENT CENTRES

Adventureland

Seacon Square, 904 Thanon Sri Nakarin. Ⓢ On Nut, then regular bus #133 from Sukhumvit Soi 77.

Mon–Fri 11am–9pm, Sat & Sun 10am–10pm; free entry, but you pay for rides and activities (B15–80) with coupons.

Fun activities and amusement rides for kids, including exciting go-kart circuits and a rollerblade rink – all equipment, including helmets and knee pads, is available for hire. There's also a "stimulator" cinema, a rollercoaster, and a "swinging ship".

Dream World

Thanon Nakhon Nayok, ten minutes' drive north of Don Muang Airport. Bus #39 or #59 from Thanon Rajdamnoen Klang in Banglamphu to Rangsit, then songthaew or tuk-tuk.

Mon–Fri 10am–5pm, Sat & Sun 10am–7pm; B120, kids B95.

Enjoyable outdoor theme park that has different zones – such as Fantasy Land, Dream Garden and Adventure Land – each of them with special rides. Most kids like the water rides best.

MBK Magic Land

Map 6, C5. Eighth floor, Mah Boon Krong Shopping Centre, at the Rama I/Phrayathai intersection. Ⓢ Central Station.

Mon–Fri 10.30am–6.30pm, Sat & Sun 10.30am–8pm; free.

Centrally located amusements centre in one of downtown Bangkok's oldest shopping centres. Contains fairly tame indoor fairground rides, costing from B15 a go.

THEME PARKS AND AMUSEMENT CENTRES

Siam Park

101 Thanon Sukhapiban 2, on the far eastern edge of town. Bus AC#14 from Victory Monument.

Mon–Fri 10am–6pm, Sat & Sun 9am–7pm; B400, kids B300.

Popular water park that boasts some of the longest waterslides in the country, along with all manner of whirlpools, swimming pools, and pools that get churned up by artificial surf. There's also a mini-zoo and a botanical garden.

ZOOS AND SAFARI PARKS

Dusit Zoo (Khao Din)

Map 2, E2. Main entrance on Thanon Rajvithi, and another one on Thanon U-Thong. Bus #56 (eastbound along Thanon Phra Sumen) from Banglamphu; or AC#10 or AC#16 from Victory Monument.

Daily 8am–6pm; B30, children B5.

The sizeable public park here is home to a fair number of creatures, including big cats, elephants, orang-utans, chimpanzees and reptiles, though conditions are fairly basic. The park also boasts a lake with pedalos, plenty of shade, and lots of food stalls.

Safari World

99 Thanon Ramindra, Minburi. Bus #26 from Victory Monument to Minburi, then a direct minibus to Safari World. Daily 9am–4.30pm; B600, kids B360.

Said to be Southeast Asia's largest wildlife park, Safari World centres on a drive-through safari park, which is home to an assortment of lions, rhinos, giraffes, zebras and monkeys. (If you don't have your own car, you can drive through the park in a Safari World coach.) There's also a sea-life area with dolphins and sea lions, and a bird park with a walk-in aviary.

Directory

AIRLINES Aeroflot, 7 Thanon Silom ☎ 233 6965; Air Andaman, 87 Nailert Bldg, 4th Floor, Unit 402a, Thanon Sukhumvit ☎ 251 4905; Air France, Unit 2002, 34 Vorwat Bldg, 849 Thanon Silom ☎ 635 1186–7; Air India, 1 Pacific Place, between sois 4 and 6, Thanon Sukhumvit ☎ 254 3280; Air Lanka, Charn Issara Tower, 942/34–35 Thanon Rama IV ☎ 236 4981; Air New Zealand/Ansett, Sirindhorn Bldg, Thanon Witthayu (Wireless Rd) ☎ 254 5440; Bangkok Airways, 1111 Thanon Ploenchit ☎ 254 2903; Biman Bangladesh Airlines, Chongkolnee Bldg, 56 Thanon Suriwong ☎ 235 7643; British Airways, 14th Floor, Abdullrahim Place, opposite Lumphini Park, 990 Thanon Rama IV ☎ 636 1747; Canadian Airlines, 6th Floor, Maneeya Centre, 518/5 Thanon Ploenchit ☎ 254 0960; Cathay Pacific, Ploenchit Tower, 898 Thanon Ploenchit ☎ 263 0616; China Airlines, Peninsula Plaza, 153 Thanon Rajdamri ☎ 253 4242–3; Egyptair, CP Tower, 313 Thanon Silom ☎ 231 0505–8; Emirates, 356/1 Thanon Vibhavadi Rangsit ☎ 531 6585; EVA Airways, 2nd Floor, Green Tower, Thanon Rama IV ☎ 367 3388; Finnair, Don Muang Airport ☎ 535 2104; Garuda, Lumphini Tower, 1168/77 Thanon Rama IV ☎ 285 6470–3; Gulf Air, Maneeya Building, 518/5 Thanon Ploenchit ☎ 254 7931–4; Japan Airlines, 254/1 Thanon Ratchadapisek ☎ 274 1401–9; KLM, 19th Floor, Thai

Wah Tower 2, 21/133 Thanon Sathorn Tai ☏ 679 1100 extn 11; Korean Air, Kongboonma Bldg, 699 Thanon Silom ☏ 635 0465; Lao Aviation, Silom Plaza, Thanon Silom ☏ 237 6982; Lauda Air, Wall Street Tower, 33/37 Thanon Suriwong ☏ 233 2544; Lufthansa, Q-House, Soi 21, Thanon Sukhumvit ☏ 264 2400; Malaysia Airlines, 98–102 Thanon Suriwong ☏ 236 4705; Myanmar Airlines, 23rd Floor, Jewelry Trade Center Bldg, Unit H1, 919/298 Thanon Silom ☏ 630 0338; Northwest, 4th Floor, Peninsula Plaza, 153 Thanon Rajdamri ☏ 254 0790; Olympic Airways, 4th Floor, Charn Issara Tower, 942/133 Thanon Rama IV ☏ 237 6141; Pakistan International PIA, 52 Thanon Suriwong ☏ 234 2961–5; Philippine Airlines, Chongkolnee Bldg, 56 Thanon Suriwong ☏ 233 2350–2; Qantas Airways, 14th Floor, Abdullrahim Place, opposite Lumphini Park, 990 Thanon Rama IV ☏ 636 1747; Royal Air Cambodge, 17th Floor, Two Pacific Place Bldg, Room 1706, 142 Thanon Sukhumvit ☏ 653 2261–6; Royal Nepal, 1/4

Thanon Convent ☏ 233 5957; Singapore Airlines, Silom Centre, 2 Thanon Silom ☏ 236 0440; Swissair, 21st Floor, Abdullrahim Place, opposite Lumphini Park, 990 Thanon Rama IV ☏ 636 2150; Thai International, 485 Thanon Silom ☏ 234 3100–19, and at 6 Thanon Lan Luang near Democracy Monument ☏ 280 0060; United Airlines, 14th Floor, Sirindhorn Building, 130 Thanon Witthayu ☏ 253 0558; Vietnam Airlines, 7th Floor, Ploenchit Center Building, Sukhumvit Soi 2 ☏ 656 9056–8.

AIRPORT ENQUIRIES General enquiries ☏ 535 1111; international departures ☏ 02/535 1254 or 535 1386; international arrivals ☏ 535 1310, 535 1301 or 535 1149; domestic departures ☏ 535 1192; domestic arrivals ☏ 535 1253.

AMERICAN EXPRESS c/o Sea Tours, 128/88–92, 8th Floor, Phyathai Plaza, 128 Thanon Phrayathai, Bangkok 10400 ☏ 216 5934–6. Amex poste restante is held for sixty days and can be collected Mon–Fri 8.30am–5.30pm, Sat

8.30am–noon. For lost cards or cheques call ☎ 273 0044 (cards, office hours), ☎ 273 5296 (traveller's cheques, office hours) or ☎ 273 0022 (after hours for both cards and cheques).

CAR RENTAL Avis Ⓦ www.avis.com: Head Office, 2/12 Thanon Witthayu (Wireless Rd; ☎ 255 5300–4); also at Don Muang International Airport ☎ 535 4052; the *Grand Hyatt Erawan Hotel*, 494 Thanon Rajdamri ☎ 254 1234; *Le Meridien Hotel*, 971 Thanon Ploenchit ☎ 253 0444; and the *Amari Airport Hotel*, Don Muang International Airport ☎ 566 1020–1. Budget Ⓦ www.budget.co.th: Head Office, 19.23 Building A, Royal City Avenue, Thanon Phetchaburi Mai ☎ 203 0250; and at *Comfort Suites Airport Hotel*, 88/107 Thanon Vibhavadi ☎ 973 3752. SMT Rent-A-Car (part of National)

Ⓔ smtcar@samart.co.th: Head Office ☎ 722 8487; and at *Amari Airport Hotel*, Don Muang International Airport ☎ 928 1525; plus numerous others on Sukhumvit and Ploenchit roads. Prices for a small car start at B1200 per day; petrol costs about B20 a litre.

CONTRACEPTIVES Condoms (known as *meechai*) are sold in all pharmacies, and you can buy international-brand birth-control pills at the Travmin Bangkok Medical Centre (see p.28).

COOKERY CLASSES Nearly all the five-star hotels will arrange a Thai cookery class for guests if requested. The most famous is held at the *Oriental* hotel (☎ 437 6211), which mainly focuses on demonstrating culinary techniques and runs for four mornings a week. The Saturday-morning Benjarong

---

Thais drive on the left, and the speed limit is 60km/h within built-up areas, 80km/h elsewhere. Theoretically, foreigners need an international driver's licence to drive in Thailand, but some companies accept national licences.

CAR RENTAL – COOKERY CLASSES

Cooking Class at the *Dusit Thani* hotel (☏ 236 6400) takes a more hands-on approach, as does the *Nipa Thai* restaurant (☏ 254 0404 ext 4823), which runs one- to five-day cookery courses on demand and regular fruit-carving lessons (daily 2–4pm) at the restaurant on the third floor of the Landmark Plaza, between sois 4 and 6 on Thanon Sukhumvit. *Mrs Balbir's* restaurant on Soi 11 Thanon Sukhumvit (☏ 651 0498) holds regular, inexpensive, classes in Indian and Thai cookery (respectively Tues 10.30am–noon & Fri 10.30–11.30am).

COURIERS DHL Worldwide, Grand Amarin Tower, Thanon Phetchaburi Mai ☏ 658 8000.

CRIME Theft and pickpocketing are two of the main problems, but by far the most common cause for concern are the burgeoning number of opportunistic con-artists. Most travellers prefer to carry their valuables at all times, but it's also sometimes possible to leave them in a hotel or guest-house locker –

the safest lockers are those which require your own padlock, as there are occasional reports of valuables being stolen by hotel staff. Padlock your luggage when leaving it in your room, as well as when consigning it to storage or taking it on public transport. Never buy anything from touts, avoid going on ridiculously cheap (under B50) tuk-tuk tours of the city (they always include a compulsory shopping stop), and ignore anyone who introduces themselves as a tourist official, especially at Hualamphong Station, as these people are con-artists. Also be warned that some tuk-tuk drivers pretend that the Grand Palace or other major sight is closed for the day, so that they get to take you on a round-city tour instead. Violent crime against tourists is not common, but it does occur. Obvious precautions include locking accessible windows and doors at night, preferably with your own padlock, and not travelling alone at night in a taxi or tuk-tuk. Drug smuggling carries a maximum penalty of death and will almost certainly result in a five- to twenty-year prison sentence.

DEPARTURE TAXES
International flights B500; domestic flights B30.

DISABLED TRAVEL
Thailand makes few provisions for its disabled citizens, and this obviously affects the disabled traveller. For example, wheelchair users will have a hard time negotiating the uneven pavements, which are high to allow for flooding and invariably lacking in dropped kerbs, and will find it difficult to board buses and trains. Even crossing the road can be a trial, where it's usually a question of climbing steps up to a bridge rather than taking a ramped underpass. However these drawbacks are often balanced out by the affordability of small luxuries such as taxis, comfortable hotels, and personal tour guides, all of which can help smooth the way considerably. Government tour guides can be hired through any TAT office and will arrange access to temples, museums and other places that may at first not seem wheelchair-friendly. Visit Ⓦ www.infothai.com/disabled for further information.

ELECTRICITY
Supplied at 220 volts AC. Several plug types are commonly in use, most usually with two round pins, but also with two flat-blade pins, and sometimes with both options.

EMBASSIES AND CONSULATES
Australia, 37 Thanon Sathorn Tai ⓣ 287 2680; Burma (Myanmar), 132 Thanon Sathorn Nua ⓣ 233 2237; Cambodia, 185 Thanon Rajdamri (enter via Thanon Sarasin) ⓣ 02/254 6630; Canada, Boonmitr Bldg, 138 Thanon Silom ⓣ 237 4125; China, 57/2 Thanon Rajadapisek ⓣ 245 7033; India, 46 Soi 23, Thanon Sukhumvit ⓣ 258 0300; Indonesia, 600–602 Thanon Phetchaburi ⓣ 252 3135–40; Ireland, either contact the UK embassy, or call the Irish embassy in Malaysia ⓣ 001-7-60-3/2161 2963; Korea, 51 Soi 26, Thanon Sukhumvit ⓣ 278 5118; Laos, 520 Ramkhamhaeng Soi 39

ⓣ 539 6667–8 extension 103; Malaysia, 35 Thanon Sathorn Tai ⓣ 287 3979; Nepal, 189 Soi 71, Thanon Sukhumvit ⓣ 391 7240; Netherlands, 106 Thanon Witthayu (Wireless Rd) ⓣ 02/254 7701–5; New Zealand, 93 Thanon Witthayu ⓣ 254 2530; Pakistan, 31 Soi 3, Thanon Sukhumvit ⓣ 253 0288–90; Philippines, 760 Thanon Sukhumvit, opposite Soi 47 ⓣ 259 0139–40; Singapore, 129 Thanon Sathorn Tai ⓣ 286 2111; Sri Lanka, 75/84 Soi 21, Thanon Sukhumvit ⓣ 261 1934–8; Vietnam, 83/1 Thanon Witthayu ⓣ 251 5835–8; UK, 1031 Thanon Witthayu ⓣ 253 0191–9; US, 20 Thanon Witthayu ⓣ 205 4000.

EMERGENCIES For all emergencies, either call the tourist police (free 24hr phoneline ⓣ 1699), visit the Banglamphu Police Station at the west end of Thanon Khao San, or contact the Tourist Police Headquarters, 23rd Floor, 26/56 TPI Tower Bldg, Thanon Chantadmai, Tungmahamek, Sathorn ⓣ 678 6800–9.

IMMIGRATION OFFICE About 1km down Soi Suan Plu, off Thanon Sathorn Tai (Mon–Fri 8am–noon 1–4pm; ⓣ 287 3101-10). Visa extensions take about an hour.

INTERNET ACCESS Most cybercafés charge B1 per minute online. Banglamphu is packed with internet cafés, in particular along Thanon Khao San and Soi Ram Bhuttri; many guest houses often have internet access too. Outside Banglamphu, mid-range and upmarket hotels also offer internet access, but at vastly inflated prices. Thanon Sukhumvit has a number of makeshift phone/internet offices, as well as several more formal and more clued-up internet cafés, including *Cybercafé*, 2nd Floor, Ploenchit Center, Soi 2 Thanon Sukhumvit (daily 10am–9.30pm); and Time

For a list of hospitals in Bangkok, see p.28.

internet Centre on the second floor of Times Square, between sois 12 and 14 (daily 9am–midnight). If you plan to email from your laptop in Bangkok, note that the usual phone plug in Thailand is the American standard RJ11 phone jack.

LANGUAGE COURSES AUA (American University Alumni), 179 Thanon Rajdamri Ⓣ 252 8398 and Union Language School, CCT Building, 109 Thanon Suriwong Ⓣ 233 4482, run regular, recommended Thai language courses.

LAUNDRIES If you don't want to entrust your clothes to a guest-house laundry service, there are a couple of self-service laundries on Thanon Khao San.

LEFT LUGGAGE At Don Muang airport (international and domestic terminals; B70 per day) and Hualamphong train station (B10–30 per day; see p.47); most hotels and guest houses will store bags by the week at much more reasonable rates (B7–10 per day).

MAIL The GPO is at 1160 Thanon Charoen Krung (New Rd), a few hundred metres left of the exit for Wat Muang Kae express-boat stop. Poste restante can be collected here Mon–Fri 8am–8pm, Sat, Sun & holidays 8am–1pm; letters are kept for three months. The parcel packing service at the GPO operates Mon–Fri 8am–4.30pm, Sat 9am–noon. If you're staying in Banglamphu, it's more convenient to use the poste restante service either at Ratchadamnoen Post Office on Soi Damnoen Klang Neua (Mon–Fri 8.30am–5pm, Sat 9am–noon), where letters are kept for two months (address them c/o Poste Restante, Ratchadamnoen PO, Bangkok 10002), or at Banglamphubon PO on Soi Sibsam Hang, just west of Wat Bowoniwes, Bangkok 10203 (Mon–Fri 8.30am–5pm, Sat 9am–noon). In the Sukhumvit area, poste restante can be sent to Nana PO, Thanon Sukhumvit, Bangkok 10112, which is between sois 4 and 6.

LANGUAGE COURSES – LEFT LUGGAGE

MASSAGE Traditional Thai massage sessions and courses are held at Wat Po (see p.79), and at dozens of guest houses in Banglamphu.

NEWSPAPERS The two daily English-language papers, the *Bangkok Post* and the *Nation*, are sold at most newsstands in the capital.

PHARMACIES There are English-speaking staff at most of the capital's pharmacies, including the numerous branches of Boots the Chemist (they have outlets on Thanon Khao San and Thanon Sukhumvit).

TELEPHONES Payphones come in three varieties: red or pale blue for local calls (use small one-baht coins; 3min per B1); dark blue or stainless steel for long-distance calls within Thailand (B5 coins); and green cardphones for local, long-distance or international calls

(B25 to B500 phonecards are sold at hotels, post offices and shops, but B5000 cards must be used for international calls). The least expensive places to make international calls are the public telephone offices in or adjacent to post offices, and the cheapest time to ring is between midnight and 5am. The largest and most convenient of these is in the compound of the GPO on Thanon Charoen Krung (New Rd), which is open 24hr and also offers a fax service and a free collect-call service (see p.253 for location details). The post offices at Hualamphong station, on Thanon Sukhumvit (see p.253) and on Soi Sibsam Hang in Banglamphu (see p.253) also have international telephone offices attached, but these close at 8pm; the Ratchadamnoen phone office on Soi Damnoen Klang Neua opens daily 8am–10pm. Many private telephone offices claim that they offer the same rates

Calling out of Thailand, dial ☏ 001, then the relevant country code. For international directory enquiries call ☏ 100. For directory assistance in English dial ☏ 1133.

as the public phone offices, but they are almost always at least ten percent more expensive. Many foreign mobile phones can be used in Bangkok, but you'll need to check with your home service provider first.

TIME Bangkok is seven hours ahead of GMT, twelve hours ahead of Eastern Standard Time and three hours behind Sydney.

TIPPING Some upmarket hotels and restaurants add an automatic ten-percent service charge to your bill. It is usual to tip hotel bellboys and porters B10–20, and to round up taxi fares to the nearest B10.

TRAVEL AGENCIES Diethelm Travel has branches all over Thailand and Indo-China; in Bangkok they're at 12th Floor, Kian Gwan Bldg II, 140/1 Thanon Witthayu (Wireless Rd) ☎255 9200, 🅕255 9192, 🅦www.diethelm-travel.com.

They sell tickets for domestic and international flights and tours, and are particularly good on travel to Burma, Cambodia, Laos and Vietnam. VC Travel and Tour, Mezzanine Floor, Hualamphong Railway Station (☎613 6725, 🅕613 6727), provide an accommodation-booking service and sell train tickets at no commission. Also recommended are Educational Travel Centre (ETC; 🅔ETC@mozart.inet.co.th), *Royal Hotel*, Room 318, 2 Thanon Rajdamnoen Klang ☎224 0043, 🅕622 1420; 180 Thanon Khao San ☎282 2958; 5/3 Soi Ngam Duphli ☎287 1477 or 286 9424; Exotissimo (🅔exotvlth@linethai.co.th), 755 Thanon Silom ☎223 1510 and 21/17 Soi 4, Thanon Sukhumvit ☎253 5240; NS Tours, c/o *Vieng Thai Hotel*, Soi Ram Bhuttri, Banglamphu ☎629 0509; and STA Travel, 14th Floor, Wall Street Tower, 33 Thanon Suriwong ☎236 0262.

EXCURSIONS
FROM BANGKOK

Bang Pa-In

Little more than a roadside market, the village of **Bang Pa-In** (map 1, H2), 60km north of Bangkok, has been put on the tourist map by its extravagant and rather surreal **Royal Palace**, even though most of the buildings can be seen only from the outside. King Prasat Thong of Ayutthaya first built a palace on this site, 20km down the Chao Phraya River from his capital, in the middle of the seventeenth century. It remained a popular royal country residence until it was abandoned a century later, when the Thai capital was moved from Ayutthaya to Bangkok. In the middle of the nineteenth century, however, the advent of steamboats shortened the journey time upriver, and the palace enjoyed a revival: Rama IV built a modest residence here, which his son King Chulalongkorn (Rama V), in his passion for Westernization, knocked down to make room for the eccentric melange of European, Thai and Chinese architectural styles visible today.

Bang Pa-In can easily be visited on a day-trip from Bangkok. At a pinch, you could also take in a visit to Ayutthaya (see p.263), though that wouldn't really leave enough time to get the most out of the extensive remains of the former capital.

THE PALACE COMPLEX

Daily 8.30am–5pm, ticket office closes 3.30pm; B50.

Set in manicured grounds on an island in the Chao Phraya River, and ranged around an ornamental lake, the **palace complex** is flat and compact – a free brochure from the ticket office gives a diagram of the layout. On the north side of the lake stand a two-storey, colonial-style residence for the royal relatives and the Italianate **Warophat Phiman** (Excellent and Shining Heavenly Abode), which housed Chulalongkorn's throne hall and still contains private apartments where the present royal family sometimes stay. A covered bridge links this outer part of the palace to the **Pratu Thewarat Khanlai** (The King of the Gods Goes Forth Gate), the main entrance to the inner palace, which was reserved for the king and his immediate family. The high fence which encloses half of the bridge allowed the women of the harem to cross without being seen by male courtiers. You can't miss the photogenic **Aisawan Thiphya-art** (Divine Seat of Personal Freedom) in the middle of the lake: named after King Prasat Thong's original palace, it's the only example of pure Thai architecture at Bang Pa-In. The elegant tiers of the pavilion's roof shelter a bronze statue of Chulalongkorn.

In the inner palace, the **Uthayan Phumisathian** (Garden of the Secured Land) was Chulalongkorn's favourite house, a Swiss-style wooden chalet painted in bright two-tone green. After passing the **Ho Withun Thasana** (Sage's Lookout Tower), built so that the king could survey the surrounding countryside, you'll come to the main attraction of Bang Pa-In, the **Phra Thinang Wehart Chamrun** (Palace of Heavenly Light). The mansion and its contents were shipped from China and presented as a gift to Chulalongkorn in 1889 by the Chinese Chamber of Commerce in Bangkok. You're allowed to take off your shoes and feast your eyes on the interior, which drips with fine porcelain and embroidery, ebony furniture inlaid with mother-of-pearl and fantastically intricate woodcarving. This residence – a masterpiece of Chinese design – was the favourite of Rama VI, whose carved and lacquered writing table can be seen on the ground floor.

The simple marble **obelisk** behind the Uthayan Phumisathian was erected by Chulalongkorn to hold the ashes of Queen Sunandakumariratana, his favourite wife. In 1881, Sunanda, who was then 21 and expecting a child, was taking a trip on the river here when her boat capsized. She could have been rescued quite easily, but the laws concerning the sanctity of the royal family left those around her no option: "If a boat founders, the boatmen must swim away; if they remain near the boat [or] if they lay hold of him [the royal person] to rescue him, they are to be executed." Following the tragedy, King Chulalongkorn became a zealous reformer of Thai customs and strove to make the monarchy more accessible.

Turn right out of the main entrance to the palace grounds and cross the river on the small cable car, and you'll come to the greatest oddity of all: **Wat Nivet Dhamapravat**. A grey Buddhist viharn in the style of a Gothic church, it was built by Chulalongkorn in 1878, complete with wooden pews and stained-glass windows.

PRACTICALITIES

The best way of getting to Bang Pa-In from Bangkok is by early-morning **train** from Hualamphong station (7.05am & 8.35am). The journey takes just over an hour, and all trains continue to Ayutthaya (20 daily; 30min). From Bang Pa-In station (notice the separate station hall built by Chulalongkorn for the royal family) it's a two-kilometre hike to the palace, or you can take a samlor (tricycle rickshaw) for about B30. Slow **buses** leave Bangkok's Northern Terminal every half-hour or so and stop at Bang Pa-In market, a samlor ride from the palace, after about two hours, before continuing to Ayutthaya (30min).

- -
Luxury cruises from Bangkok to Ayutthaya
(see p.266) make a stop at Bang Pa-In.
- -

Every Sunday, the Chao Phraya Express boat company (☏222 5330) runs a **river tour** to Bang Pa-In, taking in Wat Phailom, a breeding ground for open-billed storks escaping the cold in Siberia, plus a shopping stop at Bang Sai folk arts and handicrafts centre. The boat leaves Prachan (Maharat) pier in Ratanakosin (off Maharat Road by Wat Mahathat) at 8am, and returns at 5.30pm. Tickets, available from the piers, are B330, not including lunch and admission to the palace and the handicrafts centre (B100).

Ayutthaya

n its heyday as the booming capital of the Thai kingdom from the fourteenth to the eighteenth centuries, **Ayutthaya** (map 1, H2) was so well endowed with temples that sunlight reflecting off their gilt decoration was said to dazzle from 5km away. Wide, grassy spaces today occupy much of the atmospheric site 80km north of Bangkok, which now resembles a graveyard for temples: grand, brooding red-brick ruins rise out of the fields, satisfyingly evoking the city's bygone grandeur. A few intact buildings help form an image of what the capital must have looked like, while three fine museums flesh out the picture.

The core of the ancient capital was a four-kilometre-wide **island** at the confluence of the Lopburi, Pasak and Chao Phraya rivers, which was once encircled by a twelve-kilometre wall, crumbling parts of which can be seen at the Phom Phet fortress in the southeast corner. A grid of broad roads now crosses the island, with recent buildings jostling uneasily with the ancient remains; the hub of the modern town rests on the northeast bank of the island around the junction of U Thong and Chao Phrom roads, although the newest development is off the island to the east.

The majority of Ayutthaya's ancient remains are spread out across the western half of the island in a patchwork of parkland: two of the most evocative temples, **Wat Phra**

THE GOLDEN AGE OF AYUTTHAYA

Ayutthaya takes its name from the Indian city of Ayodhya ("invincible"), legendary birthplace of Rama (see p.74). Founded in 1351 by U Thong, later King Ramathibodi I, it rose rapidly by exploiting the expanding trade routes between India and China, and by the mid-fifteenth century its empire covered most of what is now Thailand. Ayutthaya grew into a vast amphibious city built on a 140-kilometre network of canals (few of which survive); by 1685 a million people – roughly double the population of London at the time – lived on its waterways, mostly in houseboats.

By the seventeenth century, Ayutthaya's wealth had attracted traders of forty different nationalities, including Chinese, Portuguese, Dutch, English and French. Many lived in their own ghettos, with their own docks for the export of rice, spices, timber and hides. The kings of Ayutthaya deftly maintained their independence from outside powers, while embracing the benefits of contact: they employed foreign architects and navigators, and Japanese samurai as bodyguards; even their prime ministers were often outsiders, who could look after foreign trade without getting embroiled in court intrigues.

This four-hundred-year golden age came to an abrupt end in 1767 when the Burmese sacked Ayutthaya, taking tens of thousands of prisoners. The ruined city was abandoned to the jungle, but its memory endured: the architects of the new capital on Ratanakosin island in Bangkok perpetuated Ayutthaya's layout in every possible way.

Mahathat and **Wat Ratburana**, stand near the modern centre, while a broad band runs down the middle of the parkland, containing the scant vestiges of the **royal palace and temple**, the town's most revered Buddha image at **Viharn Phra Mongkol Bopit**, and the two main **muse-**

ums. To the north of the island you'll find the best-preserved temple, **Wat Na Phra Mane**, while to the southeast lie the giant chedi of **Wat Yai Chai Mongkol** and **Wat Phanan Choeng**, still a vibrant place of worship.

Ayutthaya comes alive each year for a week in mid-December, with a festival commemorating its UNESCO World Heritage Site status. The highlight is the nightly *son et lumière* show, usually at Wat Phra Si Sanphet, a grand historical romp featuring fireworks and elephant-back fights.

ARRIVAL, INFORMATION AND TRANSPORT

Ayutthaya can easily be visited on a day-trip from Bangkok, though dedicated ruin-baggers might want to stay overnight (see p.274). The best way of **getting there** is by **train** – there are about twenty a day from the capital, via Bang Pa-In (see p.261), concentrated in the early morning and evening (1hr 30min). To get to the centre of town from the station on the east bank of the Pasak, take the two-baht ferry from the jetty 100m west of the station across to Chao Phrom pier; it's then a five-minute walk to the junction of U Thong and Chao Phrom roads.

Though frequent, **buses** to Ayutthaya are slower and less convenient, as they depart from Bangkok's remote Northern Terminal (every 15min; 2hr–2hr 30min). Most buses from Bangkok pull in at the bus station on Thanon Naresuan just west of the centre of Ayutthaya, though some, mainly those on long-distance runs, will only stop at the bus terminal 2km to the east of the centre by the *Ayutthaya Grand Hotel* on Thanon Rojana. Private air-con minibuses from Bangkok's Victory Monument finish their nonstop route opposite the Thanon Naresuan bus station (every 30min during daylight hours).

It's also possible to get there by scenic **boat tour** from Bangkok via Bang Pa-In: the *Oriental Hotel* (see p.174), among others, runs swanky day-trips for around B1500 per person, and a couple of plushly converted teak rice barges – the *Mekhala* (☎02/256 7168 or 256 7169) and the *Manohra 2* (☎02/476 0021) – do exorbitantly priced overnight cruises.

Once in Ayutthaya, the **tourist police** base (☎035/241446) and the helpful **TAT** office (daily 8.30am–4.30pm; ☎035/246076 or 246077, ⓔchedi1@cscoms.com) can be found next to the city hall on the west side of Thanon Si Sanphet, opposite the Chao Sam Phraya National Museum (map 9, F6). Under construction just to the south of the TAT office is a grandiose tourist information centre which, it's said, will house multimedia exhibits about Ayutthaya, currency exchange and bike rental facilities, a post office and a café. It's also worth asking TAT about plans to develop the facilities of the sixteenth-century kraal – into which wild elephants were driven for capture and taming – on the northeast side of town, to include a training school and hospital for elephants and public shows.

For **getting around** Ayutthaya's widespread sights, **bicycles** can be rented at the guest houses for around B40 per day (*BJ1 Guest House*, next door to *Ayutthaya Guest House*, also has a moped for B300 a day), or it's easy enough to hop on a **tuk-tuk** – B5 for a short journey if you're sharing, B30 if you're on your own. If you're short on time you could hire a tuk-tuk for a whistle-stop tour of the old city for around B150 an hour, either from the train station or from Chao Phrom market.

Big tour **boats** can be chartered from the pier outside the Chantharakasem Palace. A two-hour trip (B600 for the boat, accommodating up to eight passengers) takes in Wat Phanan Choeng (see p.273); **Wat Phutthaisawan**, a fetchingly dilapidated complex founded by Ayutthaya's first king, Ramathibodi; and the recently restored **Wat Chai Watthanaram**, which was built by King Prasat Thong in 1630 to commemorate his victory over Cambodia, taking as its model the imposing symmetry of the Baphuon temple at Angkor.

WAT PHRA MAHATHAT

Map 9, H4. Daily 8.30am–5.30pm; B30.

Heading west out of the new town centre along Thanon Chao Phrom (which becomes Thanon Naresuan), the first ruins you'll come to, after about 1km, are a pair of temples on opposite sides of the road. The overgrown **Wat Phra Mahathat**, on the left, is the epitome of Ayutthaya's nostalgic atmosphere of faded majesty.

The name "Mahathat" (Great Relic) indicates that the temple was built to house remains of the Buddha himself: according to the royal chronicles – never renowned for historical accuracy – King Ramesuan (1388–95) was looking out of his palace one morning when ashes of the Buddha materialized out of thin air here. A gold casket containing the ashes was duly enshrined in a grand 38-metre-high prang. The prang later collapsed, but the reliquary was unearthed in the 1950s, along with a hoard of other treasures including a gorgeous marble fish which opened to reveal gold, amber, crystal and porcelain ornaments – all now on show in the Chao Sam Phraya National Museum (see p.269).

You can climb what remains of the prang to get a good view of the broad, grassy complex, with dozens of brick spires tilting at impossible angles and headless Buddhas scattered around like spare parts in a scrapyard – look out for the serene head of a stone Buddha which has become nestled in the embrace of a bodhi tree's roots.

WAT PHRA MAHATHAT

WAT RATBURANA

Map 9, H4. Daily 8.30am–5.30pm; B30.

Across the road from Wat Phra Mahathat, the towering **Wat Ratburana** was built in 1424 by King Boromraja II to commemorate his elder brothers Ay and Yi, who managed to kill each other in an elephant-back duel over the succession to the throne, thus leaving it vacant for him. Four elegant Sri Lankan chedis lean outwards as if in deference to the main prang, on which some of the original stucco work can still be seen, including fine statues of garudas swooping down on nagas.

It's possible to go down steep steps inside the prang to the crypt, where on two levels you can make out fragmentary murals of the early Ayutthaya period. Several hundred Buddha images were buried down here, most of which were snatched by grave robbers, although some can be seen in the Chao Sam Phraya Museum. They're in the earliest style that can be said to be distinctly Ayutthayan – an unsmiling Khmer expression, but an oval face and elongated body that show the strong influence of Sukhothai.

WAT PHRA SI SANPHET

Map 9, E4. Daily 8.30am–5.30pm; B30.

Further west you'll come to **Wat Phra Si Sanphet**, built in 1448 by King Boromatrailokanat as his private chapel. Formerly the grandest of Ayutthaya's temples, and still one of the best preserved, it took its name from one of the largest standing metal images of the Buddha ever known, the **Phra Si Sanphet**, erected here in 1503. Towering 16m high and covered in 173kg of gold, it was smashed to pieces when the Burmese sacked the city, though Rama I rescued the fragments and placed them inside a chedi at Wat Po in Bangkok (see p.79). The three remaining grey chedis were built to house the ashes of three kings; their style is characteristic of the old capital, and they have now become the most hackneyed image of Ayutthaya.

The Wang Luang (Royal Palace) to the north of Wat Phra Si Sanphet was destroyed by the Burmese in 1767 and then plundered for bricks to build Bangkok. The only way to form a picture of this huge complex is to consult the model in the Historical Study Centre (see p.270).

VIHARN PHRA MONGKOL BOPIT

Map 9, E5. Mon–Fri 8.30am–4.30pm, Sat & Sun 8.30–5.30pm; free.
Viharn Phra Mongkol Bopit, on the south side of Wat Phra Si Sanphet, attracts tourists and Thai pilgrims in about equal measure. The pristine hall – a replica of a typical Ayutthayan viharn with its characteristic chunky lotus-capped columns around the outside – was built in 1956 (with help from the Burmese to atone for their flattening of the city two centuries earlier) in order to shelter the revered **Phra Mongkol Bopit**, one of the largest bronze Buddhas in Thailand. The powerfully austere image, with its flashing mother-of-pearl eyes, was cast in the fifteenth century, then sat exposed to the elements from the time of the Burmese invasion until its new home was built. During restoration, the hollow image was found to contain hundreds of Buddha statuettes, some of which were later buried around the shrine to protect it.

CHAO SAM PHRAYA NATIONAL MUSEUM

Map 9, F6. Wed–Sun 9am–4pm; B30.
A ten-minute walk south of the viharn brings you to the largest of the town's three museums, the **Chao Sam**

Phraya National Museum, where most of the movable remains of Ayutthaya's glory – those which weren't plundered by treasure hunters or taken to the National Museum in Bangkok – are exhibited. Apart from numerous Buddhas, it's bursting with **gold treasures** of all shapes and sizes – betel-nut sets and model chedis, a royal wimple in gold filigree, a model elephant dripping with gems and the original relic casket from Wat Mahathat.

A second gallery, behind the main hall, explores foreign influences on Thai art and is particularly good on the origins of the various styles of Buddha images. This room also contains skeletons and artefacts from the site of the Portuguese settlement founded in 1540 just south of the town on the banks of the Chao Phraya. The Portuguese were the first Western power to establish ties with Ayutthaya, when in 1511 they were granted commercial privileges in return for supplying arms.

HISTORICAL STUDY CENTRE

Map 9, G6. Mon–Fri 9am–4.30pm, Sat & Sun 8.30am–5pm; B100.
The **Historical Study Centre**, five minutes' walk from the national museum along Thanon Rotchana, is the town's showpiece, with a hefty admission charge to go with it. The visitors' exhibition upstairs puts the ruins in context, dramatically presenting a wealth of background detail through videos, sound effects and reconstructions – temple murals and model ships, a peasant's wooden house and a small-scale model of the Royal Palace – to build up a broad social history of Ayutthaya.

The centre's **annexe** (map 9, J9; same times, same ticket), 500m south of Wat Phanan Choeng on the road to Bang Pa-In, also merits a visit despite its remoteness. Built with Japanese money on the site of the old Japanese settlement, it tells the fascinating story of Ayutthaya's relations with foreign powers, using a similar array of multimedia effects, as well as maps, paintings, and historic documents prised from museums around the world.

CHANTHARAKASEM PALACE

Map 9, J2. Wed–Sun 9am–4pm; B30.

In the northeast corner of the island, the museum of the **Chantharakasem Palace** was traditionally the home of the heir to the Ayutthayan throne. The Black Prince, Naresuan, built the first *wang na* (palace of the front) here in about 1577 so that he could guard the area of the city wall which was most vulnerable to enemy attack. Rama IV had the palace rebuilt in the mid-nineteenth century, and it now displays many of his possessions, including a throne platform overhung by a white *chat*, a ceremonial nine-tiered parasol which is a vital part of a king's insignia. The rest of the museum is a jumble of beautiful ceramics, Buddha images and random artefacts.

WAT NA PHRA MANE

Map 9, E2. Daily 8.30am–4.30pm; B20 donation.

Wat Na Phra Mane, on the north bank of the Lopburi River opposite the Wang Luang, is Ayutthaya's most immediately rewarding temple, as its structures and decoration survived the ravages of the Burmese. The story goes that when the Burmese were on the brink of capturing Ayutthaya in 1760, a siege gun positioned here burst, mortally wounding their king and prompting their retreat; when they came back to devastate the city in 1767, they left the temple standing out of superstition.

The main **bot**, built in 1503, shows the distinctive features of Ayutthayan architecture: outside columns topped with lotus cups, and slits in the walls instead of windows to let the wind pass through. Inside, underneath a rich red and gold coffered ceiling representing the stars around the moon, sits a powerful six-metre-high Buddha in the disdainful, overdecorated royal style characteristic of the later Ayutthaya period.

In sharp contrast is the dark green **Phra Khan Thavaraj** Buddha which dominates the tiny viharn behind to the right. Seated in the "European position", with its robe delicately pleated and its feet up on a large lotus leaf, the gentle figure conveys a reassuring serenity. It's advertised as being from Sri Lanka, the source of Thai Buddhism, but is more likely to be a Mon image from Wat Phra Mane at Nakhon Pathom, dating from the seventh to ninth centuries.

WAT PHU KHAO THONG

Map 9, B2. No fixed hours, but generally open daylight hours; free. Head 2km northwest of Wat Na Phra Mane and you're in open country, where the fifty-metre chedi of **Wat Phu Khao Thong** rises steeply out of the fields. In 1569, after a temporary occupation of Ayutthaya, the Burmese erected a Mon-style chedi here to commemorate their victory. Forbidden by Buddhist law from pulling down a sacred monument, the Thais had to put up with this galling reminder of the enemy's success until it collapsed nearly two hundred years later, when King Borommakot promptly built a truly Ayutthayan chedi on the old Burmese base – just in time for the Burmese to return in 1767 and flatten the town.

This "Golden Mount" has recently been restored and painted toothpaste-white, with a colossal equestrian statue of King Naresuan, conqueror of the Burmese, to keep it company. You can climb 25m of steps up the side of the chedi to look out over the countryside and the town, with glimpses of Wat Phra Si Sanphet and Viharn Phra Mongkol Bopit in the distance. In 1956, to celebrate 2500 years of Buddhism, the government placed on the tip of the spire a ball of solid gold weighing 2500g, of which there is now no trace.

WAT YAI CHAI MONGKOL

Map 9, L7. Daily 8.30am–5pm; B20 donation.

To the southeast of the island, if you cross the suspension bridge over the Pasak River and the rail line, then turn right at the major roundabout, you'll pass through Ayutthaya's new business zone and some rustic suburbia before reaching the ancient but still functioning **Wat Yai Chai Mongkol**, nearly 2km from the bridge.

Surrounded by formal lawns and flower beds, the wat was established by King Ramathibodi in 1357 as a meditation site for monks returning from study in Sri Lanka. King Naresuan put up the celebrated **chedi** to mark the decisive victory over the Burmese at Suphanburi in 1593, when he himself had sent the enemy packing by slaying the Burmese crown prince in a duel. Built on a colossal scale to outshine the huge Burmese-built chedi of Wat Phu Khao Thong on the northwest side of Ayutthaya, the chedi has come to symbolize the prowess and devotion of Naresuan and, by implication, his descendants down to the present king.

By the entrance, a **reclining Buddha**, now gleamingly restored in toothpaste white, was also constructed by Naresuan; elsewhere in the grounds, the wat maintains its contemplative origins with some highly topical maxims pinned to the trees such as "Cut down the forest of passion not real trees."

WAT PHANAN CHOENG

Map 9, J8. Daily 8.30am–4.30pm; B20 donation.

In Ayutthaya's most prosperous period the docks and main trading area were located near the confluence of the Chao Phraya and Pasak rivers, to the west of Wat Yai Chai Mongkol. This is where you'll find the oldest and liveliest working temple in town, **Wat Phanan Choeng** (and the annexe to the Historical Study Centre – see p.270).

The main viharn is often filled with the sights, sounds and smells of an incredible variety of merit-making activities, as devotees burn huge pink Chinese incense candles, offer food and rattle fortune sticks. It's even possible to buy tiny golden statues of the Buddha to be placed in one of the hundreds of niches which line the walls, a form of votive offering peculiar to this temple. If you can get here during a festival, especially Chinese New Year, you're in for an overpowering experience.

The nineteen-metre-high Buddha, which almost fills the hall, has survived since 1324, shortly before the founding of the capital, and tears are said to have flowed from its eyes when Ayutthaya was sacked by the Burmese. However, the reason for the temple's popularity with the Chinese is to be found in the early eighteenth-century shrine by the pier, with its image of a beautiful Chinese princess who drowned herself here because of a king's infidelity: his remorse led him to build the shrine at the place where she had walked into the river.

ACCOMMODATION

Ayutthaya Guest House
Map 9, J4. 12/34 Thanon Naresuan ⓣ 035/232658. The best of several guest houses in this area: modern, friendly place on a quiet, unnamed lane in the town centre, with clean, wooden-floored rooms and an outdoor bar/restaurant. ❸

Krung Sri River
Map 9, K6. 27/2 Moo 11, Thanon Rojana ⓣ 035/244333–7, ⓕ 243777. Ayutthaya's newest and most upmarket accommodation is a grand affair, with swanky lobby, gym and attractive pool, occupying a prime, but noisy, position at the eastern end of the Pridi Damrong Bridge. ❼

ACCOMMODATION

PS Guest House
Map 9, I3. 23/1 Thanon Chakrapat ⊤ 035/242394. Quiet, homely and sociable spot run by a very helpful retired English teacher. The large, clean and simple rooms (one with air-con) share bathrooms, and there's a balcony to hang out on overlooking the pleasant garden. Dorm beds B75; singles B100; **②**–**❸**

Ruenderm (Ayutthaya Youth Hostel)
Map 9, K5. 48 Moo 2 Tambon Horattanachai, Thanon U Thong ⊤ 035/241978.

Large, simple rooms, with plentiful shared cold-water bathrooms, in a shambolic riverside teak house, scattered with antiques. **②**

Suan Luang
Map 9, G6. Thanon Rojana ⊤ & ⓕ 035/245537. This training ground for hotel and catering students at Rajabhat College offers functional, bright, spacious and very clean rooms with fridge, TV, air-con and cold-water bathrooms, in a quiet location that's handy for TAT and the museums. **❹**

For details of the accommodation price codes used in these listings, see p.155.

EATING

The main travellers' hangout is the small, laid-back *Moon Café*, on the same lane as the *Ayutthaya Guest House*, which serves good Western and Thai **food** and occasionally has live music. Otherwise, there's a dearth of decent places to eat: your best bet is the atmospheric *Ruenderm* riverside terrace at the youth hostel, which serves reasonable food in some weird combinations, amid gnarled wooden furniture and curios. Around the central ruins are a few pricey restaurants if you're in need of air-conditioning with your lunch.

Nakhon Pathom

Nakhon Pathom (map 1, F5) is probably Thailand's oldest town, and is thought to be the point at which Buddhism first entered the region over two thousand years ago. The modern city's star attraction is the enormous **Phra Pathom Chedi**, an imposing stupa that dominates the skyline from every direction; everything described below is within ten minutes' walk of the omnipresent chedi. The town is 56km west of Bangkok and easily reached from the capital by train or bus.

PHRA PATHOM CHEDI

Measuring a phenomenal 120m high, **Phra Pathom Chedi** stands as tall as St Paul's Cathedral in London, and is a popular place of pilgrimage for Thais from all parts of the kingdom.

Although the Buddha never actually came to Thailand, legend has it that he rested here after wandering the country, and the original 39-metre-high Indian-style chedi may have been erected to commemorate this. Since then, the chedi has been rebuilt twice; its earliest fragments are entombed within the later layers, and its origin has become indistinguishable from folklore.

Approaching the chedi from the main (northern) staircase, you're greeted by the eight-metre-high Buddha image known as **Phra Ruang Rojanarit,** standing in front of the north viharn. Each of the viharns – there's one at each of the cardinal points – has an inner and an outer chamber containing tableaux of the life of the Buddha.

Proceeding clockwise around the monument – as is the custom at all Buddhist chedis – you can weave between the outer promenade and the inner cloister by climbing through the round, red-lacquered Chinese **moon windows** that connect them. Many of the trees that dot the promenade have a religious significance, such as the bodhi tree (*ficus religiosa*) under which the Buddha was meditating when he achieved enlightenment.

The museums

There are two museums within the chedi compound and, confusingly, both call themselves **Phra Pathom Museum**. The newer, more formal setup is clearly signposted from the bottom of the chedi's south staircase (Wed–Sun 9am–noon & 1–4pm; B30). It displays a good collection of Dvaravati-era (sixth to eleventh centuries) artefacts excavated nearby, including Wheels of Law – an emblem introduced by Theravada Buddhists before naturalistic images were permitted – and Buddha statuary with the U-shaped robe and thick facial features characteristic of Dvaravati sculpture.

For a broader, more contemporary overview, hunt out the other magpie's nest of a collection, which is halfway up the steps near the east viharn (Wed–Sun 9am–noon & 1–4pm; free). More a curiosity shop than a museum, the small room is an Aladdin's cave of Buddhist amulets, seashells, gold and silver needles, Chinese ceramics, Thai musical instruments, world coins and banknotes, gems and ancient statues.

PRACTICALITIES

Trains leave Bangkok's Hualampong Station ten times a day and take about 80 minutes; there are also four trains a day from Bangkok Noi (1 hr 10min). A five-minute walk south from Nakhon Pathom's train station across the khlong and through the market will get you to the chedi. **Buses** leave Bangkok's Southern Bus Terminal every ten minutes and take about an hour. Try to avoid being dumped at the bus terminal, which is about 1km east of the town centre – most buses circle the chedi first, so get off there instead.

Nakhon Pathom's sights only merit half a day, and at any rate **accommodation** here is no great shakes. If you have to stay the night, opt for the inexpensive *Mitrsampant Hotel* (☎034/242422; ❷), opposite the west gate of the chedi compound at the Lang Phra/Rajdamnoen intersection; or for the more comfortable *Nakorn Inn Hotel* (☎034/251152, ☎254998; ❺) on Thanon Rajvithee; or the *Whale Hotel* on Soi 19, off Thanon Rajvithee (☎034/251020, ☎253864; ❹–❻).

You can change money at the exchange booth
(open banking hours only) which is one block
south of the train station on the road to the
chedi, beside the bridge over the khlong.

For inexpensive Thai and Chinese dishes, head for either *Thai Food* or *Hasang*, both located on Thanon Phraya Gong just south across the khlong from the train station, on the left. Night-time **food** stalls next to the *Muang Thong Hotel* specialize in noodle broth and chilli-hot curries, and during the day the market in front of the station serves up the usual takeaway goodies, including reputedly the tastiest *khao laam* in Thailand.

Damnoen Saduak floating markets

To get an idea of what shopping in Bangkok used to be like before most of the canals were tarmacked over, make an early-morning trip to the floating markets (talat khlong) of Damnoen Saduak (map 1, E7), 109km southwest of Bangkok. Vineyards and orchards here back onto a labyrinth of narrow canals thick with paddle boats overflowing with fresh fruit and vegetables. Local women ply these waterways every morning between 6 and 11am, selling their produce to one another and to the residents of the weatherworn homes built on stilts along the banks. Many wear the deep-blue jacket and high-topped straw hat traditionally favoured by Thai farmers. It's all richly atmospheric, which naturally makes it a big draw for tour groups – but you can avoid the crowds if you leave before they arrive, at about 9am.

The target for most groups is the main **Talat Khlong Ton Kem**, 2km west of the tiny town centre at the intersection of Khlong Damnoen Saduak and Khlong Thong Lang. Many of the wooden houses here have been expanded and converted into warehouse-style souvenir shops and tourist restaurants, diverting trade away from the khlong vendors and into the hands of large commercial enterprises. But, for the moment at least, the traditional water trade continues, and the two bridges between Ton Kem and **Talat Khlong Hia Kui** (a little further south down Khlong Thong Lang) make rewarding and unobtrusive vantage points.

Touts invariably congregate at the Ton Kem pier to hassle you into taking a **boat trip** around the khlong network, asking an hourly rate of anything from between B50 per person to B300 for the whole boat. While this may be worth it to get to the less accessible **Talat Khlong Khun Phitak** to the south, there are distinct disadvantages in being propelled between markets at top speed in a noisy motorized boat. For a less hectic and more sensitive look around, explore the walkways beside the canals.

PRACTICALITIES

One of the reasons why Damnoen Saduak hasn't yet been totally ruined is that it's a two-hour **bus** journey from Bangkok. To reach the market in good time, you'll have to catch one of the earliest buses from Bangkok's Southern Bus Terminal: the first air-con buses leave at 6am and 6.30am and take two hours; the first non-air-con bus (#78) leaves at 6.20am and takes half an hour longer.

Damnoen Saduak's **bus terminal** is just north of Thanarat Bridge and Khlong Damnoen Saduak on the main Bangkok/Nakhon Pathom–Samut Songkhram road, Highway 325. Songthaews cover the 2km to Ton Kem, but walk if you've got the time: a walkway follows the canal, which you can get down to from Thanarat Bridge, or you can cross the bridge and take the road to the right (Thanon Sukhaphiban 1, unsignposted) through the orchards. Be warned, however, that the drivers on the earliest buses from

Bangkok sometimes do not terminate at the bus station near Thanarat Bridge but instead cross the bridge and then drop unsuspecting tourists a few hundred metres down Thanon Sukhaphiban 1, into the arms of a local boat operator. To avoid this, get off with the rest of the Thai passengers at the bus station near the bridge.

The best way to see the markets is to **stay overnight** in Damnoen Saduak and get up before the buses and coach tours from Bangkok arrive – and, if possible, explore the khlongside walkways the evening before. The only **place to stay** in town is the *Little Bird Hotel*, also known as *Noknoi* (☎032/254382; ➋–➌), whose sign is clearly visible from the main road and Thanarat Bridge. Rooms here are good value: enormous, clean and all with en-suite bathrooms, and there's air-conditioning if you want it.

Phetchaburi

Straddling the Phet River about 120km south of Bangkok, **Phetchaburi** has long had a reputation as a cultural centre and became a favourite country retreat of Rama IV, who had a hilltop palace built here in the 1850s. Modern Phetchaburi has lost relatively little of the ambience that so attracted the king: the central riverside area is hemmed in by historic wats in varying states of disrepair, and wooden rather than concrete shophouses still line the river bank.

The pinnacles and rooftops of the town's thirty-odd wats are visible in every direction, but only a few are worth stopping off to investigate; the following description takes in the three most interesting, and can be done as a leisurely two-hour circular walk beginning from Chomrut Bridge, which is centrally located close to the market, about ten minutes' walk south of the air-con bus terminal. Alternatively, hop on one of the public **songthaews** that circulate round the town and charge a flat fare of B6.

Many Bangkok tour operators combine the
floating markets of Damnoen Saduak (see p.279)
with Phetchaburi as a day-trip package.

WAT YAI SUWANNARAM

Of all Phetchaburi's temples, the most attractive is the still-functioning seventeenth-century **Wat Yai Suwannaram** on Thanon Phongsuriya, about 700m east of Chomrut Bridge. The temple's fine old teak hall has elaborately carved doors, and stands near a traditional scripture library built on stilts in the middle of a pond to prevent ants destroying the precious documents.

Across from the pond and hidden behind high whitewashed walls stands the windowless Ayutthayan-style bot. Enter the walled compound from the south and pass through the statue-filled cloisters into the bot itself, which is supported by intricately patterned red and gold pillars and contains a remarkable, if rather faded, set of murals, depicting Indra, Brahma and other lower-ranking divinities ranged in five rows of ascending importance. If you climb the steps in front of the Buddha image seated against the far back wall you'll get a close-up of the left foot, which for some reason was cast with six toes.

WAT KAMPHAENG LAENG

Fifteen minutes' walk east and then south of Wat Yai, the five tumbledown prangs of **Wat Kamphaeng Laeng** on Thanon Phra Song mark out Phetchaburi as the probable southernmost outpost of the Khmer empire. Built to enshrine Hindu deities and set out in a cruciform arrangement facing east, the laterite corncob-style prangs were later adapted for Buddhist use, as you can see from the two which now house Buddha images. There has been some attempt to restore a few of the carvings and false balustraded windows, but these days worshippers congregate in the modern whitewashed wat behind these shrines, leaving the atmospheric and appealingly quaint collection of decaying prangs and casuarina topiary to chickens, stray dogs and the occasional tourist.

CHAPTER TWENTY ONE

WAT MAHATHAT

Continuing west along Thanon Phra Song from Wat Kamphaeng Laeng, across the river, you can see the prangs of Phetchaburi's most fully restored and important temple, **Wat Mahathat**, long before you reach them. The five landmark prangs at its heart are adorned with stucco figures of mythical creatures, though these are nothing compared with those on the roofs of the main viharn and the bot. Instead of tapering off into the usual serpentine *chofa*, the gables are studded with miniature figures of angels and gods, which add an almost mischievous vitality to the place. In a similar vein, a couple of gold-embossed crocodiles snarl above the entrance to the bot, and a caricature carving of a bespectacled man rubs shoulders with mythical giants in a relief around the base of the gold Buddha, housed in a separate mondop nearby. Leaving Wat Mahathat, it's a five-minute walk north up Thanon Damnoen Kasem to Thanon Phongsuriya and another few minutes back to Chomrut Bridge.

KHAO WANG

Daily 9am–4pm; B40. White songthaew from Thanon Phongsuriya to the base of the hill, then either walk up the path, or take the cable car (daily 8am–4pm; B50) from the western flank of the hill off Highway 4, quite near the non-air-con bus terminal.

Dominating the western outskirts, about thirty minutes' walk from Wat Mahathat, stands Rama IV's palace, a stew of mid-nineteenth-century Thai and European styles scattered over the crest of the hill known as **Khao Wang**. Whenever the king came on an excursion here, he stayed in the airy summer house on the summit, Phra Nakhon Khiri, with its Mediterranean-style shutters and verandas. Now a museum, it houses a moderately interesting collection of ceramics, furniture and other artefacts given to the royal family by foreign friends.

PRACTICALITIES

Air-con **buses** from Bangkok's Southern Bus Terminal (every 30min; 2hr) arrive at Phetchaburi's air-con bus terminal just off Thanon Rajwithi, from where it's about ten minutes' walk south to the town centre and Chomrut Bridge. The main station for non-air-con buses is on the southwest edge of Khao Wang, about thirty minutes' walk or a ten-minute songthaew ride from the town centre. Eight **trains** a day run from Bangkok's Hualamphong Station (3hr 15min) to Phetchaburi train station, which is on the northern outskirts of town, not far from Khao Wang, but about 1500m from the town centre.

The branch of Bangkok Bank 150m east of Wat Mahathat on Thanon Phra Song does currency exchange and has an ATM.

Most travellers **stay** at the *Rabieng Rimnum (Rim Nam) Guest House*, centrally located at 1 Thanon Chisa-in, on the southwest corner of Chomrut Bridge (℡ 032/425707, ℻ 410695; ➋). Occupying a century-old house next to the Phetburi River, it has half a dozen simple rooms with shared bathrooms and the best restaurant in town, boasting an interesting menu of inexpensive Thai dishes, from banana blossom salad to spicy crab soup. Less farang-oriented, but quieter and cheaper, is the friendly *Chom Klao* hotel across on the northeast corner of Chomrut Bridge at 1–3 Thanon Phongsuriya (℡ 032/425398; ➊–➋); it's not signed in English, but is easily recognized by its pale blue doors. Some of the rooms here give out onto the riverside walkway, and you can choose whether or not you want an en-suite bathroom.

Kanchanaburi and the River Kwai

Set in a landscape of limestone hills 121km northwest of Bangkok, Kanchanaburi (map 1, C4) is most famous as the location of the Bridge over the River Kwai, but it has a lot more to offer, including fine riverine scenery and some moving relics from World War II, when the town served as a POW camp and base for construction work on the notorious Thailand–Burma Death Railway. It's possible to see the Bridge and ride the railway on a day-trip from Bangkok, but if you have the time, the town makes a pleasant spot for an overnight stay; there are many guest houses and hotels prettily set alongside the river, including some with accommodation in raft houses moored beside the river bank.

Trains from Bangkok Noi (2hr 40min) or Nakhon Pathom (1hr 25min) are the most scenic way to get to Kanchanaburi; they depart from Bangkok twice a day at approximately 7.45am and 1.45pm, stopping at Nakhon Pathom around 9.20am and 3.05pm. The main Kanchanaburi train station is on Thanon Saeng Chuto (map 10, D2), about 2km north of the town centre, but if you're doing a day-trip and want to see the Bridge, get off at River Kwai Bridge train station (map 10, A1), a few minutes further on. Nonstop air-conditioned **buses** from Bangkok's Southern Bus Terminal are faster (about 2hr 20min) and more frequent (every 15min), arriving at the bus station off Thanon Saeng Chuto (map 10, G6). The speediest transport option is to take one of the **tourist minibuses** from Bangkok's Thanon Khao San, which take two hours.

Kanchanaburi is best explored by **bicycle**, since the town measures about 5km from north to south and all the town sights are sandwiched between the River Kwai and the busy Thanon Saeng Chuto. Bikes can be rented for around B20 per day from most guest houses and many tour agents. Alternatively, you can use the **public songthaew** (minivan) service that runs from outside the Bata shoe shop on Thanon Saeng Chuto (one block north of the bus station; map 10, F5), goes north via the Kanchanaburi War Cemetery and then up Thanon Maenam Kwai to the bridge. Songthaews leave about every fifteen minutes during daylight hours, take about fifteen minutes to the Bridge and cost about B5. Failing that, there are plenty of **samlor** (cycle rickshaws) available for hire.

The TAT office (map 10, F6; daily 8.30am–4.30pm; ☏ 034/511200) is on Thanon Saeng Chuto, a few hundred metres south of the bus station. Several banks on Thanon Saeng Chuto have ATMs and offer money changing facilities.

THE JEATH WAR MUSEUM

Map 10, E7. Daily 8.30am–4.30pm; B30.

The **JEATH War Museum** (JEATH is an acronym of six of the countries involved in the railway – Japan, England,

THE DEATH RAILWAY

Shortly after entering World War II in December 1941, Japan began looking for a supply route to connect its newly acquired territories that now stretched from Singapore to the Burma-India border. In spite of the almost impenetrable terrain, the River Kwai basin was chosen as the route for a new 415-kilo-metre-long Thailand–Burma Railway.

About 60,000 Allied POWs were shipped up from captured Southeast Asian territories to work on the link, their numbers later augmented by as many as 200,000 conscripted Asian labourers. Work began at both ends in June 1942. Three million cubic metres of rock was shifted and 14km of bridges built with little else but picks and shovels, dynamite and pulleys. By the time the line was completed, fifteen months later, it had more than earned its nickname, the Death Railway: an estimated 16,000 POWs and 100,000 Asian labourers died while working on it.

Food rations were meagre for men forced into backbreaking eighteen-hour shifts, often followed by night-long marches to the next camp. Many suffered from beri-beri, many more died of dysentery-induced starvation, but the biggest killers were cholera and malaria, particularly during the monsoon. It is said that one man died for every sleeper laid on the track.

Australia, America, Thailand and Holland) gives the clearest introduction to local wartime history, putting the notorious sights of the Death Railway in context and painting a vivid picture of the gruesome conditions suffered by the POWs who worked on the line. It includes many harrowing accounts of life in the camps, recorded in newspaper articles, paintings and photographs. The museum is housed in a reconstructed Allied POW hut of thatched palm beside the

THE DEATH RAILWAY

river, about 500m from the TAT office or a fifteen-minute walk southwest of the bus station.

KANCHANABURI WAR CEMETERY (DON RAK)

Map 10, D3. Daily 8am–4pm; free.

Many of the Allied POWs who died during the construction of the Thailand–Burma Railway are buried in the **Kanchanaburi War Cemetery**, also known as **Don Rak**, opposite the train station on Thanon Saeng Chuto. The 6982 POW graves are laid out in straight lines amid immaculate lawns and flowering shrubs. Many of the identical stone memorial slabs state simply "A man who died for his country" – at the upcountry camps, bodies were thrown onto mass funeral pyres, making identification impossible. Others, inscribed with names, dates and regiments, indicate that the overwhelming majority of the dead were under 25 years old.

THE BRIDGE OVER THE RIVER KWAI

Map 10, A1.

For most people the plain steel arches of the **Bridge over the River Kwai** come as a disappointment: it lacks drama and looks nothing like as hard to construct as it does in David Lean's famous 1957 film of the same name. But it is the film, of course, that draws tour buses here by the dozen, and makes the Bridge approach seethe with trinket-sellers and touts. To get here, either take any songthaew heading north up Thanon Saeng Chuto, hire a samlor, or cycle – it's 5km from the bus station.

The fording of the Kwai Yai at this point was one of the first major obstacles in the construction of the Thailand–Burma Railway. Sections of a steel bridge were brought up from Java and reassembled by POWs using only pulleys and derricks. A temporary **wooden bridge** was built alongside it, taking its first train in February 1943; three months later the steel bridge was finished. Both bridges were severely damaged by Allied bombers (rather than commando-saboteurs as in the film) in 1944 and 1945, but the steel bridge was repaired after the war and is still in use today. In fact the best way to see the Bridge is by **taking the train over it** – see p.291 for details. You can also walk over the Bridge to the souvenir stalls on the west bank.

The bridge forms the dramatic centrepiece of the annual *son et lumière* River Kwai Bridge Festival, held over ten nights from the end of November to commemorate the first Allied bombing of the bridge on November 28, 1944.

WORLD WAR II MUSEUM

Map 10, A2. Daily 8am–6pm; B30.

Not to be confused with the JEATH War Museum, the **World War II Museum** is a privately owned collection of rather bizarre curiosities. The war section comprises a very odd mixture of memorabilia (a rusted bombshell, the carpet used by the local Japanese commander) and reconstructed tableaux featuring emaciated POWs. More light-hearted displays include stamp and banknote collections and a gallery of selected "Miss Thailand" portraits from 1934.

RIDING THE DEATH RAILWAY

The two-hour rail journey from Kanchanaburi to Nam Tok is one of Thailand's most scenic. Leaving Kanchanaburi via the Bridge over the River Kwai, the train chugs through the Kwai Noi valley, stopping frequently at pretty flower-decked country stations.

The most hair-raising section of track begins shortly after Tha Kilen at **Wang Sing**, also known as Arrow Hill, when the train squeezes through thirty-metre solid rock cuttings, dug at the cost of numerous POW lives. Six kilometres further, it slows to a crawl at the approach to the **Wang Po viaduct**, where a three-hundred-metre trestle bridge clings to the cliff face as it curves with the Kwai Noi – almost every man who worked on this part of the railway died. Half an hour later, the train reaches its terminus at the small town of **Nam Tok**.

There are three **Kanchanaburi–Nam Tok trains** daily in both directions, so a day return is quite feasible; Kanchanaburi TAT has timetables. Many Kanchanaburi tour operators offer a day-trip that includes the impressive Hellfire Pass Memorial Museum, other war sights and waterfalls as well as a ride on the railway. It is possible to do the **Bangkok–Kanchanaburi–Nam Tok round trip** in one day – bear in mind, though, that this leaves no time for exploring, and that only third class, hard seats are available. The 7.45am train from Bangkok Noi arrives in Nam Tok at 12.50pm, then departs for Bangkok at 1pm, returning to the capital at 6.10pm.

On weekends and national holidays, the State Railway runs special day-trips along the Death Railway from Bangkok's Hualamphong Station. The trips include short stops at Nakhon Pathom, the Bridge over the River Kwai and Nam Tok, the terminus of the line. Advance booking is essential; see p.47.

RIDING THE DEATH RAILWAY

ACCOMMODATION

Felix River Kwai

Map 10, A2. On the west bank of the Kwai Yai ⓣ 034/515061, ⓕ 515095, ⓦ www.felixriverkwai.co.th. Occupying a lovely riverside spot within walking distance of the Bridge, this is the most upmarket resort in the area, with large deluxe air-con rooms and two swimming pools. ⓼

Jolly Frog Backpackers

Map 10, C3. 28 Soi China, just off the southern end of Thanon Maenam Kwai ⓣ 034/514579, ⓦ www.jollyfrog.fsnet.co.uk. Large, popular complex of comfortable bamboo huts, some with bathroom, ranged around a riverside garden. ⓶

Sam's River Raft House

Map 10, C4. 48/1 Soi Rong Heeb Oil ⓣ 034/624231, ⓕ 512023. Comfortable, thoughtfully designed, air-con raft houses and cheaper en-suite fan rooms on dry land. ⓶—⓷

Vimol Guest House

Map 10, C4. Soi Rong Heeb Oil ⓣ & ⓕ 034/514831. Unusual, two-storey, A-frame bamboo huts with sleeping quarters in the roof section and bathrooms downstairs. Friendly management and good food. ⓵

For details of the accommodation price codes used in these listings, see p.155.

EATING AND DRINKING

Beer Barrel

Map 10, B2. Thanon Maenam Kwai.
Rustic-styled outdoor beer garden serving ice-cold draft beer and a short menu of bar meals.

JR

Map 10, E7. South of Tha Chukkadon.

Floating restaurant that affords especially pretty views across the Mae Khlong and serves mid-priced Thai-Chinese dishes.

Krathom Thai

Map 10, D3. At Apple's Guest House, 293 Thanon Maenam Kwai.

Exceptionally delicious, mid-priced menu, which includes mouthwatering meat and veggie matsaman curries.

River Kwai Park Fast Food Hall

Map 10, A1. 50m south of the bridge on Thanon Maenam Kwai.

The cheapest place to eat in the vicinity of the Bridge, this is a collection of curry and noodle stalls where you buy coupons for meals that cost just B25 or B30.

EATING AND DRINKING

CONTEXTS

The historical framework

Bangkok is a comparatively new capital, founded in 1782 after Ayutthaya, a short way upriver, had been razed by the Burmese, but it has established an overwhelming dominance in Thailand. Its history over the last two centuries directly mirrors that of the country as a whole, and the city has gathered to itself, in the National Museum and elsewhere, the major relics of Thailand's previous civilizations, principally from the eras of Ayutthaya and its precursor, Sukhothai.

Early history

The region's first distinctive civilization, **Dvaravati**, was established around two thousand years ago by an Austroasiatic-speaking people known as the Mon. One of its mainstays was Theravada Buddhism, which had been introduced to Thailand during the second or third century BC by Indian missionaries. From the discovery of monastery boundary stones (*sema*), clay votive tablets and Indian-influenced Buddhist sculpture, it's clear that the

Dvaravati city states (including **Nakhon Pathom**) had their greatest flourishing between the sixth and ninth centuries AD. Meanwhile, in the eighth century, peninsular Thailand to the south of Dvaravati came under the control of the **Srivijaya** empire, a Mahayana Buddhist state centred on Sumatra which had strong ties with India.

From the ninth century onwards, however, both Dvaravati and Srivijaya Thailand succumbed to invading **Khmers** from Cambodia, who consolidated their position during the watershed reign of **Jayavarman II** (802–50). To establish his authority, Jayavarman II had himself initiated as a *chakravartin* or universal ruler, the living embodiment of the **devaraja**, the divine essence of kingship – a concept which was adopted by later Thai rulers. From their capital at **Angkor**, Jayavarman's successors took control over northeastern, central and peninsular Thailand, thus mastering the most important trade routes between India and China. By the thirteenth century, however, the Khmers had overreached themselves and were in no position to resist the onslaught of a vibrant new force in Southeast Asia, the Thais.

The earliest Thais

The earliest traceable history of the **Thai people** picks them up in southern China around the fifth century AD, when they were squeezed by Chinese and Vietnamese expansionism into sparsely inhabited northeastern Laos. Their first significant entry into what is now Thailand seems to have happened in the north, where some time after the seventh century the Thais formed a state known as **Yonok**. Theravada Buddhism spread to Yonok via Dvaravati around the end of the tenth century, which served not only to unify the Thais themselves but also to link them to the wider community of Buddhists.

By the end of the twelfth century they formed the majority of the population in Thailand, then under the control of the Khmer empire. The Khmers' main outpost, at Lopburi, was by this time regarded as the administrative capital of a land called **Syam** (possibly from the Sanskrit *syam*, meaning swarthy) – a mid-twelfth-century bas-relief at Angkor portraying the troops of Lopburi, preceded by a large group of self-confident Syam Kuk mercenaries, shows that the Thais were becoming a force to be reckoned with.

Sukhothai

At some time around 1238, Thais in the upper Chao Phraya valley captured the main Khmer outpost in the region at **Sukhothai** and established a kingdom there. For the first forty years it was merely a local power, but an attack by the ruler of the neighbouring principality of Mae Sot brought a dynamic new leader to the fore: the king's nineteen-year-old son, Rama, defeated the opposing commander, earning himself the name **Ramkhamhaeng**, "Rama the Bold". When Ramkhamhaeng himself came to the throne around 1278, he seized control of much of the Chao Phraya valley, and over the next twenty years, more by diplomacy than military action, gained the submission of most of Thailand under a complex tribute system.

Although the empire of Sukhothai extended Thai control over a vast area, its greatest contribution to the Thais' development was at home, in cultural and political matters. A famous **inscription** by Ramkhamhaeng, now housed in the Bangkok National Museum, describes a prosperous era of benevolent rule: "In the time of King Ramkhamhaeng this land of Sukhothai is thriving. There is fish in the water and rice in the fields . . . [The King] has hung a bell in the opening of the gate over there: if any commoner has a grievance which sickens his belly and gripes his heart . . .

SUKHOTHAI

he goes and strikes the bell . . . [and King Ramkhamhaeng] questions the man, examines the case, and decides it justly for him."

Although this plainly smacks of self-promotion, it seems to contain at least a kernel of truth: in deliberate contrast to the Khmer god-kings (*devaraja*), Ramkhamhaeng styled himself as a **dhammaraja**, a king who ruled justly according to Theravada Buddhist doctrine and made himself accessible to his people. A further sign of the Thais' growing self-confidence was the invention of a new **script** to make their tonal language understood by the non-Thai inhabitants of the land.

The growth of Ayutthaya

After the death of Ramkhamhaeng around 1299, however, his empire quickly fell apart. By 1320 Sukhothai had regressed to being a kingdom of only local significance, though its mantle as the capital of a Thai empire was taken up shortly after at **Ayutthaya** to the south. Soon after founding the city in 1351, the ambitious king **Ramathibodi** united the principalities of the lower Chao Phraya valley, which had formed the western provinces of the Khmer empire. When he recruited his bureaucracy from the urban elite of Lopburi, Ramathibodi set the **style of government** at Ayutthaya, elements of which persisted into the Bangkok empire and up to the present day. The elaborate etiquette, language and rituals of Angkor were adopted, and, most importantly, the conception of the ruler as *devaraja*: when the king processed through the town, ordinary people were forbidden to look at him and had to be silent while he passed.

The site chosen by Ramathibodi was the best in the region for an international port, and so began Ayutthaya's rise to prosperity, based on exploiting the upswing in **trade** in the middle of the fourteenth century along the routes between India and China. By 1540, the Kingdom of Ayutthaya had grown to cover most of the area of modern-day Thailand. Despite a 1568 invasion by the Burmese, which led to twenty years of foreign rule, Ayutthaya made a spectacular comeback, and in the seventeenth century its **foreign trade** boomed. In 1511 the Portuguese had become the first Western power to trade with Ayutthaya, and a treaty with Spain was concluded in 1598; relations with Holland and England were initiated in 1608 and 1612 respectively. European merchants flocked to Thailand, not only to buy Thai products, but also to gain access to Chinese and Japanese goods on sale there.

The Burmese invasion

In the mid-eighteenth century, however, the rumbling in the Burmese jungle to the north began to make itself heard again. After an unsuccessful siege in 1760, in February 1766 the Burmese descended upon the city for the last time. The Thais held out for over a year, during which they were afflicted by famine, epidemics and a terrible fire which destroyed ten thousand houses. Finally, in April 1767, the walls were breached and the city taken. The Burmese savagely razed everything to the ground and led off tens of thousands of prisoners to Burma, including most of the royal family. The city was abandoned to the jungle, and Thailand descended into banditry.

Taksin and Thonburi

Out of this lawless mess, however, emerged **Phraya Taksin**, a charismatic and brave general, who had been unfairly blamed for a failed counter-attack against the Burmese at Ayutthaya and had quietly slipped away from the besieged city. Taksin was crowned king in December 1768 at his new capital of **Thonburi**, on the opposite bank of the river from modern-day Bangkok. Within two years he had restored all of Ayutthaya's territories; more remarkably, by the end of the next decade Taksin had outdone his Ayutthayan predecessors by bringing Cambodia and much of Laos into a huge new empire.

However, by 1779 all was not well with the king. Taksin was becoming increasingly paranoid about plots against him, a delusion that drove him to imprison and torture even his wife and sons. At the same time he sank into religious excesses, demanding that the monkhood worship him as a god. By March 1782, public outrage at his sadism and dangerously irrational behaviour had reached such fervour that he was ousted in a coup.

Chao Phraya Chakri, Taksin's military commander, was invited to take power and had Taksin executed. In accordance with ancient etiquette, this had to be done without royal blood touching the earth: the mad king was duly wrapped in a black velvet sack and struck on the back of the neck with a sandalwood club. (Popular tradition has it that even this form of execution was too much: an unfortunate substitute got the velvet sack treatment, while Taksin was whisked away to a palace in the hills near Nakhon Si Thammarat, where he is said to have lived until 1825.)

The early Bangkok empire: Rama I

With the support of the Ayutthayan aristocracy, Chakri – reigning as **Rama I** (1782–1809) – set about consolidating the Thai kingdom. His first act was to move the capital across the river to what we know as **Bangkok**, on the more defensible east bank where the French had built a grand but short-lived fort in the 1660s. Borrowing from the layout of Ayutthaya, he built a new royal palace and impressive monasteries in the area of **Ratanakosin** – which remains the city's spiritual heart – within a defensive ring of two (later expanded to three) canals. In the palace temple, Wat Phra Kaeo, he enshrined the talismanic Emerald Buddha, which he had snatched during his campaigns in Laos. Initially, as at Ayutthaya, the city was largely amphibious: only the temples and royal palaces were built on dry land, while ordinary residences floated on thick bamboo rafts on the river and canals, and even shops and warehouses were moored to the river bank.

During Rama I's reign, trade with China revived, and the style of government was put on a more modern footing: while retaining many of the features of a *devaraja*, he shared more responsibility with his courtiers, as a first among equals.

Rama II and Rama III

The peaceful accession of his son as **Rama II** (1809–24) signalled the establishment of the **Chakri dynasty**, which is still in place today. This Second Reign was a quiet interlude, best remembered as a fertile period for Thai literature. The king, himself one of the great Thai poets, gathered round him a group of writers including the famous Sunthorn Phu, who produced scores of masterly love poems, travel accounts and narrative songs.

In contrast, **Rama III** (1824–51) actively discouraged literary development and was a vigorous defender of conservative values. To this end, he embarked on an extraordinary redevelopment of **Wat Po**, the oldest temple in Bangkok. Hundreds of educational inscriptions and mural paintings, on all manner of secular and religious subjects, were put on show, apparently to preserve traditional culture against the rapid change which the king saw corroding the country.

The danger posed by Western influence became more apparent in the Third Reign. As early as 1825, the Thais were sufficiently alarmed by **British colonialism** to strengthen Bangkok's defences by stretching a great iron chain across the mouth of the Chao Phraya River, to which every blacksmith in the area had to donate a certain number of links. In 1826 Rama III was obliged to sign the **Burney Treaty**, a limited trade agreement with the British by which the Thais won some political security in return for reducing their taxes on goods passing through Bangkok.

Mongkut

Rama IV, more commonly known as **Mongkut** (1851–68), had been a Buddhist monk for 27 years when he succeeded his brother. But far from leading a cloistered life, Mongkut had travelled widely throughout Thailand, had maintained scholarly contacts with French and American missionaries, and had taken an interest in Western learning, studying English, Latin and the sciences.

When his kingship faced its first major test, in the form of a threatening **British mission** in 1855 led by **Sir John Bowring**, Mongkut dealt with it confidently. Realizing that Thailand would be unable to resist the military might of the British, the king reduced import and export taxes, allowed British subjects to live and own land in Thailand and granted them freedom of trade. Furthermore, Mongkut quickly made it known that he would welcome diplomatic contacts from other Western countries: within a decade, agreements similar to the Bowring Treaty had been signed with France, the United States and a score of other nations.

Thus by skilful diplomacy the king avoided a close relationship with just one power, which could easily have led to Thailand's annexation. And as a result of the open-door policy, foreign trade boomed, financing the redevelopment of Bangkok's waterfront and, for the first time, the building of paved roads. However, Mongkut ran out of time for instituting the far-reaching domestic reforms which he saw were needed to drag Thailand into the modern world.

Chulalongkorn

Mongkut's son, **Chulalongkorn**, took the throne as Rama V (1868–1910) at the age of only 15, but he was well prepared by an excellent education which mixed traditional Thai and modern Western elements – provided by Mrs Anna Leonowens, subject of *The King and I*. When Chulalongkorn reached his majority after a five-year regency, he set to work on the reforms envisioned by his father.

One of his first acts was to scrap the custom by which subjects were required to prostrate themselves in the presence of the king. He constructed a new residential palace for the royal family in **Dusit**, north of Ratanakosin, and laid out that area's grand European-style boulevards. In the 1880s Chulalongkorn began to **restructure the government** to meet the country's needs, setting up a host of departments, for education, public health, the army and the like, and bringing in scores of foreign advisers to help with everything from foreign affairs to rail lines.

Throughout this period, however, the Western powers maintained their pressure on the region. The most serious threat to Thai sovereignty was the **Franco–Siamese Crisis** of 1893, which culminated in the French sending gunboats up the Chao Phraya River to Bangkok. Flouting numerous international laws, France claimed control over Laos and made other outrageous demands, which Chulalongkorn had no option but to concede. During the course of his reign the country was obliged to cede almost half of its territory, and forewent huge sums of tax revenue, in order to preserve its independence; but by Chulalongkorn's death in 1910, the frontiers were fixed as they are today.

The end of absolute monarchy

Chulalongkorn was succeeded by a flamboyant, British-educated prince, **Vajiravudh** (Rama VI, 1910–25). However, in 1912 a group of young army lieutenants, disillusioned by the absolute monarchy, plotted a **coup**. The conspirators were easily broken up, but this was something new in Thai history: the country was used to infighting among the royal family, but not to military intrigue by men from comparatively ordinary backgrounds. By the time the young and inexperienced **Prajadhipok** – seventy-sixth child of Chulalongkorn – was catapulted to the throne as Rama VII (1925–35), Vajiravudh's extravagance had created severe financial problems. The vigorous community of Western-educated intellectuals who had emerged in the lower echelons of the bureaucracy were becoming increasingly dissatisfied with monarchical government. The Great Depression, which ravaged the economy in the 1930s, came as the final shock to an already moribund system.

On June 24, 1932, a small group of middle-ranking officials, led by a lawyer, **Pridi Phanomyong**, and an army major, Luang Phibunsongkhram (**Phibun**), staged a **coup** with only a handful of troops. Prajadhipok weakly submitted to the conspirators, and 150 years of absolute monarchy in Bangkok came to a sudden end. The king was sidelined to a position of symbolic significance, and in 1935 he abdicated in favour of his ten-year-old nephew, **Ananda**, then a schoolboy living in Switzerland.

Up to World War II

The success of the 1932 coup was in large measure attributable to the army officers who gave the conspirators credibility, and it was they who were to dominate the constitutional governments that followed. Phibun emerged as prime minister after the decisive elections of 1938, and encouraged a wave of nationalistic feeling with such measures as the official institution of the name Thailand in 1939 – Siam, it was argued, was a name bestowed by external forces, and the new title made it clear that the country belonged to the Thais rather than the economically dominant Chinese.

The Thais were dragged into **World War II** on December 8, 1941, when, almost at the same time as the assault on Pearl Harbor, the Japanese invaded the east coast of peninsular Thailand, with their sights set on Singapore to the south. The Thais at first resisted fiercely, but realizing that the position was hopeless, Phibun quickly ordered a ceasefire.

The Thai government concluded a military alliance with Japan and declared war against the United States and Great Britain in January 1942, probably in the belief that the Japanese would win. However, the Thai minister in Washington, Seni Pramoj, refused to deliver the declaration of war against the US and, in co-operation with the Americans, began organizing a resistance movement called **Seri Thai**. Pridi Phanomyong, now acting as regent to the young king, furtively co-ordinated the movement under the noses of the occupying Japanese, smuggling in American agents and housing them in a European prison camp in Bangkok.

By 1944 Japan's defeat looked likely, and in July Phibun, who had been most closely associated with them, was forced to resign by the National Assembly. Once the war was over, American support prevented the British from imposing heavy punishments on the country for its alliance with Japan.

Postwar upheavals

With the fading of the military, the election of January 1946 was for the first time contested by organized political parties, resulting in Pridi becoming prime minister. A new constitution was drafted, and the outlook for democratic, civilian government seemed bright. Hopes were shattered, however, on June 9, 1946, when King Ananda was found dead in his bed, with a bullet wound in his forehead. Three palace servants were hurriedly tried and executed, but the murder has never been satisfactorily explained. Pridi resigned as prime minister, and in April 1948 Phibun, playing on the threat of communism, took over the premiership.

As communism developed its hold in the region with the takeover of China in 1949 and the French defeat in Indochina in 1954, the US increasingly viewed Thailand as a bulwark against the red menace. Between 1951 and 1957, when its annual state budget was only about $200 million a year, Thailand received a total $149 million in American economic aid and $222 million in military aid. This strengthened Phibun's dictatorship, while enabling leading military figures to divert American money and other funds into their own pockets.

Phibun narrowly won a general election in 1957, but only by blatant vote rigging and coercion. Although there's a strong tradition of foul play in Thai elections, this is remembered as the dirtiest ever: after vehement public outcry, **General Sarit**, the commander-in-chief of the army, overthrew the new government in September 1957. Believing that Thailand would prosper best under a unifying authority, Sarit set about re-establishing the monarchy as the head of the social hierarchy and the source of legitimacy for the government. Ananda's successor, **Bhumibol** (Rama IX), was pushed into an active role, while Sarit ruthlessly silenced critics and pressed ahead with a plan for economic development, achieving a large measure of stability and prosperity.

The Vietnam War

Sarit died in 1963, whereupon the military succession passed to **General Thanom**. His most pressing problem was the **Vietnam War**. The Thais, with the backing of the US, quietly began to conduct military operations in Laos, to which North Vietnam and China responded by supporting anti-government insurgency in Thailand. The more the Thais felt threatened by the spread of communism, the more they looked to the Americans for help – by 1968 around 45,000 US military personnel were on Thai soil, which became the base for US bombing raids against North Vietnam and Laos.

The effects of the **American presence** were profound. The economy swelled with dollars, and hundreds of thousands of Thais became reliant on the Americans for a living, with a consequent proliferation of prostitution – centred on Bangkok's infamous Patpong district – and corruption. What's more, the sudden exposure to Western culture led many to question traditional Thai values and the political status quo.

The democracy movement and civil unrest

Poor farmers in particular were becoming increasingly disillusioned with their lot, and many turned against the Bangkok government. At the end of 1964, the

Communist Party of Thailand and other groups formed a **broad left coalition** which soon had the support of several thousand insurgents in remote areas of the northeast and the north. By 1967, a separate threat had arisen in southern Thailand, involving **Muslim dissidents** and the Chinese-dominated **Communist Party of Malaya**, as well as local Thais.

Thanom was now facing a major security crisis, especially as the war in Vietnam was going badly. In November 1971 he imposed repressive military rule. In response, **student demonstrations** began in June 1973, and in October as many as 500,000 people turned out at Thammasat University in Bangkok to demand a new constitution. Clashes with the police ensued but elements in the army, backed by King Bhumibol, prevented Thanom from crushing the protest with troops. On October 14, 1973, Thanom was forced to resign and leave the country.

In a new climate of openness, **Kukrit Pramoj** formed a coalition of seventeen elected parties and secured a promise of US withdrawal from Thailand, but his government was riven with feuding. In October 1976, the students demonstrated again, protesting against the return of Thanom to Bangkok to become a monk at Wat Bowonniwet. This time there was no restraint: supported by elements of the military and the government, the police and reactionary students launched a massive assault on Thammasat University. On October 6, hundreds of students were brutally beaten, scores were lynched and some even burned alive; the military took control and suspended the constitution.

Premocracy

Soon after, the military-appointed prime minister, **Thanin Kraivichien**, forced dissidents to undergo anti-communist indoctrination, but his measures seem to have been too repressive even for the military, who forced him to resign in October 1977. **General Kriangsak Chomanand** took over, and began to break up the insurgency with shrewd offers of amnesty. He in turn was displaced in February 1980 by **General Prem Tinsulanonda**, backed by a broad parliamentary coalition.

Untainted by corruption, Prem achieved widespread support, including that of the monarchy. Overseeing a period of rapid economic growth, Prem maintained the premiership until 1988, with a unique mixture of dictatorship and democracy sometimes called **Premocracy**: although never standing for parliament himself, Prem was asked by the legislature after every election to become prime minister. He eventually stepped down because, he said, it was time for the country's leader to be chosen from among its elected representatives.

The 1992 demonstrations

The new prime minister was indeed an elected MP, **Chatichai Choonhavan**, a retired general with a long civilian career in public office. He pursued a vigorous policy of economic development, but this fostered widespread corruption, in which members of the government were often implicated. Following an economic downturn and Chatichai's attempts to downgrade the political role of the military, the armed forces staged a bloodless **coup** on February 23, 1991, led by Supreme Commander **Sunthorn** and General **Suchinda**, the army commander-in-chief, who became premier.

When Suchinda reneged on promises to make democratic amendments to the constitution, hundreds of thousands of ordinary Thais poured onto the streets around Bangkok's Democracy Monument in **mass demonstrations** between May 17 and 20, 1992. Hopelessly misjudging the mood of the country, Suchinda brutally crushed the protests, leaving hundreds dead or injured. Having justified the massacre on the grounds that he was protecting the king from communist agitators, Suchinda was forced to resign when King Bhumibol expressed his disapproval in a ticking-off that was broadcast on world television.

Chuan, Banharn and Chavalit

In the elections on September 13, 1992, the **Democrat Party**, led by **Chuan Leekpai**, a noted upholder of democracy and the rule of law, gained the largest number of parliamentary seats. Despite many successes through a period of continued economic growth, he was able to hold onto power only until July 1995, when he was forced to call new elections.

Chart Thai and its leader, **Banharn Silpa-archa** – nicknamed by the local press the "walking ATM", a reference to his reputation for buying votes – emerged victorious. Allegations of corruption soon mounted against Banharn and in the following year he was obliged to dissolve parliament.

In November 1996, **General Chavalit Yongchaiyudh**, leader of the **New Aspiration Party** (NAP), just won what was dubbed the most corrupt election in Thai history, with an estimated 25 million baht spent on vote-buying in rural areas. The most significant positive event of his tenure was the approval of a **new constitution**. Drawn up by an independent drafting assembly, its main points included: direct elections to the senate, rather than appointment of senators by the prime minister; acceptance of the right of assembly as the basis of a democratic society and guarantees of individual rights and freedoms; greater public accountability; and increased popular participation in local administration. The eventual aim of the new charter was to end the traditional system of patronage, vested interests and vote-buying.

The economic crisis

At the start of Chavalit's premiership, the Thai economy was already on shaky ground. In February 1997 foreign-exchange dealers began to mount speculative **attacks on the baht**, alarmed at the size of Thailand's private foreign debt – 250 billion baht in the unproductive property sector alone, much of it accrued through the proliferation of prestigious skyscrapers in Bangkok. The government valiantly defended the pegged exchange rate, spending $23 billion of the country's formerly healthy foreign-exchange reserves, but at the beginning of July was forced to give up the ghost – the baht was floated and soon went into free-fall.

Blaming its traditional allies the Americans for neglecting their obligations, Thailand sought help from Japan; Tokyo suggested the **IMF**, who in August put together a $17 billion **rescue package** for Thailand. Among the conditions of the package, the Thai government was to slash the national budget, control inflation and open up financial institutions to foreign ownership.

Chavalit's performance in the face of the crisis was viewed as inept, more concerned with personal interests and political game-playing than managing the economy properly. In November he resigned, to be succeeded by **Chuan Leekpai**, who took up what was widely seen as a poisoned chalice for his second term.

Chuan's second term

Chuan immediately took a hard line to try to restore confidence in the economy: he followed the IMF's advice, which involved maintaining cripplingly high interest rates to protect the baht, and pledged to reform the financial system. Although this played well abroad, at home the government encountered increasing hostility. Unemployment, which had been as low as 1 million before the crisis, edged past 2 million by mid-1998 – huge numbers of jobless workers were returning to their villages and swelling the ranks of the country's 6–8 million people living on the fringes of poverty. Inflation peaked at ten percent, and there were frequent public protests against the IMF.

By the end of 1998, however, Chuan's tough stance was paying off, with the baht stabilizing at just under 40 to the US dollar, and interest rates and inflation starting to fall. Foreign investors slowly began returning to Thailand, and by October 1999 Chuan was confident enough to announce that he was forgoing almost $4 billion of the IMF's planned rescue package.

The 2001 general election

The year 2000 was dominated by the build-up to the **general election**, with Chuan eventually setting the polls for January 6, 2001. It was to be the first such vote held under the 1997 constitution, which was intended to take the traditionally crucial role of money, especially for vote-buying, out of politics. However, this election coincided with the emergence of a major new party, **Thai Rak Thai** (Thai Loves Thai), formed by one of Thailand's wealthiest men, telecoms tycoon **Thaksin Shinawatra**.

Although Thaksin denied the money attraction, over one hundred MPs from other parties, including the ruling Democrats, were drawn to Thai Rak Thai as the dissolution of parliament approached. However, in September 2000, the **National Counter-Corruption Commission** announced an investigation into Thaksin's affairs, citing a failure to disclose fully his business interests in a declaration of assets when he joined Chavalit's 1997 government. The NCCC also wanted to know how members of Thaksin's household – including his maid, nanny, driver and security guard – came to hold over one billion baht's worth of stock in his businesses.

Campaigning proceeded largely regardless of the investigation, but despite the prospect of stronger anti-corruption enforcement under the new constitution, allegations of irregularities had been made against around a hundred candidates even before election day. In Bangkok, during the night before the vote, dogs were heard to howl even louder than ever – an election phenomenon Thais attribute to the commotion created by campaign bagmen on last-minute rounds. As expected, Thaksin achieved a sweeping victory, entering into a coalition with Chart Thai and New Aspiration and thus controlling 325 seats out of a possible 500.

Instead of a move towards greater democracy, as envisioned by the 1997 constitution, Thaksin's new government seemed to represent a full-blown merger between politics and big business, concentrating economic power in even fewer hands. His first cabinet was a motley crew of old-style vested interests, including former PM Chavalit, credited with having sparked Thailand's economic crisis, as deputy premier and defence minister. The regime got off to an inauspicious start: in early March: an explosion ripped through a plane at Bangkok airport on which Thaksin was meant to be travelling, killing a member of the cabin crew. At the time of writing, it appears to have been a terrible accident involving an exploding fuel tank, rather than an assassination attempt. As this book went to press, it was announced that Thaksin had beencleared of a corruption charge by a narrow margin of 8-7 in the Constitutional Court.

Religion: Thai Buddhism

Over ninety percent of Thais consider themselves Theravada Buddhists, followers of the teachings of a holy man usually referred to as the Buddha (Enlightened One), though more precisely known as Gautama Buddha to distinguish him from three lesser-known Buddhas who preceded him, and from the fifth and final Buddha who is predicted to arrive in the·year 4457 AD. Theravada Buddhism is one of the two main schools of Buddhism practised in Asia, and in Thailand it has absorbed an eclectic assortment of animist and Hindu elements into its beliefs as well. The other ten percent of Thailand's population comprises Mahayana Buddhists, Muslims, Hindus, Sikhs and Christians.

The Buddha: his life and beliefs

Buddhists believe that Gautama Buddha was the five-hundredth incarnation of a single being: the stories of these five hundred lives, collectively known as the **Jataka**, provide the inspiration for much Thai art.

In his last incarnation he was born in Nepal as **Prince Gautama Siddhartha** in either the sixth or seventh century BC. Astrologers predicted that Gautama was to become universally respected, either as a worldly king or as a spiritual saviour, depending on which way of life he pursued. Much preferring the former idea, the prince's father forbade the boy to leave the palace grounds, and took it upon himself to educate Gautama in all aspects of the high life. Most statues of the Buddha depict him with elongated earlobes, a reference to his pampered early life, when he would have worn heavy precious stones in his ears.

The prince married and became a father, but at the age of 29 he flouted his father's authority and sneaked out into the world beyond the palace. On this fateful trip he encountered successively an old man, a sick man, a corpse and a hermit, and was thus made aware for the first time that pain and suffering were intrinsic to human life. Contemplation seemed the only means of discovering why this should be so – and therefore Gautama decided to leave the palace and become a **Hindu ascetic**.

For six or seven years he wandered the countryside leading a life of self-denial and self-mortification, but failed to come any closer to the answer. Eventually concluding that the best course of action must be to follow a "Middle Way" – neither indulgent nor overly ascetic – Gautama sat down beneath the famous riverside bodhi tree at Bodh Gaya in India, facing the rising sun, to meditate until he achieved enlightenment. For 49 days he sat crosslegged in the "lotus position", contemplating the causes of suffering and wrestling with temptations that materialized to distract him, until at last he attained **enlightenment** and so became a Buddha.

The Buddha preached his **first sermon** in a deer park in India, where he characterized his Dharma (doctrine) as a wheel; Thais celebrate this event with a public holiday in

THE BUDDHA: HIS LIFE AND BELIEFS

317

July known as Asanha Puja. On another occasion 1250 people spontaneously gathered to hear the Buddha speak, an event remembered in Thailand as Maha Puja and marked by a public holiday in February. For the next forty-odd years the Buddha travelled the region, converting non-believers and performing miracles.

The Buddha "died" at the age of 80 on the banks of a river at Kusinari in India – an event often dated to 543 BC, which is why the Thai calendar is 543 years out of synch with the Western one. Lying on his side, propping up his head on his hand, the Buddha passed into **Nirvana** (giving rise to the classic pose, the Reclining Buddha), the unimaginable state of nothingness which knows no suffering and from which there is no reincarnation. Buddhists believe that the day the Buddha entered Nirvana was the same date on which he was born and he achieved enlightenment, a triply significant day that Thais honour with the Visakha Puja festival in May.

Buddhist doctrine

After the Buddha entered Nirvana, his **doctrine** spread relatively quickly across India, and probably was first promulgated in Thailand around the third century BC. His teachings, the *Tripitaka*, were written down in the Pali language – a derivative of Sanskrit – in a form that became known as Theravada or "The Doctrine of the Elders".

As taught by the Buddha, **Theravada Buddhism** built on the Hindu theory of perpetual reincarnation in the pursuit of perfection, introducing the notion of life as a cycle of suffering which could only be transcended by enlightened beings able to free themselves from earthly ties and enter into the blissful state of Nirvana. For the well-behaved but unenlightened Buddhist, each reincarnation marks a move up a vague kind of ladder, with animals at the bottom, women figuring lower down than men, and monks coming at the top – a hierarchy complicated by the very pragmatic notion that the more comfortable your lifestyle, the higher your spiritual status.

The Buddhist has no hope of enlightenment without acceptance of the **four noble truths**. In encapsulated form, these hold that desire is the root cause of all suffering and can be extinguished only by following the eightfold path or Middle Way. This **Middle Way** is essentially a highly moral mode of life that includes all the usual virtues like compassion, respect and moderation, and eschews vices such as self-indulgence and anti-social behaviour. But the key to it all is an acknowledgement that the physical world is impermanent and ever-changing, and that all things – including the self – are therefore not worth craving. Only by pursuing a condition of complete **detachment** can human beings transcend earthly suffering.

Buddhist practice

In practice most Thai Buddhists aim only to be **reborn** higher up the incarnation scale rather than set their sights on the ultimate goal of Nirvana. The rank of the reincarnation is directly related to the good and bad actions performed in the previous life, which accumulate to determine one's **karma** or destiny – hence the Thai obsession with "merit-making".

Merit-making (*tham bun*) can be done in all sorts of ways, from giving a monk his breakfast to attending a Buddhist service or donating money to the neighbourhood temple, and most festivals are essentially communal merit-making opportunities. For a Thai man, temporary ordination (see box on p.320) is a very important way of accruing merit not only for himself but also for his mother and sisters – wealthier citizens might take things a step further by commissioning the casting of a Buddha statue or even paying for the building of a wat.

BUDDHIST PRACTICE

THE MONKHOOD

In Thailand it's the duty of the 200,000-strong **Sangha** (monkhood) to set an example to the Theravada Buddhist community, by living a life as close to the Middle Way as possible and by preaching the Dharma to the people. Always the most respected members of any community, monks also act as teachers, counsellors and arbiters in local disputes. Although some Thai women do become nuns, they belong to no official order and aren't respected as much as the monks.

A monk's life is governed by 227 strict rules that include celibacy and the rejection of all personal possessions except gifts. Each day begins with an alms round in the neighbourhood so that the laity can donate food and thereby gain themselves merit (see p.319), and then is chiefly spent in meditation, chanting, teaching and study.

Monkhood doesn't have to be for life: a man may leave the *Sangha* three times without stigma and in fact every Thai male (including royalty) is expected to **enter the monkhood** for a short period at some point in his life, ideally between leaving school and marrying, as a rite of passage into adulthood. So ingrained into the social system is this practice that nearly all Thai companies grant their employees paid leave for their time as a monk. The most popular time for temporary ordination is the three-month Buddhist retreat period – **Pansa**, sometimes referred to as "Buddhist Lent" – which begins in July and lasts for the duration of the rainy season. **Ordination ceremonies** take place in almost every wat at this time and make spectacular scenes, with the shaven-headed novice usually clad entirely in white and carried about on friends' or relatives' shoulders. The boys' parents donate money, food and necessities such as washing powder and mosquito repellent, processing around the temple compound with their gifts, often joined by dancers or travelling players hired for the occasion.

One of the more bizarre but common merit-making activities involves **releasing caged birds**: worshippers buy one or more tiny finches from vendors at wat compounds and, by liberating them from their cage, prove their Buddhist compassion towards all living things. The fact that the birds were free until netted earlier that morning doesn't seem to detract from the ritual at all. In riverside and seaside wats, birds are sometimes replaced by fish or even baby turtles.

Spirits and non-Buddhist deities

While regular Buddhist merit-making insures a Thai for the next life, there are certain **Hindu gods** and **animist spirits** that most Thais also cultivate for help with more immediate problems. Sophisticated Bangkokians and illiterate farmers alike will find no inconsistency in these apparently incompatible practices, and as often as not it's a Buddhist monk who is called in to exorcize a malevolent spirit. Even the Buddhist King Bhumibol employs Brahmin priests and astrologers to determine auspicious days and officiate at certain royal ceremonies and, like his royal predecessors of the Chakri dynasty, he also associates himself with the Hindu god Vishnu by assuming the title Rama, after the seventh avatar of Vishnu and hero of the Hindu epic the *Ramayana*.

If a Thai wants help in achieving a short-term goal, like passing an exam, becoming pregnant or winning the lottery, then he or she will quite likely turn to the **Hindu pantheon**, visiting an enshrined statue of either Brahma, Vishnu, Shiva, Indra or Ganesh, and making offerings of flowers, incense and maybe food. If the outcome is favourable, devotees will probably come back to show thanks, bringing more offerings and maybe even hiring a dance troupe to perform a celebratory *lakhon chatri* as well.

Built in honour of Brahma, Bangkok's Erawan Shrine is the most famous place of Hindu-inspired worship in the country.

Whereas Hindu deities tend to be benevolent, **spirits** (*phi*) are not nearly as reliable and need to be mollified more frequently. They come in hundreds of varieties, some more malign than others, and inhabit everything from trees, rivers and caves to public buildings and private homes – even taking over people if they feel like it. So that these *phi* don't pester human inhabitants, each building has a special **spirit house** in its vicinity, as a dwelling for spirits ousted by the building's construction.

Usually raised on a short column and designed to look like a wat or a traditional Thai house, these spirit houses are generally about the size of a dolls' house, but their ornamentation is supposed to reflect the status of the humans' building – thus if that building is enlarged or refurbished, then the spirit house should be improved accordingly. Daily offerings of incense, lighted candles and garlands of jasmine are placed inside the spirit house to keep the *phi* happy – a disgruntled spirit is a dangerous spirit, liable to cause sickness, accidents and even death.

Art and architecture

A side from pockets of Hindu-inspired statuary and architecture, the vast majority of Thailand's cultural monuments take their inspiration from Theravada Buddhism, and so it is **temples** and **religious images** that constitute Bangkok's main sights. Few of these can be attributed to any individual artist, but with a little background information it becomes fairly easy to recognize the major artistic styles. Though Bangkok's temples nearly all date from the eighteenth century or later, many of them display features that originate from a much earlier time. The National Museum (see p.87) is a good place to see some of Thailand's more ancient Hindu and Buddhist statues, and a visit to the fourteenth-century ruins at Ayutthaya (see p.263), less than two hours from Bangkok, is also recommended.

The wat

The **wat** or Buddhist temple complex has a great range of uses, as home to a monastic community, a place of public worship, a shrine for holy images and a shaded meeting place for townspeople and villagers. Wat architecture has evolved in ways as various as its functions, but there remain several essential components which have stayed constant for some fifteen centuries.

The most important wat building is the **bot** (sometimes known as the *ubosot*), a term most accurately translated as the "ordination hall". It usually stands at the heart of the compound and is the preserve of the monks: lay persons are rarely allowed inside, and it's generally kept locked when not in use. There's only one bot in any wat complex, and often the only way to distinguish it from other temple buildings is by the eight **sema** or boundary stones which always surround it.

Often almost identical to the bot, the **viharn** or assembly hall is for the lay congregation, and as a tourist this is the building you're most likely to enter, since it usually contains the wat's principal **Buddha image**, and sometimes two or three minor images as well. Large wats may have several viharns, while strict meditation wats, which don't deal with the laity, may not have one at all.

Thirdly, there's the **chedi** or stupa, a tower which was originally conceived as a monument to enshrine relics of the Buddha, but has since become a place to contain the ashes of royalty – and anyone else who can afford it.

Buddhist iconography

In the early days of Buddhism, image-making was considered inadequate to convey the faith's abstract philosophies, so the only approved iconography comprised doctrinal **symbols** such as the Dharmachakra (Wheel of Law, also known as Wheel of Doctrine or Wheel of Life). Gradually these symbols were displaced by **images of the Buddha**, construed chiefly as physical embodiments of the Buddha's teachings rather than as portraits of the man.

Of the four postures in which the Buddha is always depicted – sitting, standing, walking and reclining – the **seated Buddha**, which represents him in meditation, is the most common in Thailand. A popular variation shows the Buddha seated on a coiled serpent, protected by the serpent's hood – a reference to the story about the Buddha meditating during the rainy season, when a serpent offered to raise him off the wet ground and shelter him from the storms. The **reclining** pose symbolizes the Buddha entering Nirvana at his death, while the **standing** and **walking** images both represent his descent from Tavatimsa heaven.

Hindu iconography

Hindu images tend to be a lot livelier than Buddhist ones, partly because there is a panoply of gods to choose from, and partly because these gods have mischievous personalities and reappear in all sorts of bizarre incarnations.

Vishnu has always been especially popular: his role of "Preserver" has him embodying the status quo, representing both stability and the notion of altruistic love. He is most often depicted as the deity, but frequently crops up in other human and animal incarnations. There are ten of these manifestations (or avatars) in all, of which **Rama** (number seven) is by far the most popular in Thailand. The epitome of ideal manhood, Rama is the super-hero of the epic story the *Ramayana* (see p.74) and appears in storytelling reliefs and murals in every Hindu temple in Thailand; in painted portraits you can usually recognize him by his green face. Manifestation number eight is **Krishna**, more widely known than Rama in the West, but slightly less common in Thailand. Krishna is usually characterized as a flirtatious, flute-playing, blue-skinned cowherd and is a crucial moral figure in the *Mahabarata*. Confusingly, Vishnu's ninth avatar is the **Buddha** – a manifestation adopted many centuries ago to minimize defection to the Buddhist faith.

When represented as the **deity**, Vishnu is generally shown sporting a crown and four arms, his hands holding a conch shell (whose music wards off demons), a discus (used as a weapon), a club (symbolizing the power of nature and time), and a lotus (symbol of joyful flowering and renewal). The god is often depicted astride a **garuda**, a half-man, half-bird creature.

Statues and representations of **Brahma** (the Creator) are very rare. Confusingly, he too has four arms, but you should recognize him by the fact that he holds no objects, has four faces (sometimes painted red), and is generally borne by a goose-like creature called a *hamsa*.

Shiva (the Destroyer) is the most volatile member of the pantheon. He stands for extreme behaviour, for beginnings and endings, and for fertility, and is a symbol of great energy and power. His godlike form typically has four, eight or ten arms, sometimes holding a trident (representing creation, protection and destruction) and a drum (to beat the rhythm of creation). In abstract form, he is represented by a **lingam** or phallic pillar.

Close associates of Shiva include **Parvati**, his wife, and **Ganesh**, his elephant-headed son. Depictions of Ganesh abound, both as statues and, because he is the god of knowledge and overcomer of obstacles (in the path of learning), as the symbol of the Fine Arts Department – which crops up on all entrance tickets to museums and historical parks.

Lesser mythological figures include the **yaksha** giants who ward off evil spirits (like the enormous freestanding ones guarding Bangkok's Wat Phra Kaeo); the graceful half-woman, half-bird **kinnari**; and the ubiquitous **naga**, or serpent king of the underworld, often depicted with seven heads.

The schools

For Thailand's architects and sculptors, the act of creation was an act of merit and a representation of unchanging truths, rather than an act of expression, and thus Thai art history is characterized by broad schools rather than individual names. In the 1920s art historians and academics began to classify these schools along the lines of the country's historical periods.

Dvaravati (sixth–eleventh centuries)

Centred around Nakhon Pathom, U Thong, Lopburi and Haripunjaya (modern-day Lamphun), the Dvaravati state was populated by Theravada Buddhists who were strongly influenced by Indian culture.

In an effort to combat the defects inherent in the poor-quality limestone at their disposal, Dvaravati-era **sculptors** made their Buddhas quite stocky, cleverly dressing the figures in a sheet-like drape that dropped down to ankle level from each raised wrist, forming a U-shaped hemline – a style which they used when casting in bronze as well. Nonetheless many **statues** have cracked, leaving them headless or limbless. Where the faces have survived, Dvaravati statues display some of the most naturalistic features ever produced in Thailand, distinguished by their thick lips, flattened noses and wide cheekbones.

Srivijaya (eighth–thirteenth centuries)

While Dvaravati's Theravada Buddhists were influencing the central plains, southern Thailand was paying allegiance to the Mahayana Buddhists of the **Srivijayan** empire. Mahayanists believe that those who have achieved enlightenment should postpone their entry into Nirvana in order to help others along the way. These stay-behinds, revered like saints both during and after life, are called

bodhisattva, and statues of them were the mainstay of Srivijayan art.

The finest Srivijayan *bodhisattva* statues were cast in bronze and show such grace and sinuosity that they rank among the finest sculpture ever produced in the country. Many are lavishly adorned, and some were even bedecked in real jewels when first made. By far the most popular *bodhisattva* subject was **Avalokitesvara**, worshipped as compassion incarnate and generally shown with four or more arms and clad in an animal skin. Bangkok's National Museum holds a beautiful example.

Khmer and Lopburi (tenth–fourteenth centuries)

By the end of the ninth century the **Khmers** of Cambodia were starting to expand from their capital at Angkor into the Dvaravati states, bringing with them the Hindu faith and the cult of the god-king (*devaraja*). As lasting testaments to the sacred power of their kings, the Khmers built hundreds of imposing stone sanctuaries across their newly acquired territory.

Each magnificent castle-temple – known in Khmer as a **prasat** – was constructed primarily as a shrine for a *shiva lingam*, the phallic representation of the god Shiva. Almost every surface of the sanctuary was adorned with intricate **carvings**, usually gouged from sandstone, depicting Hindu deities (notably Vishnu reclining on the milky sea of eternity in the National Museum – see p.87) and stories, especially episodes from the *Ramayana* (see p.74).

During the Khmer period the former Theravada Buddhist principality of **Lopburi** produced a distinctive style of Buddha statue. Broad-faced and muscular, the classic Lopburi Buddha wears a diadem or ornamental headband – a nod to the Khmers' ideological fusion of earthly and heavenly power – and the *ushnisha* (the sign of enlightenment) becomes distinctly conical rather than a mere bump on the head.

THE SCHOOLS

Sukhothai (thirteenth–fifteenth centuries)

Two Thai generals established the first real Thai kingdom in **Sukhothai** in 1238, and over the next two hundred years the artists of this realm produced some of Thailand's most refined art. Sukhothai's artistic reputation rests above all on its **sculpture**. More sinuous even than the Srivijayan images, Sukhothai Buddhas tend towards elegant androgyny, with slim oval faces and slender curvaceous bodies usually clad in a plain, skintight robe that fastens with a tassle close to the navel. Fine examples include the Phra Buddha Chinnarat image at Bangkok's Wat Benchamabophit, and the enormous Phra Sri Sakyamuni, in Bangkok's Wat Suthat. Sukhothai sculptors were the first to represent the walking Buddha, a supremely graceful figure with his right leg poised to move forwards.

Sukhothai era architects also devised a new type of chedi, as elegant in its way as the images their sculptor colleagues were producing. This was the **lotus-bud chedi**, a slender tower topped with a tapered finial that was to become a hallmark of the Sukhothai era.

Ancient Sukhothai is also renowned for the skill of its potters, who produced a **ceramic ware** known as Sawankhalok, after the name of one of the nearby kiln towns. It is distinguished by its grey-green celadon glazes and by the fish and chrysanthemum motifs used to decorate bowls and plates.

Ayutthaya (fourteenth–eighteenth centuries)

From 1351 Thailand's central plains came under the thrall of a new power centred on **Ayutthaya**, and over the next four centuries, the Ayutthayan rulers commissioned some four hundred grand wats as symbols of their wealth and power. Though essentially Theravada Buddhists, the kings also adopted some Hindu and Brahmin beliefs from the Khmers – most significantly the concept of *devaraja* or god-

THE SCHOOLS

kingship, whereby the monarch became a mediator between the people and the Hindu gods.

Retaining the concentric layout of the typical Khmer **temple complex**, Ayutthayan builders refined and elongated the prang into a **corncob-shaped tower**, rounding it off at the top and introducing vertical incisions around its circumference. The most famous example is Bangkok's Wat Arun, which though built during the subsequent Ratanakosin period (see p.331) is a classic Ayutthayan structure.

Ayutthaya's architects also adapted the Sri Lankan **chedi** so favoured by their Sukhothai predecessors, stretching the bell-shaped base and tapering it into a very graceful conical spire, as at Wat Sri Sanphet in Ayutthaya. The **viharns** of this era are characterized by walls pierced by slit-like windows, designed to foster a mysterious atmosphere by limiting the amount of light inside the building; Wat Yai Suwannaram in Phetchaburi has a particularly fine example.

From Sukhothai's Buddha **sculptures** the Ayutthayans copied the soft oval face, adding an earthlier demeanour to the features and imbuing them with a hauteur in tune with the *devaraja* ideology. Like the Lopburi images, early Ayutthayan statues wear crowns to associate kingship with Buddhahood; as the court became ever more lavish, so these figures became increasingly adorned, until – as in the monumental bronze at Wat Na Phra Mane – they appeared in earrings, armlets, anklets, bandoliers and coronets. The artists justified these luscious portraits of the Buddha – who was, after all, supposed to have given up worldly possessions – by pointing to an episode when the Buddha transformed himself into a well-dressed nobleman to gain the ear of a proud emperor, whereupon he scolded the man into entering the monkhood.

Ratanakosin (eighteenth century to the present)

When **Bangkok** emerged as Ayutthaya's successor in 1782, the new capital's founder was determined to revive the old city's grandeur, and the **Ratanakosin** (or Bangkok) period began by aping what the Ayutthayans had done. Since then neither wat architecture nor religious sculpture has evolved much further.

The first **Ratanakosin building** was the bot of Bangkok's Wat Phra Kaeo, built to enshrine the Emerald Buddha. Designed to a typical Ayutthayan plan, it's coated in glittering mirrors and gold leaf, with roofs ranged in multiple tiers and tiled in green and orange. To this day, most newly built bots and viharns follow a more economical version of this paradigm, whitewashing the outside walls but decorating the pediment in gilded ornaments and mosaics of coloured glass. The result is that modern wats are often almost indistinguishable from each other, though Bangkok does have a few exceptions, including Wat Benjamabophit, which uses marble cladding for its walls and incorporates Victorian-style stained-glass windows, and Wat Rajapobhit, which is covered all over in Chinese ceramics.

Early Ratanakosin sculptors produced adorned **Buddha images** very much in the Ayutthayan vein, sometimes adding real jewels to the figures; more modern images are notable for their ugliness rather than for any radical departure from type. The obsession with size, first apparent in the Sukhothai period, has plumbed new depths, with graceless concrete statues up to 60m high becoming the norm (as in Bangkok's Wat Indraviharn), a monumentalism made worse by the routine application of browns and dull yellows. Most small images are cast from or patterned on older models, mostly Sukhothai or Ayutthayan in origin.

THE SCHOOLS

Books

The following books should be available in the UK, US or, more likely, in Bangkok. Publishers' details for books are given in the form "UK publisher; US publisher" where they differ; if books are published in one of these countries only, this follows the publisher's name; if books are published in Thailand, the city follows the publisher's name. The abbreviation "o/p" means out of print – consult a library, specialist secondhand bookseller or online out-of-print-books service.

Travel

James O'Reilly and Larry Habegger (eds), *Travelers' Tales: Thailand* (Travelers' Tales). This volume of lively contemporary writings about Thailand makes perfect background reading for any trip to Bangkok.

Alistair Shearer, *Thailand: the Lotus Kingdom* (o/p in UK and US). Amusing and well-researched contemporary travelogue.

William Warren, *Bangkok's Waterways: An Explorer's Handbook* (Asia Books, Bangkok). A cross between a useful guide and an indulgent coffee-table book; attractively produced survey of the capital's riverine sights, spiced with cultural and historical snippets.

Culture and society

Vatcharin Bhumichitr, *The Taste of Thailand* (Pavilion; Collier, o/p). Glossy introduction to Thai food, including about 150 recipes adapted for Western kitchens.

Michael Carrithers, *The Buddha: A Very Short Introduction* (Oxford Paperbacks). Clear, accessible account of the life of the Buddha, and the development and significance of his thought.

James Eckardt, *Bangkok People* (Asia Books, Bangkok). A renowned expat journalist interviews a gallery of different Bangkokians, from construction-site workers and street vendors to boxers and political candidates.

Sanitsuda Ekachai, *Behind the Smile* (Thai Development Support Committee, Bangkok). Collected articles of a *Bangkok Post* journalist highlighting the effect of Thailand's sudden economic growth on the country's rural poor.

Marlane Guelden, *Thailand: Into the Spirit World* (Times Editions, Bangkok). In richly photographed coffee-table format, a wide-ranging, anecdotal account of the role of magic and spirits in Thai life, from tattoos and amulets to the ghosts of the violently dead.

Sumet Jumsai, *Naga: Cultural Origins in Siam and the West Pacific* (Oxford University Press, o/p). Wide-ranging discussion of water symbols in Thailand and other parts of Asia, offering a stimulating mix of art, architecture, mythology and cosmology.

William J. Klausner, *Reflections on Thai Culture* (Siam Society, Bangkok). Humorous accounts of an anthropologist living in Thailand since 1955.

Cleo Odzer, *Patpong Sisters* (Arcade Publishing). An American anthropologist's funny and touching account of her life with the bar girls of Bangkok's notorious red-light district.

Pasuk Phongpaichit and Sungsidh Piriyarangsan, *Corruption and Democracy in Thailand* (Political Economy Centre, Faculty of Economics, Chulalongkorn University, Bangkok). Fascinating academic study, revealing the nuts and bolts of corruption in Thailand and its links with all levels of political life. The sequel, a study of Thailand's illegal economy, *Guns, Girls, Gambling, Ganja*, co-written with Nualnoi Treerat (Silkworm Books, Chiang Mai) makes equally eye-opening and depressing reading.

Denis Segaller, *Thai Ways* and *More Thai Ways* (Asia Books, Bangkok). Two intriguing anthologies of pieces on Thai customs written by an English resident of Bangkok.

Naengnoi Suksri, The Grand Palace (Thames & Hudson; River Books). Excellent, authoritative and affordable guide, packed with maps, photos and fascinating background details.

Thanh-Dam Truong, *Sex, Money and Morality: Prostitution and Tourism in South-East Asia* (o/p in UK and US). Hard-hitting analysis of the marketing of Thailand as sex-tourism capital of Asia.

Steve van Beek, *The Arts of Thailand* (Thames and Hudson). Lavishly produced introduction to the history of Thai architecture, sculpture and painting, with superb photographs by Luca Invernizzi Tettoni.

William Warren, *Living in Thailand* (Thames and Hudson). Luscious coffee-table volume of traditional houses and furnishings; seductively photographed by Luca Invernizzi Tettoni.

History

Pasuk Phongpaichit and Chris Baker, *Thailand's Crisis* (Silkworm Books, Chiang Mai). Illuminating examination, sometimes heavy going, of the 1997 economic crisis, co-authored by the professor of economics at Bangkok's Chulalongkorn University and a farang freelance writer.

Michael Smithies, *Old Bangkok* (Oxford University Press, o/p). Brief, anecdotal history of the capital's early development, emphasizing what remains to be seen of bygone Bangkok.

William Stevenson, *The Revolutionary King* (Constable, UK). Fascinating biography of the normally secretive King Bhumibol, by a British journalist who was given unprecedented access to the monarch and his family. The overall approach is fairly uncritical, but lots of revealing insights emerge along the way.

John Stewart, *To the River Kwai: Two Journeys – 1943, 1979* (Bloomsbury). A survivor of the horrific World War II POW camps along the River Kwai returns to the region.

William Warren, *Jim Thompson: the Legendary American of Thailand* (Jim Thompson Thai Silk Co, Bangkok). The engrossing biography of the ex-intelligence agent, art collector and Thai silk magnate.

David K. Wyatt, *Thailand: A Short History* (Yale University Press). An excellent treatment, scholarly but highly readable, with a good eye for witty, telling details.

Fiction

Dean Barrett, *Kingdom of Make-Believe* (Village East Books, US). Rewarding novel about a return to Thailand following a twenty-year absence, with engaging characters and a multi-dimensional take on the farang experience.

Botan, *Letters from Thailand* (DK Books, Bangkok). Probably the best introduction to the Chinese community in Bangkok, presented in the form of letters written over a twenty-year period by a Chinese emigrant to his mother.

Alex Garland, *The Beach* (Penguin; Riverhead). Gripping and hugely enjoyable thriller about a young Brit who gets involved with a group of travellers living a utopian existence on an uninhabited Thai island.

Khammaan Khonkhai, *The Teachers of Mad Dog Swamp* (Silkworm Books, Chiang Mai). The engaging story of a young teacher who encounters opposition to his progressive ideas when he is posted to a remote village school in the northeast.

FICTION

Chart Korpjitti, *The Judgement* (Thai Modern Classics). Sobering modern-day tragedy about a good-hearted Thai villager who is ostracized by his hypocritical neighbours. Winner of the SEAwrite award in 1982.

Christopher G Moore, *God Of Darkness* (Asia Books, Bangkok). Intricately woven thriller set during Thailand's 1997 economic crisis, with plenty of detail on endemic corruption and the desperate struggle for power within family and society.

Rama I, *Thai Ramayana* (Chalermnit, Bangkok). Slightly stilted prose translation of King Rama I's version of the epic Hindu narrative.

Khamsing Srinawk, *The Politician and Other Stories* (Oxford University Press, o/p). A collection of brilliantly satiric short stories, which capture the vulnerability of Thailand's peasant farmers as they try to come to grips with the modern world.

Language

T hai belongs to one of the oldest families of languages in the world, Austro-Thai, and is radically different from many of the other tongues of Southeast Asia. Being tonal, Thai is difficult for Westerners to master, but by building up from a small core of set phrases, you'll quickly pick up enough to get by. Most Thais who deal with tourists speak some English, but you'll impress and get better treatment if you at least make an effort to speak a few words.

Thai script is even more of a problem to Westerners, with 44 consonants to represent 21 consonant sounds and 32 vowels to deal with 48 different vowel sounds. However, street signs in Bangkok are nearly always written in Roman script as well as Thai, and in other circumstances you're better off asking than trying to unscramble the swirling mess of symbols, signs and accents.

For the basics, the most useful **language book** on the market is *Thai: A Rough Guide Phrasebook*, which covers the essential phrases and expressions in both Thai script and phonetic equivalents, as well as dipping into grammar and providing a menu reader and fuller vocabulary in dictionary format (English–Thai and Thai–English). Among pocket dictionaries available in Bangkok, G.H. Allison's *Mini English–Thai and Thai–English Dictionary* (Chalermnit) has the edge over *Robertson's Practical English–Thai Dictionary* (Asia Books), although it's more difficult to find. The best **teach-yourself course** is the expensive *Linguaphone Thai*, which includes six cassettes.

Pronunciation

Mastering **tones** is probably the most difficult part of learning Thai. Five different tones are used – low, middle, high, falling, and rising – by which the meaning of a single syllable can be altered in five different ways. Thus, using four of the five tones, you can make a sentence just from just one syllable: *mái mài mâi mãi* – "New wood burns, doesn't it?" As well as the natural difficulty in becoming attuned to speaking and listening to these different tones, Western efforts are complicated by our tendency to denote the overall meaning of a sentence by modulating our tones – for example, turning a statement into a question through a shift of stress and tone. Listen to native Thai speakers and you'll soon begin to pick up the different approach to tone.

The pitch of each tone is gauged in relation to your vocal range when speaking, but they should all lie within a narrow band, separated by gaps just big enough to differentiate them. The **low tones** (syllables marked `) , **middle tones** (unmarked syllables), and **high tones** (syllables marked ´) should each be pronounced evenly and with no inflection. The **falling tone** (syllables marked ^) is spoken with an obvious drop in pitch, as if you were sharply emphasizing a word in English. The **rising tone** (marked ~) is pronounced as if you were asking an exaggerated question in English.

As well as the unfamiliar tones, you'll find that, despite the best efforts of the transliterators, there is no precise English equivalent to many **vowel and consonant**

sounds in the Thai language. The lists that follow give a rough idea of pronunciation.

Vowels

a as in dad.

aa has no precise equivalent, but is pronounced as it looks, with the vowel elongated.

ae as in there.

ai as in buy.

ao as in now.

aw as in awe.

e as in pen.

eu as in sir, but heavily nasalized.

i as in tip.

ii as in feet.

o as in knock.

oe as in hurt, but more closed.

oh as in toe.

u as in loot.

uay "u" plus "ay" as in pay.

uu as in pool.

Consonants

r as in rip, but with the tongue flapped quickly against the palate – in everyday speech, it's often pronounced like "l".

kh as in keep.

ph as in put.

th as in time.

k is unaspirated and unvoiced, and closer to "g".

p is also unaspirated and unvoiced, and closer to "b".

t is also unaspirated and unvoiced, and closer to "d".

THAI WORDS AND PHRASES

Greetings and basic phrases

Whenever you speak to a stranger in Thailand, you should end your sentence in *khráp* if you're a man, *khâ* if you're a woman – these untranslatable politening syllables will gain goodwill, and should always be used after *sawàt dii* (hello/goodbye) and *khàwp khun* (thank you). *Khráp* and *khâ* are also often used to answer "yes" to a question, though the most common way is to repeat the verb of the question (precede it with *mâi* for "no"). *Châi* (yes) and *mâi châi* (no) are less frequently used than their English equivalents.

Hello	*sawàt dii*
Where are you going? (not always meant literally, but used as a general greeting)	*pai nǎi?*
I'm out having fun/ I'm travelling (answer to *pai nǎi*, almost indefinable pleasantry)	*pai thîaw*
Goodbye	*sawàt dii/la kàwn*
Good luck/cheers	*chôk dii*
Excuse me	*khǎw thâwt*
Thank you	*khàwp khun*
It's nothing/it doesn't matter/ no problem	*mâi pen rai*
How are you?	*sabai dii reǔ?*
I'm fine	*sabai dii*
What's your name?	*khun chêu arai?*
My name is . . .	*phǒm (men)/diichǎn (women) chêu . . .*

I come from . . .	*phŏm/diichăn maa jàak . . .*
I don't understand	*mâi khâo jai*
Do you speak English?	*khun phûut phasăa angkrit dâi măi?*
Do you have . . . ?	*mii . . . măi?*
Is there . . . ?	*. . . mii măi?*
Is . . . possible?	*. . . dâi măi?*
Can you help me?	*chûay phŏm/diichăn dâi măi?*
(I) want . . .	*ao . . .*
(I) would like to . . .	*yàak jà . . .*
(I) like . . .	*châwp . . .*
What is this called in Thai?	*nĩi phasăa thai rîak wâa arai?*

Getting around

Where is the . . . ?	*. . . yùu thĩi năi?*
How far?	*klai thâo rai?*
I would like to go to . . .	*yàak jà pai . . .*
Where have you been?	*pai năi maa?*
Where is this bus going?	*rót nĩi pai năi?*
When will the bus leave?	*rót jà àwk mêua rai?*
What time does the bus arrive in . . . ?	*rót thẽ̄ung . . . kìi mohng?*
Stop here	*jàwt thĩi nĩi*
here	*thĩi nĩi*
over there	*thĩi nâan/thĩi nôhn*
right	*khwăa*
left	*sái*
straight	*trong*
near/far	*klâi/klai*
street	*thanŏn*
train station	*sathàanii rót fai*
bus station	*sathàanii rót meh*
airport	*sanăam bin*

ticket	*tŭa*
hotel	*rohng raem*
post office	*praisanii*
restaurant	*raan ahăan*
shop	*raan*
market	*talàat*
hospital	*rohng pha-yaabaan*
motorbike	*rót mohtoesai*
taxi	*rót táksîi*
boat	*reua*

Accommodation and shopping

How much is . . . ?	*. . . thâo rai/kìi bàat?*
How much is a room here per night?	*hâwng thîi nîi kheun lá thâo rai?*
Do you have a cheaper room?	*mii hâwng thùuk kwàa măi?*
Can I/we look at the room?	*duu hâwng dâi măi?*
I/We'll stay two nights	*jà yùu săwng kheun*
Can you reduce the price?	*lót raakhaa dâi măi?*
cheap/expensive	*thùuk/phaeng*
air-con room	*hâwng ae*
ordinary room	*hâwng thammadaa*
telephone	*thohrásàp*
laundry	*sák phâa*
blanket	*phâa hòm*
fan	*phát lom*

General adjectives

alone	*khon diaw*
another	*ìik . . . nèung*
bad	*mâi dii*
big	*yài*
clean	*sa-àat*

closed	*pìt*
cold (object)	*yen*
cold (person or weather)	*nǎo*
delicious	*aròi*
difficult	*yâak*
dirty	*sokaprok*
easy	*ngâi*
fun	*sanùk*
hot (temperature)	*ráwn*
hot (spicy)	*pèt*
hungry	*hiǔ khâo*
ill	*mâi sabai*
open	*pòet*
pretty	*sǔay*
small	*lek*
thirsty	*hiǔ nám*
tired	*nèu-ai*
very	*mâak*

General nouns

Nouns have no plurals or genders, and don't require an article.

bathroom/toilet	*hǎwng nám*
boyfriend or girlfriend	*faen*
food	*ahǎan*
foreigner	*fàràng*
friend	*phêuan*
money	*ngoen*
water	*nám*

General verbs

Thai verbs do not conjugate at all, and also often double up as nouns and adjectives, which means that foreigners' most un-idiomatic attempts to construct sentences are often readily understood.

come	*maa*
do	*tham*
eat	*kin/thaan khâo*
give	*hâi*
go	*pai*
sit	*nâng*
sleep	*nawn làp*
take	*ao*
walk	*doen pai*

Numbers

zero	*suŭn*
one	*nèung*
two	*sãwng*
three	*sãam*
four	*sìi*
five	*hâa*
six	*hòk*
seven	*jèt*
eight	*pàet*
nine	*kâo*
ten	*sìp*
eleven	*sìp èt*
twelve, thirteen, etc	*sìp sãwng, sìp sãam . . .*
twenty	*yîi sìp/yîip*
twenty-one	*yîi sìp èt*
twenty-two, twenty-three, etc	*yîi sìp sãwng, yîi sìp sãam . . .*
thirty, forty, etc	*sãam sìp, sìi sìp . . .*
one hundred, two hundred, etc	*nèung rói, sãwng rói . . .*
one thousand	*nèung phan*
ten thousand	*nèung mèun*

A Thai glossary

Avalokitesvara Bodhisattava representing compassion.

Avatar Earthly manifestation of a deity.

Ban Village or house.

Bencharong Polychromatic ceramics made in China for the Thai market.

Bodhisattva In Mahayana Buddhism, an enlightened being.

Bot Main sanctuary of a Buddhist temple.

Brahma One of the Hindu trinity: "the Creator".

Chedi Reliquary tower in Buddhist temple.

Chofa Finial on temple roof.

Dharma The teachings or doctrine of the Buddha.

Dharmachakra Buddhist Wheel of Law.

Erawan Mythical three-headed elephant; Indra's vehicle.

Farang A foreigner.

Ganesh Hindu elephant-headed deity.

Garuda Mythical Hindu creature – half-man half-bird; Vishnu's vehicle.

Hanuman Monkey god.

Indra Hindu king of the gods.

Jataka Stories of the five hundred lives of the Buddha.

Khlong Canal.

Khon Classical dance-drama.

Kinnari Mythical creature – half-woman, half-bird.

Lakhon Classical dance-drama.

Lak muang City pillar; revered home for the city's guardian spirit.

Meru/Sineru Mythical mountain in Hindu and Buddhist cosmologies.

Mondop Small, square temple building to house minor images.

Muay Thai Thai boxing.

Mudra Symbolic gesture of the Buddha.

Mut mee Tie-dyed cotton or silk.

Naga Mythical dragon-headed serpent in Buddhism and Hinduism.

Nirvana Final liberation from the cycle of rebirths; state of non-being.

Pali Language of ancient India.

Phra Honorific term – literally "excellent".

Prang Central tower in a Khmer temple.

Prasat Khmer temple complex or central shrine.

Rama Human manifestation of Hindu deity Vishnu.

Ramayana/Ramakien Hindu epic of good versus evil.

Ravana Rama's adversary in the Ramayana.

Rot ae/rot tua Air-conditioned bus.

Rot thammada Ordinary bus.

Samlor Three-wheeled rickshaw, usually pedal-powered.

Sanskrit Sacred language of Hinduism, also used in Buddhism.

Sanuk Fun.

Sema Boundary stone to mark consecrated ground.

Shiva One of the Hindu trinity – "The Destroyer".

Shiva lingam Phallic representation of Shiva.

Soi Alley or side-road.

Songkhran Thai New Year.

Songthaew Pick-up used as public transport.

Takraw Game played with a rattan ball.

GLOSSARY

346

Talat; Talat nam; Talat yen Market; Floating market; Night market.

Tha Pier.

Thanon Road.

Theravada Main school of Buddhist thought in Thailand.

Tripitaka Buddhist scriptures.

Tuk-tuk Motorized three-wheeled taxi.

Uma Shiva's consort.

Ushnisha Cranial protuberance on Buddha images.

Viharn Temple assembly hall for the laity.

Vishnu One of the Hindu trinity – "The Preserver".

Wai Thai greeting expressed by a prayer-like gesture with the hands.

Wat Temple.

Yaksha Mythical giant.

Yantra Magical combination of numbers and letters.

Index

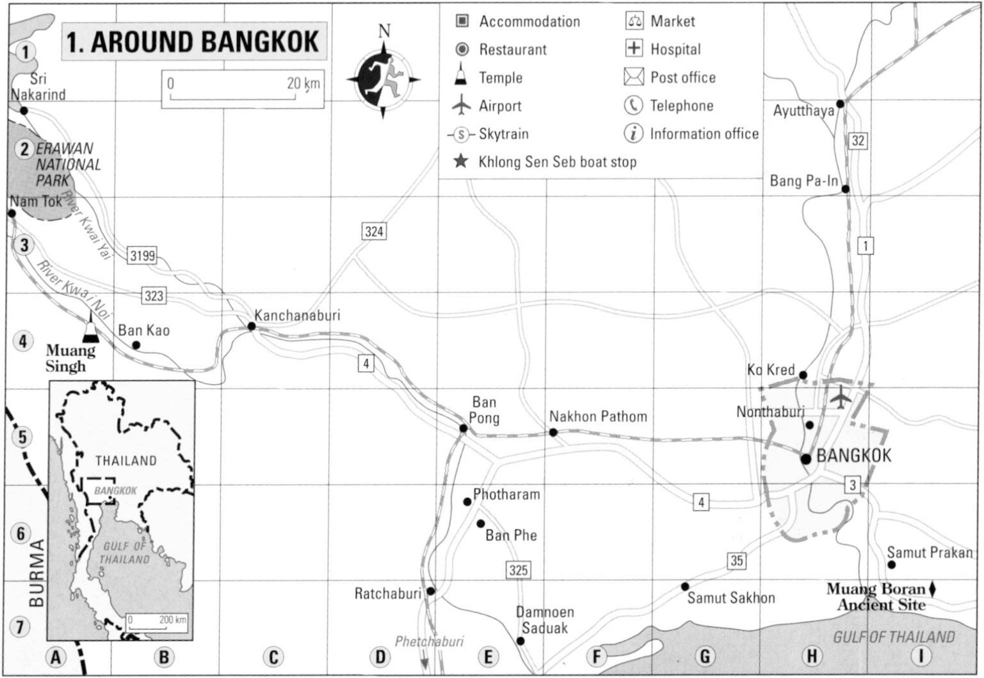
1. AROUND BANGKOK
0
20 km
N
Accommodation
Restaurant
Temple
Airport
Skytrain
Khlong Sen Seb boat stop
Market
Hospital
Post office
Telephone
Information office
Sri Nakarind
ERAWAN NATIONAL PARK
Nam Tok
River Kwai Yai
River Kwai Noi
3199
323
324
Kanchanaburi
Ban Kao
Muang Singh
4
Ban Pong
Nakhon Pathom
Photharam
Ban Phe
325
Ratchaburi
Damnoen Saduak
Phetchaburi
Samut Sakhon
35
Ayutthaya
32
Bang Pa-In
1
Ko Kred
Nonthaburi
BANGKOK
3
Samut Prakan
Muang Boran Ancient Site
GULF OF THAILAND
THAILAND
BANGKOK
GULF OF THAILAND
BURMA
0
200 km
1
2
3
4
5
6
7
A
B
C
D
E
F
G
H
I

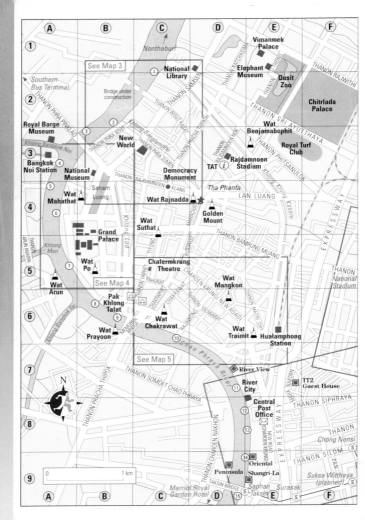

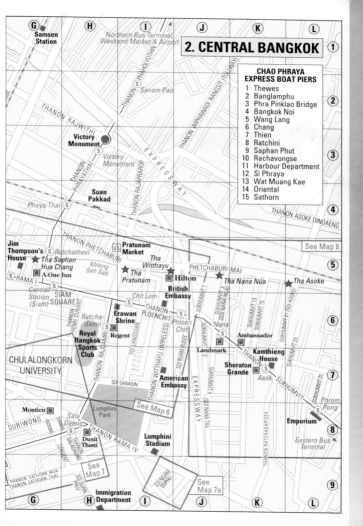

G Samsen Station

Northern Bus Terminal, Weekend Market & Airport

THANON RAJWITHI

THANON (P) PRADIPHONIDIN

Sanam Pao

THANON WIPHAWADI RANGSIT (TOLLWAY)

Victory Monument

Victory Monument

EXPRESSWAY

THANON RAJAPRAROP

THANON PHRAYATHAI

Suan Pakkad

Phaya Thai **(S)**

THANON ASOKE DINDAENG

CHAO PHRAYA EXPRESS BOAT PIERS

1 Thewes
2 Banglamphu
3 Phra Pinklao Bridge
4 Bangkok Noi
5 Wang Lang
6 Chang
7 Thien
8 Ratchini
9 Saphan Phut
10 Rachavongse
11 Harbour Department
12 Si Phraya
13 Wat Muang Kae
14 Oriental
15 Sathorn

Jim Thompson's House **(S)** Ratchathewi

THANON PHETCHABURI

Pratunam Market

Tha Saphan Hua Chang

Khlong Sen Sab

Tha Witthayu

PHETCHABURI MAI

Tha Nana Nua

Tha Asoke

(S) RAMA I

A-One Inn

Central Station (Siam) **(S)**

Tha Pratunam

Hilton

British Embassy

SIAM SQUARE

THANON HENRI DUNANT

Chit Lom **(S)**

THANON PLOENCHIT

Phloen Chit **(S)**

Nana **(S)**

SUKHUMVIT 13

SUKHUMVIT 15

Tha Asoke (SOI ASOKE)

Erawan Shrine

Ratcha-damri

Regent

THANON RAJADAMRI

SOI LANGSUAN

THANON WITTHAYU (WIRELESS)

SOI RUAM RUDEE

Ambassador

SUKHUMVIT 3

SUKHUMVIT 1

Kamthieng House

Royal Bangkok Sports Club

CHULALONGKORN UNIVERSITY

American Embassy

Landmark

EXPRESSWAY

Asok **(S)**

Sheraton Grande

THANON SUKHUMVIT

SOI SARASIN

SUKHUMVIT 23

SUKHUMVIT 31

Montien

SURIWONG

Sala Daeng **(S)**

Lumphini Park

See Map 6

THANON RAJADAPISEK

Phrom Pong **(S)**

Emporium

THANON SILOM

THANON CONVENT

SOI SALADAENG

Dusit Thani

THANON RAMA IV

Lumphini Stadium

Eastern Bus Terminal

See Map 7

THANON SATHORN NUA
THANON SATHORN THAI

SOI NGAM DUPLI

See Map 7a

G Immigration **H** Department

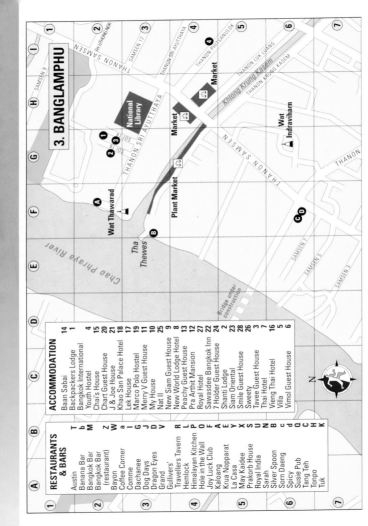

3. BANGLAMPHU

RESTAURANTS & BARS

Austin	T
Banana Bar	b
Bangkok Bar	M
Bangkok Bar (restaurant)	Z
Bayon	W
Coffee Corner	a
Comme	I
Dachanee	G
Dog Days	J
Dragon Eyes	D
Grand	V
Gullivers' Travellers Tavern	R
Hemlock	L
Himalayan Kitchen	P
Hole in the Wall	O
Joy Luck Club	F
Kaloang	E
Krua Nopparat	Y
La Casa	X
May Kaidee	S
Prakorb House	U
Royal India	N
Sarah	B
Silver Spoon	c
Sorn Daeng	d
Spicy	Q
Susie Pub	C
Tang Teh	H
Tonpo	K
Tuk	

ACCOMMODATION

Baan Sabai	14
Backpackers Lodge	1
Bangkok International Youth Hostel	4
Chai's House	15
Chart Guest House	20
J & Joe House	21
Khao San Palace Hotel	18
Lek House	17
Marco Polo Hostel	19
Merry V Guest House	11
My House	10
Nat II	25
New Siam Guest House	9
New World Lodge Hotel	8
Peachy Guest House	13
Pra Arthit Mansion	12
Royal Hotel	27
Sawasdee Bangkok Inn	22
7 Holder Guest House	24
Shanti Lodge	2
Siam Oriental	23
Smile Guest House	28
Sweety	26
Tavee Guest House	3
Thai Hotel	7
Vieng Thai Hotel	16
Villa	5
Vimol Guest House	6

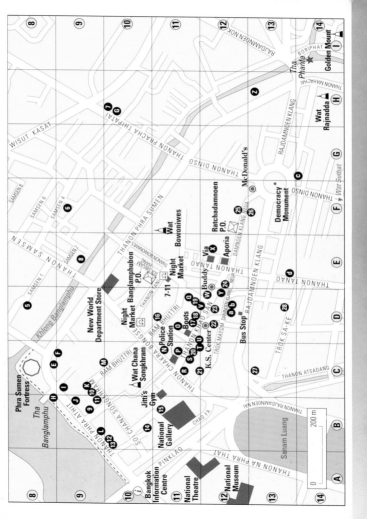

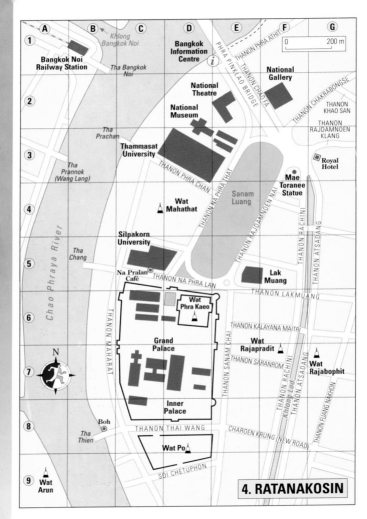

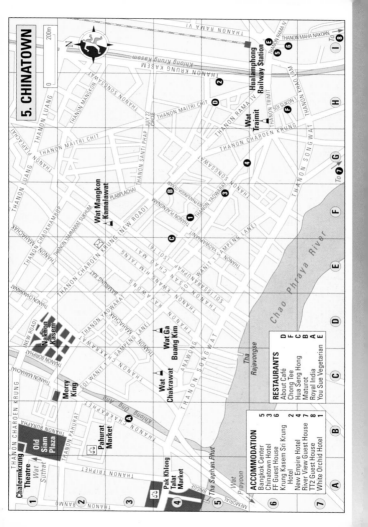

5. CHINATOWN

0   200m

THANON MAHACHAI
THANON CHAROEN KRUNG
Wat Sutthat
Chalermkrung Theatre
THANON PHAHURAT
THANON CHAKRAPHET
Old Siam Plaza
Pahurat Market
Nakhon Kasem
Merry King
THANON CHAKRAWAT
THANON CHAKKRAPHATDIPHONG
THANON BOAPHLAP
THANON CHAROEN KRUNG (NEW ROAD)
THANON CHAKKRAPHAT
Wat Ga Buang Kim
Wat Chakrawat
THANON MANGKON
Wat Mangkon Kamalawat (LABPLACHAI)
SOI WANIT 1 TAENG
SAMPENG LANE
THANON BURAPHA
THANON KRUNG KASEM
THANON LUANG
THANON LUANG
THANON PAPLACHAI
THANON MAITRI CHIT
THANON MAITRI CHIT
THANON SANTI PHAP
THANON RAMA IV
THANON SONGSAWAT
THANON YAWARAT
THANON YAOWARAT
THANON YOSSE
THANON ISSARANUPHAP
SOI ISSARANUPHAP (SOI 16)
THANON RATCHAWONG
THANON SONGWAT
THANON TRIMIT
THANON RAMA IV
Wat Traimit
Hualamphong Railway Station
THANON MAHA NAKORN
SOI SUKON
THANON MAITRI CHIT
JUW 72 CIRCLE
Khlong Krung Kasem
Khlong Ong Ang
THANON SONGWAT
THANON WANIT 2
THANON RATCHAWONG
Tha Rajavongse
Tha Saphan Phut
Wat Prayoon
MEMORIAL BRIDGE
Pak Khlong Talat Market
THANON TRIPHET
THANON ATSADANG
Chao Phraya River
To 7
N

ACCOMMODATION
Bangkok Center	5
Chinatown Hotel	3
FF Guest House	6
Krung Kasem Sri Krung Hotel	2
New Empire Hotel	4
River View Guest House	7
TT2 Guest House	8
White Orchid Hotel	1

RESTAURANTS
About Café	D
Chong Tee	C
Hua Seng Hong	B
Maturot	A
Royal India	E
You Sue Vegetarian	F

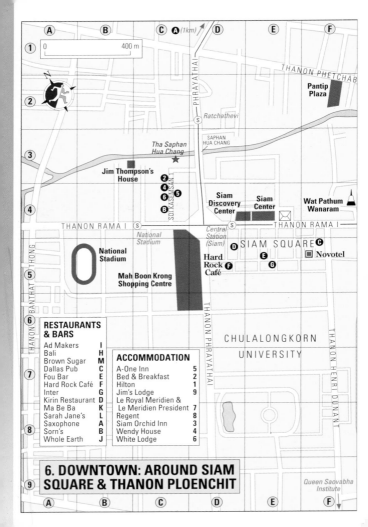

RESTAURANTS & BARS

Ad Makers	I
Bali	H
Brown Sugar	M
Dallas Pub	C
Fou Bar	E
Hard Rock Café	F
Inter	G
Kirin Restaurant	D
Ma Be Ba	K
Sarah Jane's	L
Saxophone	A
Sorn's	B
Whole Earth	J

ACCOMMODATION

A-One Inn	5
Bed & Breakfast	2
Hilton	1
Jim's Lodge	9
Le Royal Meridien & Le Meridien President	7
Regent	8
Siam Orchid Inn	3
Wendy House	4
White Lodge	6

6. DOWNTOWN: AROUND SIAM SQUARE & THANON PLOENCHIT

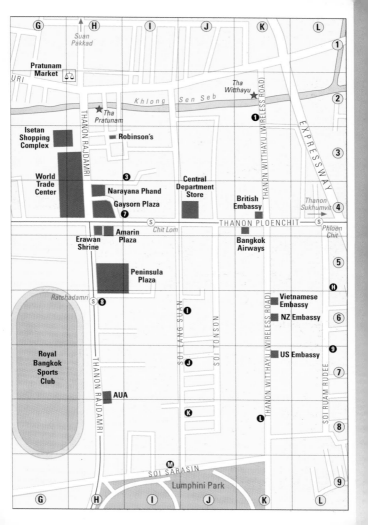

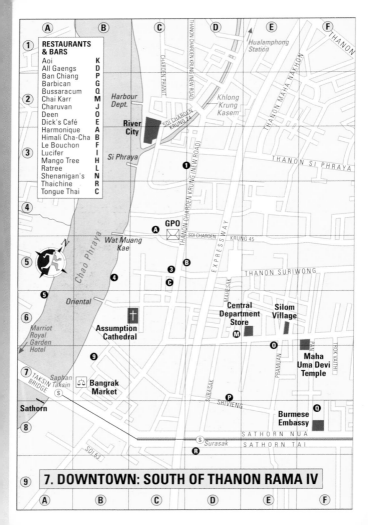

RESTAURANTS & BARS

Aoi	K
All Gaengs	D
Ban Chiang	P
Barbican	G
Bussaracum	Q
Chai Karr	M
Charuvan	J
Deen	O
Dick's Café	E
Harmonique	A
Himali Cha-Cha	B
Le Bouchon	F
Lucifer	I
Mango Tree	H
Ratree	L
Shenanigan's	N
Thaichine	R
Tongue Thai	C

7. DOWNTOWN: SOUTH OF THANON RAMA IV

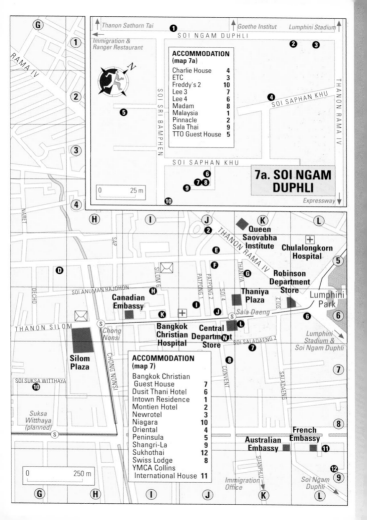

Thanon Sathorn Tai ① ↑ Goethe Institut   Lumphini Stadium ↑

SOI NGAM DUPHLI

Immigration &
Ranger Restaurant   ②   ③

ACCOMMODATION
(map 7a)

Charlie House	4
ETC	3
Freddy's 2	10
Lee 3	7
Lee 4	6
Madam	8
Malaysia	1
Pinnacle	2
Sala Thai	9
TTO Guest House	5

❺

SOI SAPHAN KHU

④

SOI SAPHAN KHU

❻ ❼
❾ ❽

0   25 m

❿

**7a. SOI NGAM
DUPHLI**

Expressway ↓

Ⓗ   Ⓘ   Ⓙ   Ⓚ   Ⓛ

②   Queen
THANON RAMA IV Saovabha
              Institute
Ⓔ   Chulalongkorn
                        Hospital
Ⓕ   Ⓖ   Robinson
SOI ANUMAN RAJDHON   Department
Ⓗ   Thaniya   Store
              Plaza   Lumphini
Canadian   Ⓛ   Park
Embassy   Ⓘ   Sala Daeng   ⑥
        Ⓚ   Bangkok Central
            Christian Department   Lumphini
Thanon Silom Hospital Store   Stadium &
Chong   SOI SALADAENG 2   Soi Ngam Duphli
Nonsi   ⑦

Silom   CONVENT
Plaza

ACCOMMODATION
(map 7)

Bangkok Christian Guest House	7
Dusit Thani Hotel	6
Intown Residence	1
Montien Hotel	2
Newrotel	3
Niagara	10
Oriental	4
Peninsula	5
Shangri-La	9
Sukhothai	12
Swiss Lodge	8
YMCA Collins International House	11

Suksa
Witthaya
(planned)

0   250 m

Ⓖ   Ⓗ   Ⓘ   Ⓙ

Australian   French
Embassy   Embassy   ⑪
                        ⑫
Immigration   ⑨
Office   Soi Ngam
            Ⓚ   Ⓛ   Duphli

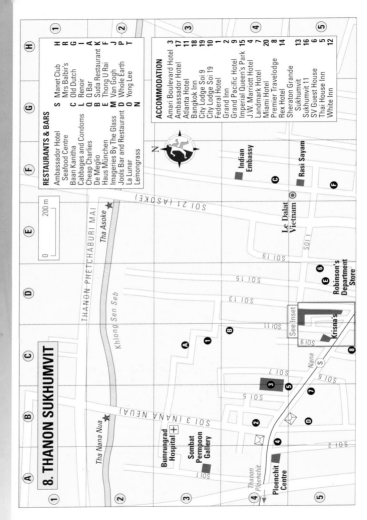

8. THANON SUKHUMVIT

RESTAURANTS & BARS

Ambassador Hotel Seafood Centre — S
Baan Kanitha — B
Cabbages and Condoms — C
Cheap Charlies — L
De Meglio — R
Haus München — Q
Imageries By The Glass — E
Jools Bar and Restaurant — D
La Lunar — M
Lemongrass — F

Manet Club — H
Mrs Balbir's — R
Old Dutch — G
Renoir — I
Q Bar — A
Suda Restaurant — K
Thong U Rai — J
Van Gogh — P
Whole Earth — T
Yong Lee — N

ACCOMMODATION

Amari Boulevard Hotel	3
Ambassador Hotel	17
Atlanta Hotel	11
Bangkok Inn	18
City Lodge Soi 9	19
City Lodge Soi 19	10
Federal Hotel	1
Grand Inn	2
Grand Pacific Hotel	9
Imperial Queen's Park	15
J.W. Marriott Hotel	4
Landmark Hotel	7
Miami Hotel	20
Premier Travelodge	8
Rex Hotel	14
Sheraton Grande Sukhumvit	13
Sukhumvit 11	16
SV Guest House	6
Thai House Inn	5
White Inn	12

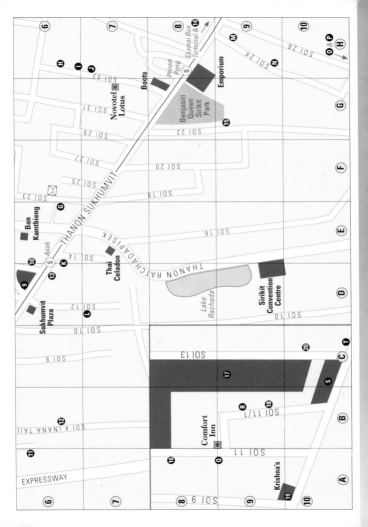

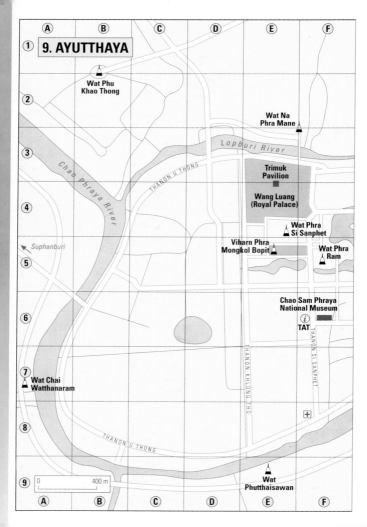

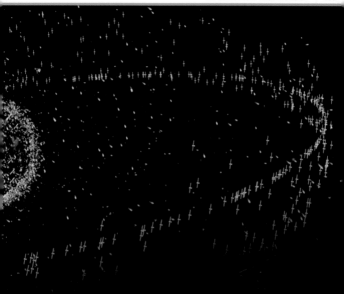

There are now more than 1,700

active artificial **satellites**.
The time they take to orbit Earth
depends on their position.

Cutting-edge technology

There are many exciting inventions in the world of technology, some of which may seem far-fetched (and some of these probably are!). This is the world of robotics, advanced biometrics, and augmented reality (to name a few). You are probably beginning to use or see some of these technologies without realizing it.

Biometrics: fingerprints

Schools, airports, and businesses are increasingly using biometrics. This technology identifies an individual based on physical traits, perhaps using a fingerprint scanner or an iris reader. The use of biometrics dates back hundreds of years – there is evidence that fingerprints were recorded in ancient China.

INVENTED BY	Unknown
WHEN	Unknown
WHERE	Unknown

Drone

Drones, or unmanned aerial vehicles (UAVs), can take the form of everything from cheap, but fun, toys to lethal military weapons. Military drones are controlled by computers, but simple drones for personal use are directed by remote control.

INVENTED BY	Unknown
WHEN	Early 1900s
WHERE	Unknown

Siri

This personal assistant is an application for the iPhone. It allows users to get things done by speaking to their phone. You can send messages, make phone calls, find a restaurant, and ask all sorts of questions.

INVENTED BY	Siri, Inc.
WHEN	2010
WHERE	USA

Augmented reality (glasses)

Augmented reality blends the real world with a virtual reality. Smart glasses are an example of an augmented reality device. A number of glasses are currently being developed by different companies.

INVENTED BY	Google
WHEN	2012
WHERE	USA

Driverless car

A driverless car may seem like a far-fetched idea, but Google has actually tested one. Sensors and cameras on the car's body transmit data to a computer, allowing the car to manoeuvre around objects. Test cars have successfully driven hundreds of kilometres – and are already legal in some states in the USA.

INVENTED BY	Many inventors
WHEN	1980s (first truly autonomous cars)
WHERE	USA

This driverless car, developed by Google in 2014, has no steering wheel and no pedals.

Artificial Intelligence (AI)

Developing robots with artificial intelligence, or AI, is a key area of robotic research. One of the first robots to be developed to interact with people was Kismet.

This is Kismet's "surprised" face

INVENTED BY Cynthia Breazeal

WHEN 1990s

WHERE USA

Agile robots

Inventors have been trying to create a walking and balancing robot for a long time, but walking is a difficult skill. One company has developed a robotic dog that can walk, run, climb and descend hills, and stay upright if physically pushed, learning as it goes.

INVENTED BY
Boston
Dynamics

WHEN
2014

WHERE
USA

Robot dog

PaPeRo robots

Partner-type-Personal-Robots (PaPeRo) were developed by a Japanese firm to interact with people and act as helpers in the home. There is now a range of PaPeRos for different tasks.

PaPeRo

INVENTED BY NEC

WHEN 1997

WHERE Japan

Invisibility cloak

A cloak that makes the wearer invisible hasn't been invented, but a means of using lenses to bend light so that something seems to disappear was revealed in 2014. It is called the Rochester Cloak.

DEVELOPED BY University of Rochester, USA

WHEN 2014

WHERE USA

Researcher demonstrating the Rochester Cloak

Exoskeleton

A robotic suit worn by a paraplegic person can allow them to walk again. British woman Claire Lomas successfully completed the London Marathon in 2012 wearing a bionic exoskeleton suit.

INVENTED BY Many inventors

WHEN 2000s

WHERE Unknown

Smart watch

One of the latest high-technology watches is Apple's smart watch. The idea is that it takes over from the phone for a lot of tasks, though it works in combination with an iPhone and not alone. It can store a huge number of apps (applications).

INVENTED BY Apple

WHEN 2015

WHERE USA

Future technologies

Some of the technologies that are being developed for the future are so cutting edge that they may never appear. However, technology moves fast and, in the future, what seems impossible now may well become a reality.

Faster travel

The Hyperloop is a proposed high-speed transport system. People enter capsules that travel through a tunnel on a cushion of air (rather than on wheels). It's proposed that the Hyperloop would reach speeds of up to 1,220 kph (760 mph). The initial design, by entrepreneur Elon Musk, was announced in August 2013.

Capsule will be around 2 m (6.6 ft) in diameter

Artwork of proposed Hyperloop, planned to run between Los Angeles and San Francisco, USA

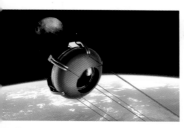

Robotic boat

The YARA *Birkeland* is expected to be the world's first autonomous ship – a ship that can sail without a crew. The container ship will be controlled remotely using on-board sensors. Powered entirely by electricity, the zero-emissions ship also helps the environment by reducing pollution as it transports fertilizer between small ports in Norway.

A line into space!

A space elevator has been imagined since 1895 as a means of reaching space, rather than in a rocket. The idea is that a spacecraft would travel into space along a tethered cable.

Universal translator

Imagine speaking into your phone and hearing your words in a different language. Universal translators are being developed that would be able to translate one language into another.

Fascinating facts

INVENTION FIRSTS

★ The first product to have a **bar code** was a packet of chewing gum, in 1974.

★ First inventions are often expensive. You could buy a car for the price of the **first microwave**.

★ Many inventions were developed for use in space. **Smoke detectors** were first used on the space station Skylab.

★ Canadian inventor Reginald Fessenden was possibly the first person to make a **spoken radio broadcast** in 1906.

★ The **first photograph** to show a person (a man cleaning shoes) is believed to have been taken by Louis Daguerre in France in 1838.

★ The **first wheelbarrow** (though it didn't have handles) is thought to have been invented in ancient China in the second century by General Jugo Liang, who needed a one-wheeled cart to carry heavy objects for the military.

★ One of the first **vehicles** designed for off-road conditions had five axles and ten wheels. It appeared in the 1930s, but it wasn't a success!

FOOD INVENTIONS

• The **first margarine** was a mixture of beef fat, a cow's udder, milk, and a pig's stomach. It won a prize as the first butter substitute.

• The **candy floss machine** was invented by a dentist in 1897.

• It took 16 years for the inventor of **sliced bread**, Otto Rohwedder, to find a way to stop it going stale.

• **Ice lollies** were invented by accident in 1905 by an 11 year old called Frank Epperson. He patented the invention as "Popsicles" 18 years later.

• It's claimed that the first **chocolate chip cookies** were an accident, when chips of chocolate were added to a cookie mix but they didn't melt.

• Chocolate had a gritty texture until 1879 when Swiss chocolatier Rodolphe Lindt created a way to make **smooth chocolate**.

WEIRD AND WONDERFUL

♦ Drink up

One industrious inventor hid a drink pouch in a tie, with the idea of carrying water in a widely worn garment.

♦ Soft robots

Researchers are currently looking into developing "soft" robots. These flexible robots would be able to move in restricted spaces (inspired by sea creatures such as the octopus!).

♦ Going up

There is a famous story about the invention of the first steel-framed skyscraper. The inventor, William Jenney, saw his wife drop a heavy book on a wire bird cage. He realized that if the cage could hold the weight of the book, there was no reason why a metal frame wouldn't support a building.

♦ Robotic fish

Robots are commonly used in many factories (such as on car production lines and in food packaging factories), but more unusual robots are being developed. Robotic fish have been developed to monitor environmental conditions. They are shaped like fish and packed with sensors that record levels of pollution and other factors that may affect the survival of marine life.

♦ Walking on water

Wouldn't it be fun to walk on water! Leonardo Da Vinci sketched an idea for doing just this in around 1480, using air-filled leather bags and balancing poles. The idea wouldn't have worked.

♦ Which way?

An early car navigation system existed in the 1930s. It was a box, fixed to the dashboard, containing a map that was mounted on rollers. The driver or passenger simply rolled the map up or down to show the car's location. There was also a version that could be worn on the wrist (the "Plus Fours Routefinder").

Edison's lightbulb came with a warning: "Do not attempt to light with a match."

♦ Oldest wheel

The earliest wheels we know of belong to a stone toy that has been dated back to around 5500 BCE. It was found in modern-day Turkey.

♦ Passenger lifts

The first passenger lift operated in a New York department store in 1857. It climbed five storeys in one minute. The world's fastest lifts, in a skyscraper in Taiwan known as Taipei 101, shoot up 84 storeys in just 37 seconds.

YOU'VE PROBABLY SEEN...

▶ Silly putty
This was invented by James Wright in 1943. He was trying to create a hard rubber and one of the mixtures he made bounced. However, it was only in the 1950s that a toy shop owner saw its potential as a toy.

▶ No-spill cup
The Anywayup Cup was invented by Mandy Haberman in 1990, as a leak-proof training cup for toddlers. It was to prove a runaway success.

▶ Square-bottomed paper shopping bags
Surprisingly, these were first patented in 1872 by American inventor Luther Childs Crowell. He patented many other paper-related inventions, including one for a machine that could fold newspapers.

▶ Metal bottle caps
The crimped metal caps that seal fizzy drinks bottles have a history that dates back to 1891 and an inventor called William Painter. The caps were patented as "crown corks".

▶ Disposable nappies
These were first patented in 1951 by American inventor Marion Donovan.

She sold the rights to the patent for one million US dollars as she couldn't manufacture the quantities that were being ordered.

▶ Banknotes
Paper banknotes are commonly used, but the use of polymer (or plastic) banknotes is increasing. They were invented and developed in Australia in the 1960s.

The world's first vending machine was designed by Hero of Alexandria in around 60 CE.

▶ Football
Early footballs were made from animal bladders, blown up and popped in a leather sack. The spherical leather football, more similar in shape to those used today, was invented in the 1860s by the English leatherworker Richard Lindon. He went on to develop an oval rugby ball. Footballs today are made from synthetic materials.

▶ Teddy bears
These toys were named after an American president, Theodore "Teddy" Roosevelt, who refused to shoot and kill a bear cub. They were first sold by a New York shop owner in 1903 who called them "Teddy's Bears".

▶ Jigsaw puzzle
Early jigsaw puzzles were cut from wood. One of the first was made by a cartographer (a person who draws or makes maps) in the 1760s. It was a map of the world, and was used for teaching geography.

NEVER GIVE UP

• **Thomas Edison** tried many materials for the filament in his light bulb, including cork, wood, rubber, grass, and even human hair.

• Thomas Edison invented his light bulb after **thousands of failed attempts**. He famously said: "Genius is one per cent inspiration and 99 per cent perspiration."

• When iRobot launched a robotic vacuum cleaner in 2002, some people thought it was a silly idea that wouldn't last, but the **Roomba** continues to sell.

• An oil-based spray called **WD-40** failed 39 times before its inventors hit on a final product. WD-40 stands for "Water Displacement 40th Attempt". It gained fame for having multiple and unusual uses, such as preventing guitar strings from rusting and removing crayon marks.

• One of the most unusual inventors is an American called **Ron Popeil**. He has invented all sorts of household and leisure gadgets, including a chop-o-matic that chops vegetables and a pocket fisherman (a fishing rod that folds to fit into a pocket).

• The inventor of **bubble gum** said his invention was "an accident". He sold his first batch in one afternoon.

WHO SAID THAT?

"Invent something that will be used once and then thrown away. Then the customer will come back for more." William Painter, inventor of the crown cork bottle cap.

"To invent, you need a good imagination and a pile of junk." Thomas Edison

"If I have seen further than others, it is by standing upon the shoulders of giants." Isaac Newton

"If birds can glide for long periods of time, then... why can't I?" Orville Wright

WHAT'S IN A NAME?

★ The name **Lego®** comes from the Danish words "leg godt" meaning "play well".

★ **Zips** were named after the sound the first zips made as they opened and closed.

★ **Duct tape** is also widely known as "duck" tape because of its ability to repel water.

★ **Coca-Cola** was named after the coca leaves and kola berries from which it was originally made.

Glossary

Alloy A material made of two or more metals, or from a metal combined with another material. Bronze is an alloy, made from a mixture of copper and tin.

Artificial Intelligence (AI) Robots that are developed to learn are described as having artificial intelligence (as opposed to the natural intelligence that people enjoy).

Braille A system of reading and writing that uses raised dots. There is now a braille code for every widely spoken language in the world, as well as one for music and for mathematics. There is even a braille system for use with computers.

Browser (web) An application that is used to find information on the World Wide Web.

Codex The earliest form of a book, made from manuscripts stitched together along one side.

Compound machine A machine, such as a bicycle or wheelbarrow, which uses two or more simple machines.

Fibre optics A means of sending information in the form of light impulses along glass or plastic fibres.

Filament The part of a light bulb that glows when an electric current passes through it. Thomas Edison famously experimented with thousands of substances to try and find a suitable filament.

Force A push or pull that can make something move, prevent something moving, or change an object's motion.

Four-stroke cycle engine The most common type of engine. Each piston in the engine works in four stages, or strokes: intake (taking in a mixture of air and petrol), compression (squeezing the mixture), combustion (a spark ignites the mixture, which burns rapidly and pushes the piston down), and exhaust (the spent mixture leaves the cylinder).

Gears Toothed wheels that mesh together as they turn. Gears are used to change the speed or force with which wheels turn, allowing the efficient use of power.

Generator A machine that produces (or generates) electricity.

Global Positioning System (GPS) A navigation system that relies on information from satellites to provide precise location details. GPS depends on the satellites linking with ground-based receivers. Many cars are fitted with GPS receivers.

Industrial Revolution A period of rapid industrial expansion in Britain and, later, in rest of Europe and the USA. It started in the late 1700s and saw a huge amount of innovation and invention. This is the time that factories began to emerge and people moved away from the countryside to form towns around these factories.

Information Age Also referred to as the Computer or Digital Age, this defines the time we are living in, whereby we are reliant on information technology with economies that depend on computers.

Innovation The means by which an idea or invention is developed and improved in a new way.

Internal combustion engine An engine that burns fuel inside one or more cylinders, rather than in an exterior furnace. Most vehicles are powered by internal combustion engines.

Internet The global network that links millions of computers.

Joystick A means of controlling the cursor for a computer game to make the game seem more realistic.

Lens A curved piece of glass. Lenses can be found in telescopes, glasses, and cameras, among other things.

Lever A rigid bar, pivoted at one point along its length. This means it can be used to transmit and change force. An oar is an example of a simple lever.

Maglev This is short for "magnetic levitation". Maglev trains depend on magnets to lift the train and move it forwards.

Mesopotamia An ancient region that stretched through modern-day Iraq and Kuwait, as well as parts of modern-day Turkey and Iran. Mesopotamia has been widely termed the "cradle of civilization".

Microprocessor The complicated circuits at the heart of a computer that carry out instructions and calculations, and communicate with other parts of the computer. The microprocessor is a computer's brain.

Monorail A railway with a single rail track. Many monorails operate with the train suspended from the rail but others run on it. Monorails are widely used at airports.

Monowheel A vehicle with a single wheel. The rider sits next to the wheel, or within it (unlike a unicycle).

Movable type A system of printing in which letters or words are created on individual blocks, so they can be moved into position to form a word or sentence.

Nanotechnology The science of creating materials and machines that are too small to see – far smaller than the fullstop at the end of this sentence. They can only be seen under powerful microscopes. Nanotechnology is being applied to an increasingly wide range of items.

Papyrus A fragile material made from the stem of the papyrus plant and used to write on in ancient Egypt before the invention of paper. It was also used for objects such as baskets, ropes, and sandals, among other things.

Patent A legal document that grants sole rights to an individual or company to make, use, and sell an invention. Patents have a set time period and they do expire. Patent applications are given a number if successful and a year of issue.

Pendulum A hanging weight that swings to regulate the workings of a clock such as a Grandfather clock.

Piston A round metal part that fits snugly in a cylinder and moves up and down. Car engines usually have four pistons, each one in its own cylinder.

Power line A cable that carries electrical power. It is usually supported by a pylon.

Projector A device for projecting an image onto a screen.

Radar A system used to detect aircraft, ships, and other objects. It works by emitting pulses of radio waves, which are reflected off the object.

Radio waves A type of energy that is invisible, travels in waves, and can be used to send information.

Robot A machine that is controlled by a computer, and that can do work

previously done by people. Car factories, for example, use robot assembly lines to build cars as well as to paint them.

Satellite An object in orbit around a body in space. Thousands of artificial satellites orbit Earth, aiding communication and navigation, taking part in research, providing weather forecasts, as well as being used in spying.

Sextant Sailors have used sextants for hundreds of years. These tools measure the angle between the horizon and objects in the sky, helping determine a boat's position.

Simple machine The simplest ways in which a force can be applied. A lever, wedge, and screw are all simple machines.

Smartphone A mobile phone that can perform many of the functions of a computer, in addition to its use as a telephone. Most smartphones have a touch-screen interface.

Steam engine An engine that uses steam, created by heating water to boiling point. It is used to drive machinery.

Supercomputer A computer that is used

by large organizations for handling huge amounts of data. Weather forecasting depends on the operation of supercomputers.

Technology The means by which knowledge and inventions are put to practical use.

Telecommunication Communication over a distance by electronic means such as a telephone or television.

Transistor A tiny electronic component that is used to switch or amplify electric signals. It is a means of controlling an electrical current.

World Wide Web (WWW) The part of the Internet that contains websites, which are navigated by a web browser and are made up of documents that are linked together.

Index

Acknowledgments

Dorling Kindersley would like to thank:
Annabel Blackledge for proofreading; Helen Peters
for indexing; Jessica Cawthra, Priyanka Kharbanda,
Fleur Star, Vatsal Verma, Kingshuk Ghoshal, and
Francesca Baines for editorial assistance; Chrissy
Barnard, Kanupriya Lal, Ira Sharma, Govind Mittal,
and Philip Letsu for design assistance; Saloni Singh
for the jacket; Pawan Kumar and Balwant Singh for
DTP assistance; Surya Sarangi for picture research
assistance; and Robert Dunn for pre-production.

The publishers would also like to thank the
following for their kind permission to reproduce
their photographs:

(Key: a-above; b-below/bottom; c-centre; f-far; l-left;
r-right; t-top)

1 **Dreamstime.com:** Apreciindere. 2-3 **Dreamstime.
com:** Inokos. 3 **Dreamstime.com:** Dimitry Romanchuck
(br). 4 **Corbis:** Dr. Albert J. Copley / Visuals Unlimited
(cl). 4-5 **Science Photo Library:** KTSDesign (c). 5
Corbis: National Archives - digital vers / Science Faction
(tr). **Dorling Kindersley:** The Science Museum, London
(cr). **Dreamstime.com:** Photomall (br); Rise2rise (bc).
6 **Getty Images:** Grant Faint (br). **Rex Features:** Brian
Smith (t). 7 **123RF.com:** de2marco (cr). **Dreamstime.
com:** Aleksandrs Samuilovs (br); Candybox Images (t);
Angelo Gilardelli (br). **Science Museum, London:** (bc).
8 **Getty Images:** DeAgostini (cl). 8-9 **Corbis:** Gianni Dagli Orti
(c). 9 **Alamy Images:** Mostardi Photography (br). **Corbis:**
Sander de Wilde (bc). **TopFoto.co.uk:** Dinodia (cr). 10
Getty Images: Yale Joel / The LIFE Picture Collection
(cl). 10-11 **Corbis:** Transtock (c). 11 **Alamy Images:**
Historic Collection (br). **Corbis:** (tr). 13 **Corbis:** Mark
Alberhasky / Science Faction (b); Michael Rosenfeld /
Science Faction (br). **Dorling Kindersley:** Powell-Cotton
Museum, Kent (r). **Getty Images:** Fine Art Images /
Heritage Images (cb). 14 **123RF.com:** Matouš Vinš. 15
Corbis: Charles Fortwei (tl). 16 **Dorling Kindersley:**
The Science Museum, London (b). **Getty Images:** SSPL
(cb). 16-17 **Getty Images:** Sean Gallup (c). 17 **Getty
Images:** Encyclopaedia Britannica / UIG (br); Stocktrek
(t). 18 **Getty Images:** Danita Delimont (b). 19 **Alamy
Images:** age fotostock (bc); Stockxpert (br). **John
Cairns** (cr). **Corbis:** Walter Bibikow / JAI (b). 20
Corbis: Onne DiBackground); Evgeny
Glyaneko (t). 20-21 **Courtesy of WaterCar.** 22 **Corbis:**
Michael Dalder / Reuters (b). 23 **Getty Images:** SSPL
(bc). **Courtesy Mercedes-Benz Cars, Daimler AG:** (t).
24 **Dorling Kindersley:** National Cycle Collection (br).
(b). 24-25 **Alamy Images:** Howard Barlow. 25 **Alamy
Images:** Marc Tielemans (cr). **Corbis:** infusta-207 /
INFphoto.com (br). 26 **Getty Images:** SSPL (t). 26-27
Corbis: Hulton-Deutsch Collection (b). 27 **123RF.com:**
philipus (br). **Alamy Images:** Robert Mullan (tr). 28
Corbis: Piotr Wittman / epa (b). 28-29 **Science &
Society Picture Library:** (b). 29 **Corbis:** Bettmann (cr).
Dreamstime.com: Kaspars Grinvalds (tl); Bob Phillips /
Digital69 (tr). **Photoshot:** Mike Stocker (tc). 30 **NASA:** (b).
31 **NASA:** (t, br). 32-33 **Getty Images:** Stockside.
Images. 34 **Dreamstime.com:** Jochenschneider (br).
Getty Images: De Agostini Picture Library (br). 35
123RF.com: Andrej Polivanov (t). **Dorling Kindersley:**
National Maritime Museum, London (b). **Dreamstime.
com:** Diana Rich (br). 36 **Corbis:** Jutta Klee. 38 **Alamy
Images:** Carlos Mora (c, br). **Dreamstime.com:** Viktor
Pravdica (bl). 39 **Alamy Images:** victor cea (tr). **Getty
Images:** Sanna Berg (b). 40 **Alamy Images:** dbimages
(cr). **Dreamstime.com:** Gaby Kooijman (cla); Sergiyn
(cb). 41 **Dorling Kindersley:** The Science Museum,
London (cra). **Dreamstime.com:** Showface (br). 42
Science Source (c). 42-43 **Getty Images:** SSPL. 43
Science Photo Library: NYPL /
Science Source (c). 43 **Getty Images:**
MyLoupe / UIG (b). 43 **Science & Society**

Picture Library. 44 **Dreamstime.com:** Steven
Jones (t). 45 **Dreamstime.com:** Monika Wisniewska (tr);
Porapak Apichodilok (br). **Getty Images:** SSPL (bc). 46
Corbis: (br). **Getty Images:** Hoberman Collection (b).
47 **123RF.com:** cokeromo (ca). **Dreamstime.com:**
Zsfl123 (t). 48 **Getty Images:** Tetra Images (cla).
Science Photo Library: New York Public library (bc).
48-49 **Alamy Images:** David J. Green (t). **Getty Images:**
SSPL (b). 49 **Getty Images:** Kolett (br). 50 **Dreamstime.
com:** Alexander Shalamov (br). **Photoshot:** imago
sportfotodienst (b). 52-53 **Dreamstime.com:** Dmires.
54 **Dreamstime.com:** Aleksandr Kurganov (br);
Voyagerix (br). 55 **Dreamstime.com:** Edwardgerges
(t). **iStockphoto.com:** studiocasper (br). 56 **Dorling
Kindersley:** Board of Trustees of the Royal Armouries
(bc). **Dreamstime.com:** Goce Risteski (bl). **Scott
Norsworthy Flickr.** 56-57 **Dreamstime.com:** Jilang
Zhang. 58 **Alamy Images:** www.BibleLandPictures.com
(tr). 59 **Corbis:** Zero Creatives (br). **Dreamstime.com:**
Hamsterman (tl); Kmitu (bl). 60 **iStockphoto.com:**
cristiani. 61 **Corbis:** Mark Cooper (cb). 62 **Dreamstime.
com:** Paul Lecha. 63 **123RF.com:** Antron Havelaar (bl).
Dorling Kindersley: The Trustees of the British Museum
(cra). **Dreamstime.com:** Tuayai (tc). 64 **Alamy Images:**
The Art Archive (ca). **Dorling Kindersley:** The Science
Museum, London (bc). 65 **123RF.com:** Sandra Van Der Steen
(tr). **Getty Images:** DEA Picture Library (bl). 66 **Corbis:**
Bettmann (b). **Dorling Kindersley:** The Science
Museum, London (br). 67 **Alamy Images:** Chris Willson
(br). **Dorling Kindersley:** Museum of the Moving Image,
London (tr). 68-69 **Alamy Images:** ClassicStock. 70
Dreamstime.com: Sdtower (bl). **Getty Images:**
Science & Society Picture Library (cra). 70-71 **Getty
Images:** Cate Gillon. 71 **123RF.com:** Elnur Amiklishiyev
(br). **Alamy Images:** Chris Willson (ca). 72 **Getty
Images:** SSPL (t). 73 **Corbis:** Paul Almasy (cr).
Dreamstime.com: Denlarkin (b); Pavel Losevsky
(cr); Kurgyverjucky (cla); Keith Bell (cra); Luhuanfeng
(cb). **Getty Images:** SSPL (t). 74 **Dreamstime.com:**
Shariff Che' Lah (cb). 76-77 **Alamy Images:** Deyan
Georgiev - Rbf content. 79 **Corbis:** Gianni Dagli Orti
(tr). **Dreamstime.com:** Aprecindere (crb); Feng Cheng
(tc). 80 **Alamy Images:** Chris Hellier (bc). **Wild Places
Photography** (cr). **Dreamstime.com:** Ewa Walicka (t).
Science & Society Picture Library: (br). 81 **Alamy
Images:** Finnbarr Webster (ca). **Marc Tielemans** (tr);
Gallo Images (bl). 82 **Getty Images:** William West / AFP
(b). 83 **Dreamstime.com:** Robert Kneschke (cb). 84 **Getty
Images:** SSPL (b). **Science & Society Picture Library:**
Science Museum (cla). 86 **Dreamstime.com:**
Andreadonetti (tr); Motorolka (tl); Anna Kucherova (tc).
Science Photo Library: Peter Menzel (b). 86 **Dorling
Kindersley:** CONACULTA-INAH-MEX (cb); Thackeray
Medical Museum (cla). **iStockphoto.com:** Yasl. (crb).
86-87 **Alamy Images:** BSIP SA (ca). 87 **Alamy Images:**
Hero Images (tc). (cra). **Science Photo Library:** Philippe
Psaila (bl). 88 **Getty Images:** Marwan Naamani / AFP
(cla). **Science Photo Library:** Sovereign / ISM (b).
89 **Alamy Images:** MixPix (br). **Dreamstime.com:**
Andrelsaiko (cla). 90-91 **Science Photo Library.** 92
Alamy Images: Katraina Images. 93 **Dreamstime.com:**
Tab1962 (cb). 94-95 **Alamy Images:** Juice Images (b).
95 **Alamy Images:** Radharc Images (cla). **Corbis:** (b).
Dreamstime.com: Eng101 (ca). 96 **Dorling Kindersley:**
Museum of English Rural Life, The University of Reading
(cb). **Dreamstime.com:** Daniel Baker (c). **Dmitar
Marinov (cla); Marlee (bl).** 97 **Alamy Images:** The Art
Archive (cra). **Getty Images:** Paul Quayle / Design Pics
(br). 98 **Corbis:** (br). **Dorling Kindersley:** Museum of
English Rural Life, The University of Reading (t). **Getty
Images:** SSPL (br). 99 **Getty Images:** SSPL (r). 100
Alamy Images: gaphotos.com. 101 **Alamy Images:**
Doug Steley A (b). **Corbis:** (cra). **Dreamstime.com:** SSPL
(cra). 102-103 © **CERN .** 104 **Corbis:** Reuters (br). **Getty**

Images: SSPL (t). 105 **Dreamstime.com:** Darkworx
(tc); Meredith Lamb (t). **Getty Images:** Joshua Roberts /
Bloomberg (b). 106 **Alamy Images:** (bl). **Dorling
Kindersley:** The Science Museum, London (br).
Dreamstime.com: Peter Sobolev (cb). 107 **NASA.**
108 **Dreamstime.com:** Buttet (bl); Leung Cho Pan
(cla); Emel82 (cl). 109 **Alamy Images:** travelib (ca).
Dreamstime.com: Aleksandr Kirsik (cb); Ravindran
John Smith (t). 110-111 **Alamy Images:** gary warnimont
(t). 110 **Getty Images:** De Agostini / C. Marchelli (br).
111 **Alamy Images:** The Art Archive (t). **Dorling
Kindersley:** The Combined Military Services Museum
(CMSM) (b). **Dreamstime.com:** Chode (cb). 112
Dorling Kindersley: Natural History Museum, London
(bc). 113 **Alamy Images:** Zoonar GmbH (br). **Dorling
Kindersley:** Museum of English Rural Life, The
University of Reading (b); The Science Museum,
London (cla). **Dreamstime.com:** Wendy Kaveney (ca).
114-115 **Getty Images:** Eman Jamal. 116 **Science
Photo Library:** Spencer Sutton. 117 **Alamy Images:**
Kuttig - People (bl); David Bleeker Photography (crb).
118 **Science Photo Library:** Power and Syred (tr). 118 **Getty
Images:** Francis Miller. 119 **Getty Images:** Apic (cb).
120 **123RF.com:** emevil (cla). **Corbis:** Imaginechina (bl).
121 **NASA:** (b). 122 **Getty Images:** DEA / S. Vannini (cb).
123 **Alamy Images:** The Art Archive (tr); D. Hurst (ca).
Dreamstime.com: Alfonsodetomas (br). 124-125 **Getty
Images:** Datacraft Co Ltd. 126 **Getty Images:** SSPL
(br). 127 **Alamy Images:** War Archive (t). **Corbis:**
Oleksiy Maksymenko / All Canada Photos (br); Jason
Szenes / epa (tc). 128 **Science Photo Library:** CCI
Archives (b). 129 **Dorling Kindersley:** Natural History
Museum, London (bc). 130 **Dreamstime.com:** Marc
Slingerland (t); Sardonl (br). 131 **Alamy Images:**
NASA Archive (b). **Dreamstime.com:** Andrei
Malov (tr). 132 **Alamy Images:** Brian Harris (bc).
Dreamstime.com: Kirill Shalmanov (cb). 133 **Corbis:**
Roger Du Buisson (br); Bob Rowan / Progressive
Image (tl). **Dreamstime.com:** Alexandr Malyshev
(tl). **Getty Images:** SSPL (cb). 134 **Dreamstime.com:**
O'Rear (bc). 134-135 **Dreamstime.com:** Hayati
Kayhan (ca); Sourabil (bc). 135 **Dreamstime.com:**
Paul Hakimata / Phakimata (br). 136 **Corbis:** Hank
Morgan - Rainbow / Science Faction (b). 136-137
Dreamstime.com: Lukasz Bialko (b). 138-139 **NASA.**
140 **Getty Images:** Bobi (cr); Ed Jones / AFP (b). 141
Alamy Images: Richard Levine (cla). **Corbis:** John
Chapple / Splash News (br); Timothy Fadek (cra). 142
Alamy Images: Daniel Santos Megina (crb). **Corbis:**
George Steinmetz (t). **Dreamstime.com:** Andrey Volokin
Stage (bc). 143 **Alamy Images:** Pawan Kumar (br).
Corbis: Kerim Okten. **University of Rochester:** (tr).
144-145 **Science Photo Library:** Claus Lunau. 145
Getty Images: Visuals Unlimited, Inc. / Victor Habbick
(b). **iStockphoto.com:** Tuomas Kujansuu (br). **The Eye
Tribe:** (tr).

Jacket images: Front: 123RF.com: Cokemomo (8:5).
Dorling Kindersley: Australian National Maritime
Museum, Sydney (8:3), Museum of the Moving Image,
London (Main), National Cycle Collection (3:1), National
Motor Museum, Beaulieu (6:1), National Motorcycle
Museum (6:2), The Science Museum (Main), Science
Museum, London (9:2), Natural History Museum, London
(3:4), Stephen Oliver (9:3), Science Museum, London
(3:2), Stephen Oliver (9:3), Science Museum, London (9:3),
Science Museum, London (8:1), The Science Museum, London
(2:6), The Science Museum, London (3:3), Wallace
Collection, London (3:5), Whipple Museum of History
of Science, Cambridge (2:3). **Dreamstime.com:**
Denlarkin (4:6), Diana Rich (1:2), Goce Risteski (1:2),
Thommeo (1:4), Titovstudio (3:3). **NASA:** Bill Ingalls (7:6).

All other images © Dorling Kindersley

For further information see:
www.dkimages.com